THE BEST PLAYS OF RACINE

THE
BEST PLAYS
OF
RACINE

TRANSLATED INTO ENGLISH RHYMING VERSE
WITH INTRODUCTIONS AND NOTES BY

LACY LOCKERT
A.M., PH.D.

PRINCETON
PRINCETON UNIVERSITY PRESS

PRINTED IN THE UNITED STATES OF AMERICA

To My Father

CHARLES LACY LOCKERT

NO WORDS CAN TELL WHAT HIS LOVE, HIS
INFLUENCE, AND HIS COMRADESHIP
HAVE MEANT IN MY LIFE

CONTENTS

". . . the four great masterpieces of Racine: *Andromaque, Britannicus, Phèdre, Athalie*."—N.-M. Bernardin in L. Petit de Julleville's *Histoire de la Langue et de la Littérature française*.

". . . *Andromaque* . . . *Britannicus* . . . *Phèdre* . . . if we except *Athalie*, which is manifestly a type by itself, it is by these three dramas that Racine must be judged."—C. E. Vaughan in *Types of Tragic Drama*.

". . . looking at Racine's theatre through the cool grey spectacles of old age, I find that I prefer *Athalie, Phèdre, Britannicus*, and . . . *Andromaque*."—Mary Duclaux in *The Life of Racine*.

". . . among the works of Racine . . . the four miracles . . . are, in my opinion, *Andromaque, Britannicus, Phèdre*, and *Athalie*."—Émile Faguet in *Propos de Théâtre*.

RACINE, the greatest of French tragic dramatists and in the judgment of his own countrymen the equal of Molière in magnitude of genius and achievement, has never been appreciated by the English-speaking world. The reason for this fact is not merely, as we commonly hear it said, that he is too artificial for our taste; the fault is less one-sided. His plays are artificial in respects in which our literary tradition demands naturalness; they are natural in respects in which our literary tradition demands artificiality.

In depicting the life of other lands and days than his own, Racine, like most writers prior to the age of romanticism, makes little use of "local colour." This in itself would not repel us. It is scarcely less true of Shakespeare; his Hamlet is essentially an Elizabethan in an Elizabethan world. But Racine's world, the Court of Louis XIV, happens to have been a peculiarly artificial one—its speech and manners modelled on those of the absurd, high-flown pastoral romances which were in great favour then; a world of strained conventions, preciosity, gallantry, decorum, and preoccupation with love-making. It jars upon us that the dramatist's Greek heroes and Roman citizens wear the masks of such a world. We are prone not to realize that under those masks are emotions as poignant and passions as savage as literature can show. We are repelled by a love-jargon of "sighs" and "flames" and "conquests"—all the more so because such stereotyped phrasing is associated in our minds with the frigid, declamatory, insincere English tragedies of the age of Dryden and Pope.

On the other hand, we expect poetry (even dramatic poetry) to be full of figurative, heightened language. We find it so in Shakespeare, and in Aeschylus and Calderon and

x

Goethe. Almost all literature accepts this convention. Macbeth can speak of

> pity, like a naked new-born babe,
> Striding the blast, or heaven's cherubim horsed
> Upon the sightless couriers of the air,

without our being offended by the consideration that no man ever actually talked like that. But Racine nearly always puts in the mouths of his characters only those metaphors and similes which would be natural under the circumstances of their utterance. Here it is he who is the severe realist; and hence we, who are accustomed to splendid imagery in poetry, think his lines flat and unpoetic. Their poetry is of another sort, rare in English literature: the sort that we occasionally find in lines of Wordsworth like

> For old, unhappy, far-off things,
> And battles long ago;

or in Rossetti's translation of a line of Dante,

> We were alone and without any fear,

—a perfect union of precision, clarity, and euphony.[1]

---

[1] John C. Bailey in his volume of condescending criticism, *The Claims of French Poetry,* points out that Racine has no sense of the infinite with its wonder and its mystery, no deep and broad view of life, no strange or great thoughts, no fine surprises of language, no detailed and intimate delight in nature such as we encounter in Homer, Virgil, Shakespeare, Aeschylus, Sophocles, Dante, and Goethe, and maintains that writing which lacks these characteristics is not the highest poetry. That is doubtless true, but writing which lacks them may at least be poetry. Bailey would perhaps admit that the opening lines of Tennyson's *Oenone,*

> There lies a vale in Ida, lovelier
> Than all the valleys of Ionian hills,

are poetry, though little save the sheer music of the words distinguishes them from the bald prose statement, "There is a valley in East Tennessee more beautiful than any in Vermont." A whole poem could conceivably be made up of lines as simple as those quoted from Tennyson, and yet be charming, if it were all equally musical. And when lines of no less exquisite

Effective verse translation, especially in the case of a poet of such alien genius, must be content to compromise and approximate. In rendering Racine, I have used the rhymed iambic pentameter couplet. It is the best English analogue of the French alexandrine. It was the prevalent verse form in our own "classical" period, when English literature was somewhat under the influence of French "classical" literature, of which Racine was the culmination; and hence it naturally associates itself in our minds with the ideas and art of French classicism. Moreover, the same consideration which led Gilbert Murray to employ it in translating Greek tragedies is of still greater importance in translating Racine: its rhymes retain for it some effect of poetry even where the language is very simple, whereas in English blank verse as a rule "the language has to be tortured a little, or it will read like prose."

For most of us, the old "heroic couplet" of Dryden, Pope, and Dr. Johnson is distasteful because of its monotonous swing and heavily clashing rhymes. These unpleasant features can be avoided in two ways: by making the pauses occur in the middle instead of at the end of a line, and by using imperfect rhymes. I have freely availed myself of both devices.

As regards the "language of gallantry" which we find so difficult to accept in Racine, I have somewhat toned it down, occasionally by omitting it altogether, and frequently by employing a conventional English turn of expression which better conveys to us the effect of Racine's phrasing on French ears than literal translation could succeed in doing. Thus

verbal melody are the vehicle of plays in which masterful dramaturgic skill presents gripping situations and acutely psychologized characters, no formula of any critic can gainsay the immense value of the achievement or the extreme greatness of the author.

"glance" has been used conventionally in English much as Racine uses "eye" or "eyes."

I have appropriated words or phrases now and then from the old Bohn Library blank verse translation of Racine by R. B. Boswell—e.g. in the heroine's address to the sun in Act I of *Phèdre*; but I find, on subsequent comparison of Boswell's version of the plays with mine, that much more often we have quite independently made the same or closely similar departures from a literal rendering of our original.

Stage directions are at times altered, enlarged, or added for the sake of greater clearness or vividness.

To M. Georges Bally, Assistant Professor of French at Vanderbilt University, and to Miss Louise Allen my indebtedness for assistance in this translation of Racine's masterpieces is very great. Without M. Bally's encouragement it would not have been attempted, and he has overseen it throughout with unfailing patience and kindness. In putting Racine into English verse I have been guided by Miss Allen's fine sense of literary values to only a slightly less extent than in my translation of the *Inferno* of Dante. I wish to express also my appreciation of the assistance of Miss V. O. King in proof-reading.

LACY LOCKERT.

ANDROMAQUE
(ANDROMACHE)

INTRODUCTION

AS a memorable event in the history of the French stage, the first performance of *Andromaque* yields in importance only to that of Corneille's *Cid* and perhaps that of Victor Hugo's *Hernani*. The enthusiasm which Racine's play aroused was scarcely less great than the furor created by the *Cid*; the fashionable theatre-goers of 1667-8 could think of nothing but the Trojan heroine and her sorrows. In the nineteenth century *Andromaque* was acted more times than any other tragedy of its author.

Few dramas have achieved such continuous tension and so many startling effects with an equal economy of means. Each of the four major characters is ruled by a single emotion. Orestes loves Hermione to distraction, who in turn is infatuated with Pyrrhus, her betrothed, who has conceived an overmastering passion for his Trojan captive, Andromache, whose own heart is with her dead husband, Hector. Pyrrhus tells Andromache that he will kill her child if she will not marry him, and on her hesitation to take this step, to which her fears as a mother urge her, and from which her instincts as a devoted widow make her shrink, the action of the play depends. When she encourages Pyrrhus, he forsakes Hermione, who in wild frenzy of outraged pride and jealous love has to fall back upon Orestes, who thereupon is beside himself with joy and hope; when she repulses Pyrrhus, she drives him into the arms of the enraptured Hermione, who then disdains Orestes, who becomes frantic with rage and despair. Notwithstanding the decorous language and the smooth flow of the polished alexandrines in which they speak, the struggle of these tormented souls is nothing less than that of "wildcats in a red-hot iron cage." Unfriendly critics of French classical drama have complained that it portrays types rather than individuals. But Orestes, Pyrrhus, and Hermione are living, individualized figures, were it only by reason of their appalling vileness, pettiness, and malevolence. Suffering makes them hateful. When it seems that Hermione is to wed Pyrrhus after all, Orestes plans to abduct her that she may not be happy while he himself is miserable. Pyrrhus, in announcing his decision to marry her, wantonly tortures Orestes; and later, when he has broken his word and is about to espouse Andromache instead, he cannot keep away from the woman he has betrayed. As for Hermione, her position is piteous, but she is no "sympathetic" victim of man's perfidy. The strain and agony of the situation in which she is placed have keyed her nerves to the snapping-point and brought out all the hardness and unloveliness in her nature. It was she who, before the play opens, incited Greece to demand the life of the infant Astyanax. In the face of all evidence and argument, she persists in regarding Andromache as her voluntary "rival," and hates her accordingly. She tries to hold Orestes that she may have some one in reserve if her hopes are finally defeated; but her claws are quick to wound him when he maladroitly says that Pyrrhus disdains her; and when she presently feels that her wedding is sure to take place, she dismisses him and his anguish from her mind with the impatient question, "Have we no theme, except his sighs, for cheer?" and in that hour of her seeming triumph, when Andromache implores her to save Astyanax, nothing could be more venomous than her sweetly-phrased refusal.

The character of Hermione is, in fact, the finest thing in the play; she may almost be said to "make" the play; Racine has done scarcely anything else so brilliant. She is one quivering compound of intense emotions, veering impulses, unreason, and vicious spite—utterly feminine and eternally real.

Pyrrhus and Orestes, also, are in essence true to life, though in their case universal human nature is tricked out in the garments of a highly mannered, artificial civilization, as different as can well be imagined from that heroic and legendary age of Greece to which they properly belong. There is not much "local colour" in the secular dramas of Racine. Some of his characters, like Hermione, have few traits peculiar to people of his own land and times; some have many; but none of them has an appreciable number which are *not* those of seventeenth century French men and women but are instead distinctive of the country and period in which the scene is laid. Taine and Benjamin W. Wells have pointed out that Pyrrhus's conception of love is "that of the *précieux* salons of Paris and of the courtiers of Versailles, with a certain decorum in its outward expression, with happily turned phrases, and insinuating attenuations that mask with a certain courtliness the fundamental brutality of his absolute power." Orestes, indeed, is something more than a conventional young prince of the dramatist's own day who is disappointed in love; but that something more is not ancient but, strange to say, prophetically modern. As Jules Lemaître has shown in a very acute piece of critical writing, Orestes is an anticipation of the characteristic hero of the age of romanticism, a melancholy egoist who considers himself uniquely persecuted by heaven and hence a man apart, not subject to the same responsibilities as other men. But his creator, unlike Chataubriand, Hugo, and the elder Dumas, does not solicit our admiration for such a person; he represents him, rightly, as a potentially criminal weakling.

It is a commonplace of criticism that after the two plays of his novitiate, *La Thébaïde* and *Alexandre le Grand,* Racine attained to full stature of genius at a single bound and gave to his country a new type of tragedy, his own peculiar type, with simple plot, natural characters swayed by universal human passions, and (for the French "classical" stage) a minimum of conventions;—that this type was at once originated and perfected in *Andromaque,* a masterpiece which stands on an essential parity with his very best subsequent work. The truth is somewhat less spectacular, as truth is wont to be. Others before Racine—notably Rotrou and Tristan l'Hermite—had portrayed with considerable success men and women mastered by genuine, passionate love; Tristan had used simple plots, with no more conventions than Racine and with far greater regard for certain kinds of realism. And, moreover, *Andromaque* has a larger share of the artificialities which then characterized French tragedy than can be found in any subsequent play of Racine.

This is true, for instance, as regards its preciosity of diction, marked by "an incredible abuse of the word *yeux*"[1] and such extravagances of the language of gallantry as the declaration of Pyrrhus that the flames of love with which he burns for Andromache are fiercer than the flames of burning Troy. Again, with each of the four chief characters—Andromache, Pyrrhus, Hermione, and Orestes—is associated one of those insipid, colourless figures known to the French stage as "confidants," who have no personality of their own but exist solely to listen to their respective principals, to inform them, advise them, and sympathize with them, and to do their bidding. And the very dilemma of Hector's widowed wife, which is the mainspring of the action, owes its poignancy to feelings which are not of all time but of an age.

Andromache might, indeed, not unnaturally have found it very difficult to bring herself to wed Pyrrhus, because he was associated in her memory with the horrors of the sack of

---

[1] In the present translation frequently rendered not "eyes" but "glance" or in some other way.

Troy. She alleges this obstacle once in a brief reference to it in the first act and once at length in an eloquent speech near the end of Act III. That it was what she felt she ought to feel, rather than what she did feel, and that she did not instinctively shrink from Pyrrhus for this or any other reason, is made sufficiently clear by the rest of the play. In the first place, as critics have frequently pointed out, she appeals constantly to his love for her in every way that she can without committing herself; she would find such a course intolerable if he really were repulsive to her. Furthermore, Pylades' report indicates that after the murder of Pyrrhus she mourns him with genuine affection; and this fact was brought out unmistakably in a scene which the author included in his original version of Act V but afterwards suppressed as dramaturgically defective. It was because of her belief that to wed again would be a disloyalty to Hector's ashes that she refused marriage with Pyrrhus even when it seemed the only way to save the son whom she had borne to Hector. The best that can be said for such a viewpoint is that it was in keeping with the ideas of the pastoral and gallant romances, with the notions of the salons of Paris, which are reflected in the drama as well as in the social life of the period. Natural, rational, sane, it is not. The more Andromache loved Hector, the more precious should the life of their child have seemed to her, and the more readily should she have sacrificed any personal repugnances with the feeling that by the preservation of that child she could be most truly loyal to its father.[2]

When the issue presently becomes unescapable, the solution which Andromache finds for it is no less preposterous than

[2] Cf., in contrast, Euripides' beautiful portrait of Andromache in *The Trojan Women*. Faced with the prospect of having to be not Pyrrhus' wife in honourable marriage but his mere concubine, she, too, shrinks from

was her attitude which drew its lines so sharply. She will consent to wed Pyrrhus, she tells her confidante, and will make him swear in turn to protect her son, and then, as soon as the marriage ceremony is over, she will kill herself. It never seems to occur to her that Pyrrhus may very probably, and reasonably, think that he is in no way obligated to keep a bargain of which she has kept only the letter, not the spirit at all; or that he, too, might keep only the letter of it and find a savage satisfaction in thus amply revenging his disappointed hopes—perhaps, for instance, by guarding the child "safely" in a tower, without food or drink, like Ugolino and his sons. It does not seem even to occur to her that Pyrrhus, who for her sake must become irrevocably embroiled with the whole of Greece, will not be thankful for merely being able to call himself her husband for a few minutes. In contrasting *Andromaque* with the extravagant dramas which immediately preceded it, Jules Lemaître selects as an example of their absurdities the rapture of the hero of Thomas Corneille's

such a sequel to her dear union with Hector, but is advised by Hecuba to make the best of the inevitable, so as to ensure her son's being well treated. Then she is told that the Greeks have decided to kill him. Her first, immediate words are: "Oh, I could have borne mine enemy's bed!"

The "dilemma" of Racine's Andromache is taken straight from *Pertharite*, one of the most far-fetched and unnatural of Corneille's tragedies in the period of his degeneration as a dramatic artist. This and other parallels in the relations of four of its characters with each other to those of the four major characters in *Andromaque* were first pointed out by Voltaire. Like similarities can be found with Thomas Corneille's *Mort de l'Empereur Commode* and *Camma*. H. C. Lancaster, in his *History of French Dramatic Literature in the Seventeenth Century*, Part IV, pp. 54-55, has noted these and many more parallels between details in *Andromaque* and in earlier French "classical" plays, and there are yet others. Daniel Mornet has tried to show that all of Racine's tragedies draw heavily upon the work of his immediate predecessors, but Mornet can assemble no such list of similarities in the case of any of the rest of them. The fact is that in *Andromaque* Racine took details right and left from these predecessors, and into this body of romanesque material breathed a fierce breath of life.

Timocrate when he finds that he will be wedded to the woman he loves and then be killed directly afterwards. But almost the identical absurdity which Lemaître ridicules in *Timocrate* is to be found in *Andromaque*! In charging Cephissa, who will survive her, to see that Pyrrhus does not break his word, Andromache says:

> Make him appreciate
> The marriage which I grant him.[3]

At the end of the drama "all who gave way to passion have perished in body or in mind," observes B. W. Wells. "Andromache alone remains, because she alone has not been passion's fool." But soberly considered, Andromache might with justice be described in the phrase of Shakespeare's Thersites as "a fool positive."

And yet—so strangely wise is genius even when most perversely astray—the folly of Andromache is self-consistent. If any woman could be capable of one phase of it, she might perhaps be capable of it all. It all admits of a single explanation: that Andromache's mind deals almost entirely—as every one's does to some extent—with words, which are but the names of real things, instead of dealing with the realities themselves. Pyrrhus wants to marry her; well, if she "marries" him, she satisfies his wish! She will have "kept her bargain" (the words of it); he will keep his. If, in spite of herself, she should live after the wedding (as in fact she does), Pyrrhus, alive or dead, is her "husband," and that makes her love him. She loved Hector and cannot bear to "be

---

[3] In their point of likeness, the heroine of *Andromaque* is really more absurd than the hero of *Timocrate*. He, like many lovers but to a greater degree than they, *feels* extravagantly; she bases her plans on the *belief* that some one else will feel thus, and thinks it only natural and right that he should.

untrue to his memory"; it would be "untrue to his memory" to "wed another husband"; therefore she cannot "wed another husband"—circumstances make no difference. Her eventual decision, to marry Pyrrhus and then immediately take her own life, is not at variance with the rest; her suicide would punish and atone for her "disloyalty" to Hector in submitting to the ceremony, and she would be dead (she thinks) before she could begin to love Pyrrhus as "her husband." So bizarre a figure is not very convincing, yet is perhaps sufficiently plausible to be allowed in a drama; but to fill the rôle of the sympathetic heroine—that is another matter! The tragedy in which this character is presented in that rôle cannot rightly be accounted a genuine masterpiece and one of the great plays of the world; it is, rather, a superb, an astonishing *tour-de-force*.[4]

---

[4] Émile Faguet maintains that Racine purposely represented Andromache as "passion's fool," and that he did not intend her "stratagem" to be regarded as a well-advised plan but merely as the utmost concession to which she can force herself for her son's sake, and one in the efficacy of which she believes because she wishes to believe in it. In answer it may be said: (1) that Cephissa's failure to point out the absurdity of Andromache's plan shows that Racine did not think it absurd or expect his audiences to do so; (2) that her plan was in keeping with the fantastic conceptions prevalent in the upper-class seventeenth century French society that read Madeleine de Scudéry's romances and went to plays like *Timocrate*; and (3) that even if Faguet's interpretation is correct, Racine has none the less blundered, for among people who are not steeped in the pseudo-classical tradition a "heroine" who is so foolish and self-indulgent and unmotherly will elicit irritation or disgust more often than such sympathy as the artistic effect demands for her.

CHARACTERS IN THE PLAY

ANDROMACHE, *widow of Hector; captive of Pyrrhus.*

PYRRHUS, *son of Achilles; King of Epirus.*

ORESTES, *son of Agamemnon; former suitor of Hermione, whom he still loves.*

HERMIONE, *daughter of Menelaus and Helen, the King and Queen of Sparta; affianced bride of Pyrrhus.*

PYLADES, *friend of Orestes.*

CLEONE, *female attendant of Hermione.*

CEPHISSA, *faithful friend of Andromache.*

PHOENIX, *aged counsellor of Pyrrhus.*

FOLLOWERS OF ORESTES.

The scene is laid in the palace of Pyrrhus at Buthrotum, a city of Epirus.

ANDROMACHE

ACT I

The scene shows a palace with columns, and in the back-
ground the sea, with some ships. Enter ORESTES *and*
PYLADES.

ORESTES.

Yes, now that I regain so true a friend,
My fortune wears a new face, and doth mend
With wrath already softened, since her care
Was taken thus to re-unite us here.
Who would have thought that when I reached a shore
Fatal to all my longings, 'twould restore
Pylades to Orestes' sight?—that when
Six months I had lost thee, Pyrrhus' court again
Would give thee back to me?

PYLADES.

                            Thanks render I
For this to heaven, which persistently
Had thwarted me, until it seemed quite barred
Was my return to Greece, since that ill-starred
Day when the waves waxed angry to divide
Our vessels, with Epirus nearly spied.
Parted from thee, ah, what anxieties
I suffered! Tears how many have mine eyes
Given to thy misfortunes and the fear
Thou mettest new dangers which I could not share.
I most of all dreaded that gloom wherein
Thy soul was plunged, as I so long have seen.

I dreaded lest heaven should offer, cruelly kind,
The death to thee for which thy heart has pined
Always. But I once more behold thee, sir;
And (dare I say it?) the fate is happier
That leads thee to Epirus. The rich train
Following thy steps is not of one who fain,
Since he is so unfortunate, would die.

ORESTES.

Alas, who can divine the destiny
That brings me hither! Love constraineth me
To seek a heartless woman, but its decree
Who knoweth, or if I life or death shall find?

PYLADES.

What! is thy soul a slave whom love doth bind,
That on it thus thy whole existence hangs?
How art ensorcelled that, with all the pangs
Forgot that once were thine, thou art disposed
To wear again its chains? Hast thou supposed
That, though in Sparta cruel, Hermione
Will in Epirus be more kind to thee?
Ashamed of having with thy prayers addressed her
In vain so long, thou camest to detest her,
Until thou wouldst not even speak of her
To me. 'Tis clear, thou didst deceive me, sir.

ORESTES.

Myself did I deceive. Friend, do not tread
On one forlorn who loves thee. Have I hid,
Ever, my heart from thee, or my desire?
Thou sawest me first with longing set on fire;
And when his daughter Menelaus gave
To Pyrrhus who avenged him,[1] sawest me rave

In my despair; and hast observed me since,
The while from sea to sea I dragged my chains
Of love and sorrow. I regretfully
Beheld thee ever fain to follow me
In this sad state, my frenzy's rage to stay,
And from myself to save me every day.
But when I thought of how, while I endured
Such agonies, Hermione outpoured
On Pyrrhus all her store of bounties, then
Thou knowest how anger seized me; her disdain
I would requite with my forgetfulness.
I convinced others, and myself no less,
That I was mine own master, now. I thought
My passion that of hate. I held as naught
Her charms, and cursed her for her cruelty,
Defied her glance again to trouble me,
And deemed that I had quenched my love.
                                                   To Greece
Did I return with soul that seemed at peace,
And found her princes were together met
As though disturbed by dangers new and great.
I flew to them. I hoped, 'mid glorious wars,
To fill my mind with different, nobler cares,
To gain anew my spirit's former zest,
And love's last remnant drive from out my breast.
But join with me to marvel how the fate
That ever hounds me made me hurry straight
Into the snare I fain would shun. I heard
Everywhere threats 'gainst Pyrrhus. He had stirred
To murmurs the whole land. Complaint is loud
That, heedless of his blood and what he vowed,
He rears the foe of Greece beside his throne,
Astyanax, the hapless little son

Of Hector, and the last of all that race
Of kings who have 'neath Troy their resting place.
Andromache, to save his life, beguiled
The shrewd Ulysses, and another child,
Supposed to be Astyanax, let him tear
From her and put to death.[2] All this I hear,
And more: that Pyrrhus for Hermione
Cares little, and that elsewhere offers he
Both heart and crown. Though Menelaus will
Not credit the report, he likes it ill,
And that the marriage is so long delayed.

E'en while his soul with trouble is o'erweighed,
A secret joy is born in mine, and yet
I tell myself at first that naught is it
But vengeance that so thrills me. Very soon
Within my breast reigned the disdainful one
Again. Too well I knew that smouldering fire.
I saw 'twould not be long before mine ire
Had run its course. Rather, I saw instead
I had always loved her. I solicited
The choice of all the Greeks. So was I sent
To Pyrrhus; I assumed the charge, and went.
I am to try to wrest from out his arms
This child whose life so many States alarms;
But oh, if I, made bold by passion's sway,
Instead of Hector's son might bring away
My princess! Dream not any peril could
Dampen mine ardour, now twofold renewed.
Since all my struggles have proved vain, I let
Myself be blindly driven on by fate.
I love Hermione; I am seeking her
Here in these halls to move her heart, to bear
Her hence, or die before her eyes. Thou who

Dost Pyrrhus know, what thinkest thou he will do?
What taketh place within his Court, within
His breast? Does my Hermione retain
Her power o'er him, Pylades, or will he
Give back the prize that he hath snatched from me?

PYLADES.

I should deceive thee, dared I promise, sir,
That to thy hands he would surrender her,
Although his pride at winning her is scant.
His soul on Hector's widow is intent.
He loves her. But that cold, bereavèd one
As yet repayeth his love with hate alone,
And each day seeth him try every art
To melt or gain by fear his captive's heart.
He hides her child from her, threatens his life,
Makes flow, then staunches straight, her tears of grief;
And many a time Hermione hath viewed
Her lover turn to her again in mood
Exasperate and lay before her feet
The homage of his vows, impelled by heat
Of love less than of rage. Expect not, then,
Assurance of a heart that nowise can
Control itself. He may, to madness moved,
Wed one he loathes and injure one beloved.

ORESTES.

But tell me how Hermione sees now
Her marriage deferred, her charms esteemed so low.

PYLADES.

Hermione appeareth outwardly
Heedless of her betrothed's inconstancy,
As sure that never need she bend her pride,

For he will beg her yet to be his bride;
But she with tears hath unto me complained.
She weeps in secret that she is disdained.
Always will she depart, hath always stayed.
Sometimes she calls Orestes to her aid.

ORESTES.

Ah, if I could believe it, I would fly
To cast myself . . .

PYLADES.

Discharge thine embassy.
Thou dost await the King. 'Gainst Hector's son
Let thy words show him, sir, Greece leagued as one.
Far from surrendering unto them the child
Of her he loves, he will be only filled
With tenderer passion by their hate. The more
'Tis sought to part them, they are joined more sure.
Urge him. Insist on everything, to gain
Nothing. He comes.

ORESTES.

So be it! But go, then,
And move anew my cruel torturer
To see a lover who seeks only her.
[*Exit* PYLADES. *Enter* PYRRHUS *and* PHOENIX.

ORESTES (*to* PYRRHUS).

Ere all the Greeks address thee by my voice,
Let me declare myself, in being their choice,
Fortunate, sir, and tell thee of my joy
To see Achilles' son, taker of Troy.
Thy deeds, like his, we view admiringly:
Hector fell before him, Troy before thee;

And thou hast shown, by bravery and success,
None but Achilles' child could fill his place.
    But that which he would ne'er have done, with grief
Doth Greece behold thee do: afford relief
To the misfortunes of the Trojan strain,
Be touched with ill-timed pity, and sustain
The remnant which long war hath left their cause.
Hast thou forgotten, sir, what Hector was?
Our decimated folk remember well.
His name alone makes wives and daughters quail,
And in all Greece there are no families
Who do not from this wretched son of his
Demand a reckoning for sire or spouse
Whom they have lost through Hector. And who knows
To what his offspring may some day set hand?[3]
We yet may see him on our ports descend
And burn, as we have seen his father do,
Our ships, and brandishing a torch, pursue
Their flight across the waves. Sir, shall I dare
To speak my thought? Thou thyself for thy care
Of him shouldst dread the recompense. Fear lest
This serpent which thou rearest in thy breast,
For saving him, shall some day serve thee ill.
Then give thou unto all the Greeks their will.
Assure their vengeance. Thine own life assure.
Destroy a foe from whom thou hast the more
Danger since he, ere war with them, would make
Trial of arms 'gainst thee.

PYRRHUS.

      Greece for my sake
Is much too anxious. I imagined her
Concerned o'er things of greater moment, sir,

And thought her projects would be grander far,
Hearing the name of her ambassador.
Who would suppose, indeed, that this affair
Deserved the intervention of the heir
Of Agamemnon, or that an entire
People, so oft victorious, would conspire
Against a child's life? As a sacrifice
To whom, then, must I slay him? Unto Greece?
Hath Greece some right still o'er him, and alone
Of Greeks can I not deal with, as mine own,
A captive given me by lot, withal?
Yea, sir, when underneath the smoking wall
Of Troy the blood-stained conquerors divided
Their spoil, the lot that each man's share decided
Then gave Andromache and her son to me.
Ulysses filled the cup of misery
For Hecuba.[4] Thy sire to Argos bore
Cassandra. Have I yet o'er them or o'er
Their captives claimed authority? Have I
E'er touched the guerdon of their bravery?
    'Tis feared, forsooth, that Hector and hence Troy
May live again some day, and that this boy,
Hector's, may rob me of the light I spare
Unto his eyes. Sir, 'tis excessive care
That such great prudence showeth. I have no skill
Thus to conceive a so-far-distant ill.
I call to mind how stood that city once
With her proud ramparts and heroic sons,
Mistress of Asia; then consider I
What lot was Troy's and what her destiny.
I see but prostrate towers covered o'er
With ashes, now, a river red with gore,
Waste fields, a child in chains; nor can I deem

That Troy, so fallen, cherishes a dream
Of vengeance. Yet if death had for the son
Of Hector truly been resolved upon,
Why hath it been deferred this whole year past?
Could not the sword have pierced him on the breast
Of Priam? With so many others dead,
'Neath ruined Troy he should have slept instead.
All was permitted then. Both infancy
And age alike on weakness did rely
Vainly to shield them. Victory and night,
More cruel than we, were potent to incite
Our hearts to slaughter, and to wanton blows
Our swords. My wrath against our vanquished foes
Was but too fierce. Yet shall my cruelty
Outlive my rage? Must I deliberately,
Though now my soul, touched with a milder mood,
Feels pity, dip my hands in a child's blood?
Nay, sir; let Greece find other prey. Let her
Pursue the remnant left of Troy elsewhere.
My hate hath run its course; 'tis at an end.
What war hath spared, Epirus will defend.

ORESTES.

Full well thou knowest, sir, by what trickery
A false Astyanax was sent to die
Instead of Hector's only son. 'Tis not
The Trojans, it is Hector that is sought.
Yea, the Greeks hound the father in the child.
He won their wrath with blood too freely spilled.
Naught can efface it save his blood alone,
And e'en to Epirus it can lead them on.
Do thou act first.

PYRRHUS.

Nay, I accept with joy
That prospect. Let them seek another Troy
Here in Epirus. Let them in blind hate
Distinguish him no longer who of late
Made them be conquerors, from the conquered. This
Is not the first injustice wherewith Greece
The service of Achilles did repay.[5]
It availed Hector once, sir, and some day
It may avail his offspring equally.

ORESTES.

So Greece hath a rebellious child in thee?

PYRRHUS.

And is it but to follow at her beck
That I have triumphed?

ORESTES.

Hermione will check
Thy course, my lord. Her glance will interfere
Between her sire and thee.

PYRRHUS.

However dear
Hermione may always be to me,
To love her does not mean that I must be
Her father's slave. I still may reconcile
The claims of love and honour. Yet some while
Shalt thou see Helen's daughter. I know what tie
Of blood unites you. After that, sir, I
Shall not detain thee further; and thou mayst
Say to the Greeks I will not do their hest.

[*Exit* ORESTES.

PHOENIX.

Thou sendest him thus to his belovèd's feet!

PYRRHUS (*with casual indifference*).

Long did he languish for the princess, it
Is said.

PHOENIX.

But what, sir, if that fire now were
Rekindled, and he gave his heart to her
Again? What if he won her heart thereby?

PYRRHUS.

Ah, let them love each other, Phoenix! I
Oppose it not. Let her go hence. Aflame
With mutual madness each for each, let them
Return to Sparta. All our ports give free
Exit to him and her alike. For me
How much constraint and weariness 'twould heal!

PHOENIX.

My lord . . .

PYRRHUS.

Another time I shall reveal
My soul to thee. Andromache is here.
[*Exit* PHOENIX. *Enter* ANDROMACHE *and* CEPHISSA.
Thou seekest me, madam? May a hope so fair
Be mine?

ANDROMACHE.

I go but to the place where they
Keep my son.[6] Seeing thou only once a day
Permittest me to look on the single joy
Left to me still from Hector and from Troy,

I go to weep with him a little space.
Not yet since yesterday hath my embrace
Clasped him.

PYRRHUS.

Nay, if I did but heed their fears,
The Greeks would give thee soon new cause for tears,
Madam.

ANDROMACHE.

And what is this anxiety
With which their hearts are smitten? Can it be,
My lord, some Trojan hath escaped?

PYRRHUS.

Not dead
Yet is their hate toward Hector; and they dread
His son.

ANDROMACHE.

O worthy cause for their dismay—
A hapless child, who knows not to this day
That he is Hector's offspring, nor that thou,
Sir, art his master!

PYRRHUS.

Howsoever, now
All Greece demands that he shall die. The son
Of Agamemnon comes to importune
His death at once.

ANDROMACHE.

Wilt thou accord so grim
A sentence? Ah, is it my love for him
That makes him guilty? No one is afraid

He will some day avenge his father dead.
'Tis feared that he will from his mother's face
Wipe the tears. He could take for me the place
Of sire and husband. But I needs must lose
All, and at thy hands always.[7]

PYRRHUS.

I did refuse,
Madam, and therefore needless are thy tears.
Greece threatens me already with her spears.
But though a thousand ships o'erpass the sea[8]
Once more to seek thy son,—yea, even though he
Cost all the blood that Helen made to flow,—
Though I behold my palace halls laid low,
After ten years, in ashes, still would I
Not falter; still I to thine aid would fly.
I would defend his life, though with mine own!
    But 'mid these perils to be undergone
For thy sake, look more kindly upon me!
Still must I strive against thy cruelty,
Now, when assailed on all sides and abhorred
By all the Greeks? I offer thee my sword.
May I not hope that thou wilt also take
A heart that worships thee? When for thy sake
I battle, shall not this be mine: nowise
To number thee among mine enemies?

ANDROMACHE.

My lord, what makest thou? What will Greece say?
Must a heart so magnanimous needs display
Such weakness? Wouldst thou have so brave and good
A purpose laid to a mad lover's mood?
Wouldst fain Andromache, a captive, grieving

Eternally and wearied out with living,
Should love thee? Those unhappy eyes of hers,
Which thou hast doomed to everlasting tears,—
What charms do they possess for thee? No, no!
To reverence the misery of a foe,
To save the unfortunate, to render back
A son unto his mother and for his sake
To oppose a hundred peoples' cruelty
Without requiring that my heart shall be
The price of saving him—'gainst my will, if needs
Must, to protect him—these, my lord, are deeds
Worthy of Achilles' son.

PYRRHUS.

What! Hath thine ire
Not run its course? Can any without tire
Hate and for ever punish? True, much teen
I wrought, and oft these hands hath Phrygia seen
Dyed with the blood of those akin to thee.
But oh, how sore thine eyes have wounded me![9]
How very dearly they have made me pay
For tears they shed! have rendered me the prey
Of what remorse! I suffer all the pain
I dealt at Troy. Vanquished, with chain on chain
Fettered, torn by regrets, burning with fires
Fiercer than those I kindled, such desires
Unquiet, such tears, and such anxiety—
Alas! so cruel as thou, was ever I?
But each of us in turn sufficient woes
Hath on the other brought. Our common foes
Ought to unite us. Grant me nothing more,
Madam, save only hope. I will restore
Thy son to thee. I will be to him now

A father. I myself will teach him how
To avenge his countrymen. I will requite
Greece for your wrongs and mine. Give me the light
Of one glance, and I all can undertake.
Thine Ilium shall from the dust awake
Once more. The Greeks less swiftly cast them down
Than I within those walls new-reared shall crown
Thy child.

ANDROMACHE.

Such honours can no longer stir
My heart. I vowed them his when lived his sire.
Nay, ye look not to see us any more,
Dear, sacred walls that did not have the power
To save my Hector! Wretches are content
With lesser boons. It is our banishment
I ask of thee with tears. Oh, suffer me
Far from the Greeks to go, far even from thee,
To hide my son and for my husband mourn.
Thy love doth win us too much hate. Return,
Return to Helen's daughter!

PYRRHUS.

Madam, can
I do so? Ah, thou rackest me with what pain!
How shall I give her back a heart which thou
Dost captive hold? I know that I did vow
Its empery to her. I know that she
Came to Epirus as the queen-to-be.
Fate chose to bring you both together here,
Her to give slavery's chains, and thee to bear
Its yoke. But have I sought to make her glad?
Would not one rather say, on seeing instead

Thy charms supreme and hers held in disdain,
That she is captive here, and thou dost reign?
Oh, with what joy one sigh of all I breathed
For thee, if given her, would be received!

ANDROMACHE.

Wherefore unwelcome would she find thy sighs?
Hath she forgotten thy past services?
Do Troy and Hector make her shrink from thee,
And oweth she to a husband's memory
Her love? And what a husband, too! Ah, dire
To think of: 'twas *his* death that gave thy sire
Immortal fame! He gained his whole renown
From Hector's blood. Both thou and he are known
But at my tears' expense![10]

PYRRHUS.

So be it! so!
I must obey thee, must forget thee—no,
Rather must hate thee, for my passion's force
Hath grown too frenzied to end now its course
In mere indifference. Think well hereof:
My heart henceforward, if it doth not love
To madness, shall to madness hate. No stay
My righteous wrath shall know. The son must pay
The reckoning for his mother's scorn to me.
Greece doth demand him, nor as formerly
Do I intend to find my glory in
Preserving the ungrateful.

ANDROMACHE.

Alas, then,
He needs must die. He hath for his defence
His mother's tears and his sweet innocence—

Naught else. And after all, this lot of mine
Being what it is, perchance his death shall win
A speedier end of all my sorrows. I
Have borne for him my life and misery.
But in his steps now I shall follow close
To see once more his father. We shall thus,
All three of us, by thee again made one,
To thee . . .

PYRRHUS.

       Go, madam, go unto thy son.
Mayhap thy heart, when once thine eyes have spied
His face, will grow more timorous, nor a guide
Make of its wrath for ever. I shall return
Unto thee presently, that I may learn
Our fates. When thou within thine arms fast caught
Dost hold him, let his safety be thy thought.

                    [Exeunt severally.

ACT II

The scene is the same. HERMIONE *and* CLEONE *are discovered.*

HERMIONE.

I do as thou desirest. I consent
That he shall see me. I will yield, and grant
This joy still to him. Pylades will lead
His footsteps hither soon. But did I heed
Mine own misgivings, I would shun his sight.

CLEONE.

And what ill doth his face portend, what blight,
For thee? Is he not that Orestes yet
Whose constancy and love thou wouldst regret,
Madam?—for whose return thou oft hast prayed?

HERMIONE.

That love, which I have all too ill repaid,
It is which maketh his presence in this place
So hard for me to bear. Ah, what disgrace
For me, what triumph for him, now to behold
Mine evil fortune match his woes of old!
"Is this the proud Hermione?" he will scoff.
"Once she disdained me; she hath been cast off,
Herself now, by another. She must learn,
Who set a high price on her heart, in turn
To suffer scorn." Ah gods!

CLEONE.

                Nay, give thou o'er
These empty fears. He knoweth too well the power
Of thy fair charms. Dost thou suppose that he

Who loves thee comes with insults unto thee?
He bringeth back to thee a soul whereout
He could not tear thee. But thou sayest not
What is thy sire's command.

HERMIONE.

If Pyrrhus still
Doth make delays, and if consent he will
Not give to put the Trojan boy to death,
Home with the Greeks my father ordereth
That I return.

CLEONE.

Sayst thou? Then, madam, hear
Orestes. Seeing that Pyrrhus doth his share
Of these things, fail not thou to do the rest.
To anticipate him would indeed be best.
Didst thou not own thou hatest him to me?

HERMIONE.

Hate him, Cleone? All my dignity,
My honour, is at stake, such kindness I
Have shown to him, whereof all memory
He yet hath lost—yea, e'en he that was so
Dear to me, and who could betray me. Oh,
Too much I have loved him, not to hate him now!

CLEONE.

Take flight, then, madam, from him; and since thou
Art worshipped . . .

HERMIONE.

Nay, give my wrath time to swell
Yet greater. Let me find a heart of steel.
Cleone, it is terrible to bring

Myself to leave him. And that very thing
Contrives he but too well, the faithless one!

CLEONE.

What! Waitest thou some fresh insult to be shown?
To love a captive—yea, before thine eyes
To love her—cannot even this suffice
To make him odious to thee? What more
Than he hath done, thinkest thou is in his power?
He would have angered, could he anger thee!

HERMIONE.

O cruel, why wilt thou further torture me?
I do not dare to think upon the plight
In which I am. Of all that meets thy sight,
Strive thou to credit naught. Believe that I
No longer love, and vaunt my victory.
Believe that in contempt for him my heart
Is hard. Alas, and if thou hast the art,
Make me believe it!
                    Thou wouldst have me flee
From him? So be it! Nothing hinders me.
Away then! Let us envy not again
His shameful prize. Let her that wears the chain
Bind him in bondage with it. Let us fly . . .
    But what if to his duty by and by
He should return; if faith should find once more
Place in his breast; if he should come to implore
His pardon at my feet; if 'neath my sway,
Love, thou couldst bind him; if he wished . . . But nay!
He only seeks to flout me. None the less,
Let us bide here to mar their happiness.
Let us find some delight in thwarting them,

Or make him clearly seen, by driving him
To break his solemn oath, a perjured one
In the eyes of all the Greeks. Upon the son
Already I have drawn their hate. I would
Have them yet ask of him the mother's blood.
The torments she hath caused me, let us pay
Back to her. May she be his ruin! May
He, better still, cause her to die, instead!

CLEONE.

Thinkest thou that eyes, then, which for ever shed
Tears would contest thy beauty's sovereignty,
Or that a heart so bowed by misery
Soliciteth her persecutor's love?
Look if her sorrows have found help thereof.
Nay, wherefore is her spirit thus sunk in woe?
Why doth she to a favoured suitor show
Such coldness?

HERMIONE (*disregarding* CLEONE'S *questions*).

Ah, 'tis mine unhappy lot,
Too well I have hearkened to him![11] I did not
Through silence clothe myself with mystery.
I deemed that without danger I could be
Sincere. I did not arm my glance with pride.
I asked but of my heart, yea, naught beside,
What words to say to him. And who, in truth,
Would not have trusted in his solemn oath
And bared her soul like me? In other days
Was it his wont to look upon my face
With the same eye wherewith he views me now?
Everything wrought for him, as still must thou
Recall: our family avenged, the joy

Of Greece, our vessels with the spoils of Troy
All laden, his sire's deeds by his outdone,
His love that seemed more ardent than mine own,
My heart, thou thyself dazzled finally
By his renown. Ere yet betrayed he me,
All these betrayed me. But too much is this,
Cleone, and whatever Pyrrhus is,
Hermione is not a thing of stone.
Orestes hath his merits. He hath shown
That he can love, e'en though he win no love.
Perhaps he can make himself beloved. Enough!
Let him come, then.

CLEONE.

Good madam, he is here.

HERMIONE.

Nay, I had not supposed he was so near!

[*Enter* ORESTES.

(*To* ORESTES) Shall I believe, my lord, that some last trace
Of old affection brings thee to this place
To an unhappy princess, or must I
Ascribe thy visit but to courtesy?

ORESTES.

Such is the fatal blindness of my heart.
Thou knowest it, madam; 'tis Orestes' part
Ever to come, thy beauty to adore,—
Ever to swear that he will come no more.
I know thy glance will make love's wounds to bleed
Again in me; that all my steps which lead
Toward thee are perjured: I know and blush at this.
But I invoke those gods as witnesses
Who saw my frenzy when we parted last

That I have rushed where'er destruction best
Might quit me of mine oaths and of my pain.
I have begged death from savage tribes who stain
The altars of their gods with human gore
Only.[12] They have shut 'gainst me their temple door;
These barbarous folk spilled not the blood that I
Freely offered them. I have finally
Come to thee, and I see that from thine eyes
I needs must seek the doom that ever flies
When I would grasp it. My despair doth need
But their indifference. Let them but forbid
My last hope. To advance the fatal hour
Wheretoward I haste, let them but say once more
What they have always said to me. Alone
This thought it is that now hath led me on
For a year past. Madam, 'tis for thy glance
To slay a victim whom the Scythians
Would have made theirs ere thou couldst strike the blow,
If any could be found as cruel as thou.

HERMIONE.

Have done, my lord, with all this talk of death.
For cares more pressing, Greece hath claimed thy faith.
Why prate of Scythia and my cruelty?
Think of those kings who must all speak through thee.
Their vengeance—shall it hang on a wild mood
Of thine? Do they require Orestes' blood,
Forsooth? Discharge thou thine appointed task.

ORESTES.

Pyrrhus refuses that which Greece doth ask,
And thereby sets me free. He sends me back
Home, for some power makes him undertake
To defend Hector's son.

HERMIONE.

The false wretch!

ORESTES.

So,
Ready now to depart, I come to know
From thy lips what is mine own destiny.
Methinks I hear already the reply
Which silently thy hatred doth accord
Unto me.

HERMIONE.

What! Always unjust, my lord,
In thy sad words? Always wilt thou complain
That I abhor thee? Where is that disdain
With which thou oft hast charged me? Lo, I went
Forth to Epirus, whither I was sent.
My father ordered it. But who doth know
If I have ne'er in secret shared thy woe?
Dost think thou only hadst anxieties?
That this land saw no tears fall from mine eyes?
And who hath told thee I have not, in spite
E'en of my duty, sometimes wished I might
See thee?

ORESTES.

Wished thou mightest see me! Ah, divine
Princess! . . . But say, in pity's name, are mine
The ears to which thy words are spoken? See:
This is Orestes standing before thee!—
Orestes, long the object of thy scorn!

HERMIONE.

Yes, it is thou, whose love first taught me, born
As it was of my glance, that glance's power,—

Thou whom much worth made me esteem,—thou o'er
Whom I have felt compassionate, and whom
I fain would love.[18]

ORESTES.

I understand. My doom
Is this : that Pyrrhus hath thy heart ; thy head
Orestes.

HERMIONE.

Ah, do not desire instead
The lot of Pyrrhus ! I would all too sore
Hate thee.

ORESTES.

And thou wouldst love me even more.
O that thou couldst look on me differently !
Thou wishest to love me, and it cannot be ;
But didst thou wish to hate me, love alone
Would rule thee, and thy heart would be mine own.
Ah gods ! such reverence, a regard so dear—
How they would plead for me if thou couldst hear !
Thy mind is fixed on Pyrrhus, it may be
Against thy will—against his, certainly.
For indeed he loathes thee ; his soul, otherwhere
Enslaved, no longer . . .

HERMIONE.

Who hath told thee, sir,
That he disdains me ?[14] Hath his speech, his glance
Informed thee of it ? Dost thou think, perchance,
That my charms win me scorn ; that they can light
But brief fires in a man's breast ? Others might
Judge me more favourably than thou.

ORESTES.

Go on.

'Tis well to insult me thus. O cruel one,
Is it I, then, that scorn thee here? Hast thou
Not proved my constancy enough ere now?
Am I a witness of thy weak charms? I
Have scorned them? Ah, thou wouldst how eagerly
Behold my rival scorn their power to move
E'en as I scorn it!

HERMIONE.

For his hate or love
What do I care, sir? Go, and arm all Greece
Against a rebel. Bring the fatal price
Of his rebellion home upon his head.
Let a new Troy be of Epirus made.
Away! Still sayst thou that he hath my heart?

ORESTES.

Madam, do more, and hence thyself depart.
Wouldst thou remain a hostage in this place?
Come, that to every soul may speak thy face.
Unite a common wrath.

HERMIONE.

But what if he
In the meantime, sir, should wed Andromache?

ORESTES.

Madam!

HERMIONE.

Think what shame 'twould be for us
If he became a Phrygian woman's spouse.

ORESTES.

And thou dost hate him! Nay, confess it, love
Cannot be locked within one's breast. Thereof
Speaks all, the voice and silence and the eyes,
And so betrays us, and the flames but rise
The higher which we vainly would conceal.

HERMIONE.

Sir, thy soul's prejudice, I see full well,
Gives to my words the poison whence it takes
Death, in my reasoning for ever seeks
Some ruse, and deemeth hate springs from love in me.
I must explain, and thou accordingly
Wilt act. Thou knowest my duty led me here.
Here duty holdeth me, and I can ne'er
Go hence until my father shall desire,
Or Pyrrhus, that I go. As from my sire,
Make Pyrrhus see that never can the foe
Of Greece become his son-in-law, and so
He must between the Trojan boy and me
Decide. Let him consider which one he
Would keep and which relinquish. Let him send
Me home, or give the child at thy demand.
Farewell. If he permits, I instantly
Will follow thee.

[*Exeunt* HERMIONE *and* CLEONE.

ORESTES.

Yes, thou wilt follow me.
'Tis beyond doubt. I am already sure
Of his consent. I fear not, any more,
That Pyrrhus will withhold thee. He hath eyes
Only for his dear Trojan princess, flies

The sight of every other, and perchance
Awaits but some excuse to speed thee hence.
One word, and all is done. What joy to bear,
Epirus, from thy shores a prize so fair!
Shield what is left of Troy. Keep Hector's son,
His widow, and a thousand others. One
Thing ask I: that Hermione, restored
To me, no more shall see thy land or lord.

　　　　　　　　　　　　[*Enter* PYRRHUS *and* PHOENIX.

　　Good fortune sends him hither. I will speak!
Love, blind him to her beauty!

PYRRHUS.

　　　　　　　　　　　　'Twas to seek
Thee, sir, I came.[15] Anger, I will confess,
Armed me against thy words with stubbornness;
But since I left thee, I have seen their force
And justice. I, like thee, feel that my course
In brief ran counter to the cause of Greece,
My father, and myself; that I gave peace
And aid to Troy, bringing thereby to naught
All that Achilles wrought and I have wrought.
A righteous vengeance I no more condemn.
The victim shall be yielded to thy claim.

ORESTES.

My lord, this choice is prudent . . . and stern, too.[16]
The blood of a poor wretch buys our concord.

PYRRHUS.

　　　　　　　　　　　　　　　　True;
But I would fain insure it further still.
Of our eternal concord and good will
Hermione is the pledge. I wed with her.

It seemed that such a glad occasion, sir,
Waited but thee for witness. Here all Greece
Thou representest and her sire, who sees
His brother live again in thee. Go seek
Her presence, then. Go. Tell her I shall take
To-morrow peace and her hand's gift from thee.[17]

ORESTES (to himself).

Oh, gods!

[Exit ORESTES, wildly.

PYRRHUS.

How now! Hath love the mastery,
Phoenix? Dost thou not know me still?

PHOENIX.

Ah, sire,

Now I indeed do know thee. Thy just ire
Restores thee to thyself and to all Greece.
This is no slave of bonds ignoble; this
Is Pyrrhus, Achilles' son and rival, who
At last to honour's path is drawn anew
And over Troy a second triumph wins.

PYRRHUS.

Say, rather, that my victory begins
To-day when all my joy lies in good fame,
And when my heart, proud as it once was tame,
Deems it hath quelled, in love, a thousand foes.
Bethink thee, Phoenix, of the thronging woes
I shun which follow in love's train; what ties,
What duties I had chosen to sacrifice;
What perils . . . For one glance I would have lost
The memory of all. The leaguèd host

Of Greece entire would on a rebel son
Have fallen. I would gladly have undone
Myself for her.

PHOENIX.

Yes, I can bless, my lord,
The kind severity that hath restored
Thy . . .

PYRRHUS.

Thou hast seen, then, how she dealt with me?
I deemed, beholding her anxiety
For her child's sake, she must from him return
Disarmed of hate. I sought her, this to learn.
I found her all in tears and racked with throes
Of anguish, made more bitter by her woes;
And wildly and more wildly Hector's name
A hundred times burst from her lips. In vain
I promised her that I would shield her son.
" 'Tis Hector," she cried ever and anon
While still she clasped him. "Here are his dear eyes,
His mouth, and his brave mien already. This
Is Hector. Ah, my husband, 'tis to thee
I cling!" What is her thought? Supposeth she
That I will leave a son to her this day
To nourish her love?[18]

PHOENIX.

Doubtless she would repay
Thy mercy thus. But let her be, my lord.

PYRRHUS.

'Tis by her beauty she is reassured.
That heartens her. She proudly thinketh yet,

Despite my wrath, to find me at her feet.
I shall unmoved behold her, Phoenix, lie
Clutching mine. She is Hector's widow; I
Am the son of Achilles. Too much hate, I see,
Stands between Pyrrhus and Andromache.

PHOENIX.

Then speak of her no more to me. Go, sir,
Unto Hermione, and in pleasing her
Have thou content, and even thine anger quite
Forget. Thyself for this your marriage rite
Prepare her. To a rival must thou leave
That task? 'Tis but too well he loves her.

PYRRHUS.

                                        If
I wed her, thinkest thou that Andromache
May not at heart be pricked with jealousy?

PHOENIX.

What! Always to Andromache doth turn
Thy thought? Her joy or grief—of what concern,
O gods, are they to thee? What magic spell,
Strive as thou wilt, draws thee to her?

PYRRHUS.

                                    I still
Have not said everything that should be said
To her. My hate hath been but half displayed
Before her eyes. As yet she doth not know
To what extent I have become her foe.
Let us return to her. 'Tis my desire
To flout her to her face and give mine ire
Free scope. Come, Phoenix; see me humble all
Her charms. Let us begin.

PHOENIX.

　　　　　Go, sir, to fall
Before her feet, and swearing unto her
Thou lovest her, still further scorn incur.

PYRRHUS.

'Tis plain thou thinkest that, with forgiveness filled,
My heart seeks her and would be reconciled.

PHOENIX.

Thou lovest her; 'tis enough.

PYRRHUS.

　　　　　　　　I love her?——one
Who the more hates me as my love is shown,—
Who hath no kindred, friends, nor hope save me?
I can destroy her son; and, it may be,
I should. A stranger . . . what say I? a slave
Here in Epirus; if she would but have,
I offered her that son, my heart, my throne,—
And yet her persecutor's place alone
In her ungrateful heart can I secure!
No, I have sworn it; my revenge is sure.
For once I needs must justify her hate.
I will protect her child no longer. Great
Shall be her weeping. By what name will she
In anguish call me? What sight will she see
This day! 'Tis certain, Phoenix, she will die
Thereat, and I shall be her slayer—I,
As though I plunged a dagger in her breast!

PHOENIX.

Why, then, proclaim thy purpose? Were it not best
To have considered well thy strength ere now?[19]

PYRRHUS.

I take thy meaning. Pardon a last show
Of weakness. Doth so slight a struggle seem
Dangerous to thee? It was the final gleam
Of an expiring love. Come. I shall yield
Unto thy counsels, Phoenix. Must the child
Be given up? Must I see Hermione?

PHOENIX.

Yes, go to her, and very earnestly
Solicit her with humble vows, my lord . . .

PYRRHUS.

All shall be done to which I pledged my word.

ACT III

The scene is the same. ORESTES *and* PYLADES *are discovered.*

PYLADES.

Sir, temper this mad passion, I implore.
I know thee not; thou art thyself no more.
Let . . .

ORESTES.

        Thy advice no longer is in season,
For I am tired of hearkening to reason,
Pylades. Thus my life and misery
End never. I must bear her off, or die.
The plan hath been determined on, and 'tis
My will to execute it. I say, it is
My will!

PYLADES.

        Then must she needs be carried off.
I give consent thereto. But 'neath what roof
Thou art, consider meantime. What will men
Think of thee, seeing thy demeanor? Feign;
Make calm thy restless violence; bid thy face
Keep well its secret. These armed guards, this place,
The air about thee—all are Pyrrhus's,
And most of all Hermione. From her gaze
Especially conceal thy rage. Oh, why
In this state wast thou seeking her?

ORESTES.

                      Do I
Know? Was I master of myself? A fit

Of frenzy swept me headlong and I might
Have uttered threats against both him and her.

PYLADES.

What fruit would such an outburst surely bear?

ORESTES.

And what heart, tell me, would not, at that blow
That shook but now my very reason, grow
Desperate? He weds, he says, Hermione
To-morrow; and he fain, to honour me,
Would from my hand receive her! Ah, that hand
Shall sooner with his cruel blood be stained . . .

PYLADES.

Thou blamest him for this strange fatality;
Yet, tortured by his own devices, he
May well deserve compassion, even as thou.

ORESTES.

Nay, nay, my pangs but feed his pride, I know.
Until he saw me—saw my love—disdain
Was all he felt for her. Her charms till then
Could move him not. He only taketh her
To snatch her from me. Gods! all was so sure!
Hermione, made mine, would never see
His face again. To give itself to me,
Her spirit, wavering betwixt love and hate,
Did only for a last refusal wait.
Her eyes were opened, Pylades. She heard,
She spake to me. She pitied me. One word
Would have completed all.

PYLADES.

       Thou fanciest so.

ORESTES.

What! with her rage against a faithless . . .

PYLADES.

No.

Her love was never more intense for him.
Had Pyrrhus yielded her to thee, canst deem
She would not have found some excuse to stay?
Nay, credit me, and bear her not away,
But flee for ever from her treacherous lure.
Wilt thou make thine a fury who is sure
To loathe thee and regret through all thy years
The longed-for marriage that was almost hers,
And wish . . .

ORESTES.

'Tis therefore I resolve to seize
Upon her. For else all things, Pylades,
Would smile on her; and as my portion, then,
Must I bear hence but empty rage?—again
Go far from her and struggle to forget?
No, I will make her the associate
Of *my* pain. Too much have I grieved alone.
I am tired of being pitied. In mine own
Turn I will make her fear me, and condemn
Her cruel eyes to weeping till each name
That I have given her, she will give to me.

PYLADES.

Behold the issue of thine embassy:
Orestes is a kidnapper!

ORESTES.

And what
Avails it, Pylades, though our States have got

Revenge and find joy in my skilfulness,
If *she* rejoiceth at my tears, no less?[20]
What gain have I that Greece admireth me,
When I have in Epirus come to be
A mockery? What wouldst thou? Be it known
Plainly to thee, mine innocence hath grown
A heavy load for me to bear.[21] Some power
Unjust there is, that leaveth wrong secure
And houndeth innocence. Whate'er the phase
In which I view my life, I see always
Misfortune that doth shame the gods on high.
I will deserve their wrath, yea, justify
Their hate, and win the reward of crime before
Its punishment. But thou, thou as of yore
By what fatuity wouldst bring upon
Thyself an anger that seeks me alone?
My friendship hath o'erburdened thee too long.
Fly from one hapless, one who doeth wrong.
Dear Pylades, compassion blinds thy sense.
Trust my words. Leave me to those perils whence
I await the outcome. Bear to Greece this child
Whom Pyrrhus to my hands will shortly yield.
Go!

PYLADES.

We shall carry off Hermione![22]
Come, sir; a great heart showeth gloriously
In the midst of dangers. What cannot friendship do
When led by love? Now let us go unto
Our men and fire their souls. Our ships are all
Ready for sailing, and the wind doth call.
I know this palace—every maze unlit.
Thou seest the sea doth wash the walls of it;

And this night, by a way hid from all eyes,
Safe to thy vessel thou shalt bear thy prize!

ORESTES.

I wrong, dear friend, thy too great loyalty.
Forgive as thou alone hast pitied me.
Pardon a wretch who loses all he sets
His heart on, whom the world hates, and who hates
Himself. Might I in turn some happier day . . .

PYLADES.

Mask well thy mind, sir; that is all I pray
Of thee. Take care the stroke be not revealed
Before it fall. Remember not how steeled
Against thee is Hermione. Forget
Thy love. But see, she cometh!

[*Enter* HERMIONE *and* CLEONE.

ORESTES.

Go, then, straight.
Assure thou me of her, and, be assured,
I answer for myself.

[*Exit* PYLADES.

(*To* HERMIONE) I have restored
Thy lover to thee, madam, by my care.
I have seen Pyrrhus, and they now prepare
Your marriage.

HERMIONE.

So I have been told, and more:
That thou didst seek me that I might therefor
Be ready.[23]

ORESTES.

And thy spirit will not rebel?

HERMIONE (*disregarding his question*).
Who would have dreamed that Pyrrhus might be still
Faithful; that love could lie cold in his heart
So long, and only when I would depart
Kindle again for me? Like thee I deem
That he fears Greece, that prudence urgeth him
More than doth love, and that my glance hath stronger
Sway over thee than him.[24]

ORESTES.

Nay, I no longer
Deny he loves thee. Hath thy glance not wrought
All that it would in him? . . . And thou, no doubt,
Also—thou dost not wish to thwart him now.

HERMIONE.
And what, sir, can I do? I pledged my vow.
Shall I snatch from him what I ne'er made his?
Love does not rule the life of princesses.
The glory of obedience is all
That hath been left us. Yet was I, withal,
About to go with thee, and 'twas thine to see
How I relaxed e'en duty's claims, for thee.

ORESTES.
Ah, cruel one, well thou knowest . . .[25]
(*Controlling himself*) But every heart
Hath choice of its disposal. 'Tis thy part
To dispose of thine. I cherished hopes, but thou
Hast given it elsewhere, nor hast wronged me. Now
I blame thee, after all, far less than fate.
Why vex thee with laments importunate?

Thou doest thy duty, I must needs confess.
'Tis mine to spare thee words of bitterness.

[*Exit* ORESTES.

HERMIONE.

Thoughtest thou his wrath would be so well suppressed?

CLEONE.

The grief that speaks not is the deadliest.
I pity him—the more since of his woe
He is himself the author, and the blow
That hath destroyed him falls from his own hand.
Think for how long thy marriage had remained
Unconsummated! When he spoke, then straight
Pyrrhus declared himself.

HERMIONE.

Thou deemest that
Pyrrhus is afraid. But what is it he fears?
Those who fled before Hector for ten years;
Who oft, in absence of Achilles' aid,
Sought refuge in their burning ships, dismayed;
And who, save that his son had helped them, would
Still seek for Helen from Troy unsubdued?
Nay, Pyrrhus is nowise his own enemy.
He does but what he wishes, and if he
Weds me, he loves me. Let Orestes, though,
Charge me, if so he likes, with all his woe.
Have we no theme, except his sighs, for cheer?
Pyrrhus returns to me! Ah, Cleone dear,
Canst guess the rapture of Hermione?
Dost thou know Pyrrhus? Have they told to thee
The number of his mighty deeds? . . . But who
Can count them? Brave, all-conquering, handsome, true

Also,—he lacketh naught for his fair fame.
Think . . .

[*Enter* ANDROMACHE *and* CEPHISSA.

CLEONE.

Hide thy feelings. She whom thou didst name
Thy rival comes in tears, perchance to outpour
Her woes to thee.

HERMIONE.

Gods! Can I not give o'er
My soul to joy? Let us go. What should I
Say to her?

ANDROMACHE.

Madam, whither dost thou fly?
Is not this sight, then, to thine eyes full sweet:
The widow of Hector weeping at thy feet?
I come not here with tears of jealousy,
Envying thee him who yields his heart to thee.
I have beheld the one man cruelly slain,
Alas, on whom I e'er would look. Love's flame
Was kindled by Hector in my breast of yore;
'Tis sealed up in his tomb for evermore.
A son is left me. Some day thou wilt know,
Madam, how women love a son. But oh,
Thou ne'er—at least that is my hope—wilt learn
What anguish we can suffer through concern
For him when he remains the one thing which
Is left us still of all those blessings rich
That soothed our hearts erewhile and it is sought
To take him from us. Ah, when wearied out
With ten years' miseries the Trojans would
Threaten thy mother in revengeful mood,

I gained her the support of Hector. Thou
Hast equal power over Pyrrhus now.
What can be feared if Hector's child live still?
Let me go hide him on some lonely isle.
His mother's care will be his guaranty.
My son will learn but how to weep, with me.

HERMIONE.

I know thy grief, but speech of mine were ill
Now when my father hath declared his will.
'Twas he that stirred the wrath of Pyrrhus. Who,
If it must needs be quenched, can better do
That task than thou? His soul hath long by thee
Been ruled. Make him decide. I will agree.[26]

> [*Exeunt* HERMIONE *and* CLEONE.

ANDROMACHE.

How cruel and scornful her refusal was!

CEPHISSA.

I would accept her counsel, and bear my cause
To Pyrrhus. Thy one look would put to rout
Hermione and Greece. . . .

> [*Enter* PYRRHUS *and* PHOENIX.
> He seeks thee out,

Himself!

PYRRHUS (*to* PHOENIX).

Where is the Princess? Didst thou not
Tell me that she was here?

PHOENIX.

So had I thought.

ANDROMACHE (*to* CEPHISSA, *in sad irony*).

Thou seest my power o'er him!

PYRRHUS (*whispering*).
                    What is she
Saying now, Phoenix?

ANDROMACHE.
                Help is none. Ah me!

PHOENIX (*to* PYRRHUS).
Come; let us find Hermione, my lord.

CEPHISSA (*to* ANDROMACHE).
Why waitest thou? Be not stubborn. Though 'tis hard,
Speak!

ANDROMACHE.
        He hath promised to give up my son.

CEPHISSA.
He hath not given him yet.

ANDROMACHE.
                 No, no! my moan
And pleading would be utterly in vain.
His death has been decreed.

PYRRHUS (*to* PHOENIX).
                 Will she not deign
To bestow upon us even a single glance?
What haughty pride!

ANDROMACHE.
            Cephissa, let us hence.
I only vex him further.

PYRRHUS (*to* PHOENIX).
          Let us go
To give to the Greeks the son of Hector.

ANDROMACHE (*with a convulsive cry*).

Oh!
Stay, my lord! What dost thou intend to do?
Give them the son? Then give the mother, too!
So kindly were thy promises of late!
Now art thou not at least compassionate?
Ah gods! Have I no hope of pardon, even?

PYRRHUS.

Phoenix will tell thee that my word is given.

ANDROMACHE.

And thou it was who wouldst have braved for me
All perils?

PYRRHUS.

I was blind then; now I see.
Mercy could have been his at thy request.
Thou ne'er didst ask for it. The time is past.

ANDROMACHE.

My lord, thou must have understood full well
The sighs that feared to be repulsed and fail.
Forgive the trace of pride, born of the estate
Once mine, that would not be importunate.
Thou knowest that but for thee Andromache
Would never have to a master bent the knee.

PYRRHUS.

Nay, thou dost loathe me, and thou art afraid
Within thy heart to owe me aught. Indeed,
This child for whom thou feelest such distress—
If I had saved him, thou wouldst love him less.
Anger, disdain—against me both are joined.

Thou hatest me more than all the Greeks combined.
Enjoy such noble wrath at leisure, then.
Come, Phoenix.

ANDROMACHE (*to herself*).
I shall go to meet again
My husband.

CEPHISSA.

Madam . . .

ANDROMACHE (*to* CEPHISSA).
What is it thou wishest me
Still to say to him? Dost thou think that he
From whom my woes proceed doth know them not? . . .
[*To* PYRRHUS.
Behold the state to which I have been brought
By thee, my lord. I have seen my father die
And our home burn. I have seen my family
All cut off, and my husband's bleeding frame
Dragged in the dust,[27] his son (a slave the same
As I) alone being left me. But what does not
A son make possible? I live; my lot
Of slavery I accept. Nay, more than that,
I am glad sometimes that 'tis here that fate
Hath exiled me instead of otherwhere,[28]
And that (since he must serve who was the heir
Of many kings) so fortunate was he
In his misfortune that he should have thee
For master. I had dreamed his prison would
Yet be his place of refuge. Priam could
In suppliance win Achilles' grace erewhile.
I thought his son would be more generous still.
Forgive, dear Hector, such blind trust and hope!

I ne'er suspected that thy foe would stoop
To crime. In spite of all that he could show,
I judged him noble. Would he were but so
Enough to lay us 'neath the monument[29]
I reared here to thine ashes, and thus vent
His hate and end at last our sorrows there,
And nowise sunder mortal dust so dear!

PYRRHUS.

Go and await me, Phœnix.

[Exit PHŒNIX.

        (To ANDROMACHE) Madam, stay.
Unto thine arms the son thou weepest may
Yet be restored. I find, regretfully,
That moving thee to tears but armeth thee
'Gainst me. I thought to bring more wrath here. . . . Nay,
Vouchsafe at least to turn thine eyes this way.
Look if my face be of a merciless
Judge, or a foe that seeketh thy distress.
Why force me to be recreant to thee? Let
Us both, in thy son's name, have done with hate.
'Tis I who plead with thee to save him—I!
To beg of thee his life, have *I* to sigh
And cling to *thy* knees in behalf of *him*?
Save him and save thyself: for the last time
I say it.
        I know what pledges I shall break
For thee;—what hatred I shall for thy sake
Invoke upon me. I shall send back now
Hermione, and set upon her brow,
Instead of a queen's crown, a seal of shame
Eternal. I shall lead thee to the fane
Where for her wedding-rites folk busy them,
And shall invest thee with the diadem

That is made ready for her head. But this
Offer of mine no longer, madam, is
One which thou canst afford but to disdain.
I tell thee, thou must either die or reign.
A year's ingratitude makes desperate
My heart; it cannot leave in doubt its fate.
Too long is this to threaten, fear, and sigh;
I die if I must lose thee, but I die
No less if I must wait. Take thought. Alone
I leave thee now, but I shall come back soon
To bring thee to the temple, where the child
Will be. There shalt thou see me—either mild
Or raging—either crown thee or destroy
Before thine own eyes, madam, this thy boy.

[*Exit* PYRRHUS.

CEPHISSA.

I had foretold thee that in spite of Greece
Thou still wouldst be thy fortune's arbitress.

ANDROMACHE.

Alas, thy words have what fulfilment won!
No choice is left me but to doom my son.

CEPHISSA.

Thou hast clung, madam, to thy husband long
Enough. To be too constant, would be wrong.
He would himself not counsel this excess.

ANDROMACHE.

What! I must needs set Pyrrhus in his place?

CEPHISSA.

The safety of his son demands it, whom
The Greeks would snatch from thee. Within his tomb

Will he blush, thinkest thou, at such a thing?
Will he indeed scorn a victorious king
Who would restore thee to a royal seat
Like thy forefathers' and beneath his feet
Trample for thee thy conquerors in his ire;
Who would forget Achilles was his sire,
Disown his deeds, and bring them all to naught?

ANDROMACHE.

Though he remembers them no longer, ought
I to forget them? Ought I to forget
Hector deprived of burial and in hate
Dragged shamefully around our walls? Ought I
To forget how I beheld his father lie
Stretched at my feet, staining the altar red
To which he clung? Recall that night of dread
That plunged a whole race in eternal night.
See Pyrrhus bursting, with fierce eyes alight,
Into the glare our burning palace shed,
Trampling upon the forms of all my dead
Brethren, and, blood-bedewed from head to foot,
Urging the slaughter on; recall the shout
Of the victors and the screams of those devoured
By flames or perishing beneath the sword;
And picture to thyself Andromache
Racked by these horrors. That is verily
How 'twas that Pyrrhus first before me came;
Those are the deeds that won his crown of fame;
And he whom thou wouldst have me wed is this!
No, I will join not with such crimes as his.
For his last victims let him, if he choose,
Take us; for otherwise I needs must lose
All, all my memories!

CEPHISSA.

As thou wilt. Then let
Us go to see thy son die. They but wait
For thee. Thou shudderest, madam.

ANDROMACHE.

Ah, thou art
With what reminders buffeting my heart![30]
Now, after all my trials, I must go
And see my child die, my one joy in woe
And Hector's image, this my child, whom he
Left as the token of his love to me!
Alas, the hour again comes to my mind
In which his courage made him seek to find
Achilles, or death, rather. For his son
He asked, and took him in his arms. "Mine own
Dear wife," he said, wiping my tears away,
"I know not what success fate hath this day
In store for me. I leave this babe to thee
As my faith's warrant. If he loseth me,
Let him in thee find me again. If thou
Dost cherish the memory of our marriage, show
My son how loved his father was erewhile."
And blood so precious can I see men spill,
And shall I let his whole race with him die?
Must *my* fault doom him, barbarous king? If I
Hate thee, is *he* guilty of *my* hate? Hath
He blamed thee yet for all his kinsmen's death?
Did he reproach thee for the ills he knew not?

Yet thou, my child, shalt perish if I do not
Stay the cruel sword that hangs above thy head.
And I *can* stay it, and I shall instead
Give thee thereto? No, no! thou shalt not die.

I cannot suffer it. Let us instantly
Go and find Pyrrhus. But nay, go thou, my dear
Cephissa; find him for me.

CEPHISSA.

I shall bear
What message to him?

ANDROMACHE.

Tell him that the love
Wherewith I love my son is strong enough . . .
Thinkest thou that in his soul he hath indeed
Sworn he will slay him? Can his passion breed
Such rigour?

CEPHISSA.

He will soon return, most wroth.

ANDROMACHE.

Then go, assure him . . .

CEPHISSA.

Of what thing? thy troth?

ANDROMACHE.

Alas! is that still mine to plight him so?
O Hector's ashes! O ye Trojans! O
My father! O my son! how very dear
Thy life doth cost thy mother!

(To CEPHISSA) Come!

CEPHISSA.

Nay, where,
Madam? and to what end?

ANDROMACHE.

I will beside
My husband's cenotaph ask him to guide.

ACT IV

The scene is the same. Enter ANDROMACHE *and* CEPHISSA.

CEPHISSA.

Ah, 'tis thy husband, madam; I can doubt
It not; 'tis Hector who hath brought about
A miracle within thee.[31] He would fain
That Troy might yet be lifted up again
Together with this child so blest whom he
Inspires thy heart to save. Pyrrhus to thee
Hath promised, even as thou thyself hast heard
But now. He waited only for one word
To give him back to thee. Trust in his love.
Sire, sceptre, allies—deeming thy heart enough,
He casts all at thy feet. He makes thee queen
Over himself and all his land. Does, then,
This conqueror deserve such enmity?
Indignant with the Greeks, already he
Is careful of thy son as thou, keeps ward
Against their hate, gives him his bodyguard,
And to protect the child's life, risks his own.

But at the temple all things have been done
In preparation. Thou hast promised.

ANDROMACHE.
                    Yes,

I shall be there. But let us go apace
To see my son.

CEPHISSA.
            Nay, but why hastenest thou?
It is enough that seeing him is now

Forbidden thee no longer. Thy caresses
Can soon be lavished on him. Your embraces
No grudging eye will number. What delight
To rear a child that grows before thy sight
No more as doth a slave reared by his lord,
But is to kingship like his sires restored!

ANDROMACHE.

Cephissa, it is for the last time now
I go to look on him.

CEPHISSA.

What sayest thou?

O gods!

ANDROMACHE.

Ah, dear Cephissa mine, 'tis not
From thee that I would ever hide my thought.
Thy loyalty hath been displayed to me
In all my woes. But I had looked for thee
In turn to know me better. Didst thou, pray,
Deem that Andromache would e'er betray
Falsely a husband that hoped still to live
In her; that she would cause the dead to grieve
Again, and trouble them for her repose?
Is this the ardour that inspired my vows
To Hector's ashes? But his son was doomed
To die. How shield him? Pyrrhus will have assumed,
In wedding me, the task of his defence.
'Tis well. I gladly place my confidence
In him for this. I know what manner of man
He is. Sincere though violent, better than
He promiseth, Cephissa, will he do.
Upon the wrath of Greece I reckon, too.

Her hate will give to Hector's child a sire.
I go, then, since necessity doth require
That I should sacrifice myself, to give
To Pyrrhus whatso time I yet shall live.
When we are joined before the altar, I
Shall bind with an indissoluble tie
My son and him together; but my hand,
That harms none else, will then cut short my strand
Of life forthwith, that is no longer true,[32]
Will save my honour, and render what is due
To Pyrrhus, my son, my husband—yea, and me.
My heart hath planned this innocent trickery.
'Tis this that Hector bids me do. Alone
I set forth to rejoin him and mine own
Forefathers. Thou, Cephissa, needs must close
Mine eyes for me in death.

CEPHISSA.

Ah, ne'er suppose
That I could bear to live . . .[33]

ANDROMACHE.

No, no! thou must
Not follow me, Cephissa. I entrust
To thee mine only treasure. If I was worth
Living for, live for Hector's child henceforth.
Sole guardian of the Trojans' hopes art thou.
Think of the line of kings that needs thee now.
Keep watch on Pyrrhus. See he doth not break
His word. If it be needful, thou mayst speak
To him of me. Make him appreciate
The marriage which I grant him. Tell him that
I was united with him ere I died;

That his resentment should be laid aside;
And that I proved, in leaving him my son,
In what esteem I held him. Make thou known
Unto my child the heroes of his race.
Lead him as best thou canst to tread the ways
Their footsteps trod. Tell him the deeds that won
Glory for them,—rather what they have done
Than what they were. Talk to him every day
Of the virtues of his sire, and sometimes say
Something about his mother, too, to him.
But of revenge for me, he must not dream.
I leave a master over him, whom he
Should honour. Let him recall temperately
His forefathers. He is of Hector's breed,
But he is all of it, and I, indeed,
Myself in one day for the sake thereof
Give up my life, my hatred, and my love.

CEPHISSA.

Alas!

ANDROMACHE.

Come not with me, if thou hast fears
Thy heart is powerless to restrain thy tears. . . .
Some one draws nigh. . . . Cephissa, dry thine eyes.
Remember that Andromache relies
Upon thy faith. . . . It is Hermione.
Let us begone and from her violence flee.

[*Exeunt* ANDROMACHE *and* CEPHISSA. *Enter* HERMIONE
and CLEONE.

CLEONE.

My wonder at thy silence knows no bounds.
Thou sayest naught, and this shameful wrong confounds

Not in the least thy spirits, madam. Lo:
Thou bearest tranquilly so cruel a blow,—
Thou who wast seen to quiver formerly
Even at the mention of Andromache?—
Thou who without despair couldst not endure
That Pyrrhus should so much as glance at her?
He weds her; he will give her with his crown
The troth that was an hour ago thine own;
And still thy lips are mute and will not deign
In thy distress against him to complain.
I fear a calm so ominous of doom.
'Twere better . . .

HERMIONE.
Didst thou bid Orestes come?

CLEONE.
He will come, madam; he will come; and thou
Mayst well believe that he at once will bow
Before thee, without hope of recompense
Yet always fain to serve thee, for thy glance
Only too surely charms his heart.

[*Enter* ORESTES.

But he
Is here.

ORESTES.
Ah, madam, is it verily
True that for once Orestes hath obeyed
Thy will in seeking thee? Am I not misled
By flattering hopes? My presence here thou hast
Desired? Shall I believe thy heart, at last
Disarmed, can wish . . .

HERMIONE.

I wish to know if thou
Lovest me, sir.

ORESTES.

Love thee? O gods! Each vow
I made and broke, my flight and my return,
My reverence, the reproaches thou didst earn,
My wild despair, mine eyes for ever drowned
In tears—what witnesses are to be found,
If thou believe not these, that will avail?

HERMIONE.

Avenge me. I believe them all.

ORESTES.

'Tis well.
Come, madam. Let us set all Greece aflame
Once more. To exalt my prowess and thy fame
Let us adopt, thou Helen's rôle and I
Agamemnon's and renew the misery
Of Troy here in this land, and even as were
Our sires, be named of men. Come, let us fare
Forth. I am ready.

HERMIONE.

Nay, sir, let us stay.
I would not carry affronts so far away.
What! crown the insolence of my foes and go
To await elsewhere a vengeance all too slow?
And shall I trust my fate to war's decree,
Which might, indeed, not give us victory?
I would have all Epirus weep when I
Depart. Avenge me ere the hour go by,

If thou art to avenge me. Seek delay,
And thou refusest. Run to the temple. Slay . . .

ORESTES.

Whom?

HERMIONE.

Pyrrhus.

ORESTES (*recoiling*).

Pyrrhus, madam?[34]

HERMIONE.

Ah, so slack

In hate? Run quickly, lest I call thee back.
Speak not of rights that I would fain deny him.
'Tis surely not for thee to justify him.

ORESTES.

I? I would justify him? Ah, thy kind
Favours have graven too deeply in my mind
His crimes. Let us take vengeance—I agree—
But in some other manner. Let us be
His foes, not his assassins, and withal
By righteous conquest bring about his fall.
What! to the Greeks shall I for answer bear
His head? and have I taken on me the care
Of the State's business to accomplish it
By murder? In the name of heaven, permit
Greece to be heard, that he may die weighed down
Beneath the hate of all. He wears a crown,
Remember, and the brow whereon it lies . . .

HERMIONE.

I have condemned him; doth not that suffice
For thee? And doth it not suffice for thee

That my offended pride demands for me
A victim all mine own; that thou canst gain
Hermione only if the King be slain;
That I hate Pyrrhus; and, sir, finally
That I have loved him—yea, I do not try
To conceal this; the faithless wretch knew how
To charm my heart, it nowise mattereth now
Whether love moved me or my father's hest,
But act thou on that knowledge as seems best.
Though he betrayed my trust, sir, shamefully,—
Though with just horror his crime filleth me,—
So long as yet he lives, beware lest I
Forgive him. Be not sure, till he shall die,
Of an uncertain wrath; for if to-day
He doth not perish, I to-morrow may
Love him!

ORESTES.

Then must I kill him, and forestall
His pardon,—must . . . nay, must do what, withal?
How shall I serve thy hate so quickly? How
Shall my sword find his breast? I am but now
Come to Epirus. Thou wouldst have me bring
A throne to the dust, wouldst have me slay a king,
And grantest me, to punish him, but one day,
One hour, one moment. Thou wouldst have me slay
Thy victim before all his people's eyes.
Then let me lead him like a sacrifice
To the altar. I resist no more. I fain
Would view the place where he must needs be slain.
This night I shall attempt his life for thee.

HERMIONE.

But he this day weddeth Andromache.
In the temple is already set his throne.
My shame is manifest; his crime is done.
For what awaitest thou? Lo, he presents
His bosom to thy blows. Without defence
He goeth to the ceremony—without
His guards. He hath disposed all these about
The son of Hector and abandoneth
Himself unto the hand that by his death
Seeks to avenge me. Art thou careful, then,
Despite him, of his life? Arm thine own men
And all my followers. Rouse to thine aid
Thy friends. Mine wait thy word. He hath betrayed
Me, deceived thee, and scorned us all. In sooth
Their hate already equals mine. 'Tis loath
To spare a Trojan woman's wedded lord.
Speak, and my foe cannot escape thy sword.
Thou needest but to let them strike the blow.
Lead or be led by rage so noble. Go,
And return covered with the traitor's gore.
It is thus only that thou canst be sure
To keep me thine.

ORESTES.

But, madam, think . . .

HERMIONE.

Ah, this,
Sir, is too much. Debate so lengthy is
An insult to my wrath. I was most fain
To put within thy power the means to gain
My favour and content thee; but I find

That thou wouldst rather mourn thy fate unkind,
Always, than merit aught. Go, go, and boast
Elsewhere about the constancy thou show'st,
And leave the care of my revenge to me!
It shames me that I have so abjectly
Been gracious to thee. I have had to face
Rebuffs too many times in one day's space.
I—I alone—shall to the temple where
Their marriage waits, and where thou dost not dare
To go and merit my love, and there shall I,
All alone, somehow to mine enemy
Win passage. I shall stab the heart I could
Not touch; and then my hands, bedewed with blood,
Shall be against myself turned, and in spite
Of him shall instantly our fates unite.
All faithless as he is, 'twill be to me
Sweeter to die with him than live with thee!

ORESTES.

Nay, I will rob thee of this pleasure grim.
None but Orestes' arm shall deal to him
His death. By me thy foes are to be slain,
And if thou wilt, thou canst reward me then.

HERMIONE.

Go. Trust thy fortunes to my oversight.
Let all thy ships be ready for our flight.

[*Exit* ORESTES.

CLEONE.

Thou workest thy ruin, madam; and there is need
For thee to think . . .

HERMIONE.

Whether I work indeed
My ruin or no, I think of vengeance! I

Even yet know not if I should rely
On any save myself, whate'er he might
Promise me. Pyrrhus stands not in *his* sight
So guilty as in mine. More sure than his
Would *my* blows be, I truly deem. What bliss
To avenge with mine own hand the wrongs I bore,
To lift an arm red with the traitor's gore,
And both my pleasure and his pain to enhance
By hiding my rival from his dying glance!
Alas, if, paying his crime's penalty,
He should be spared the knowledge that through me
Death comes to him! Go, find Orestes. Bid
Him tell him 'tis for me that he doth bleed,
And not for Greece. Run, my Cleone! I
Should lose my whole revenge, were he to die
Ignorant that through me it is he dies.

CLEONE.

I shall obey. But what is this mine eyes
Behold? O gods! Who would have dreamed this thing
Would ever come to pass? It is the King.[35]

[*Enter* PYRRHUS *and* PHOENIX.

HERMIONE.

Ah! run, Cleone, to Orestes. Say
That till he sees me again, he must essay
Nothing!

[*Exit* CLEONE.

PYRRHUS.

Thou art surprised that I am here,
Madam; and that I now intrude, is clear.
I do not come armed with unworthy wiles
To cover my wrong-doing o'er with veils

Of righteousness. Enough that silently
My heart condemns me, and but ill should I
Pretend what I do not believe. I wed
A Trojan woman. And to thee instead
I pledged the faith erewhile that I swear now
To her. Yea, madam, all this I avow.
Another man would tell thee that our sires,
Without consulting either my desires
Or thine, had plighted us upon the plain
Of Troy, and in our absence forged a chain
Which bound us to each other lovelessly.
That I consented is enough for me.
My faith was promised thee by mine own envoys.
Far from disowning, I approved the choice.
I saw thee to Epirus come with them,
And though another's eyes' resistless flame
Had now left thine no power to subdue
My heart, I bowed not to this ardour new.
I stubbornly determined to be leal
To thee. I greeted thee as queen, and till
This very day I deemed mine oath would prove
Stronger than love to bind me. But my love
Conquers, and by a cruel destiny
Andromache receives a heart from me
Which she abhors. One by the other led,
We fly unto the altar, to be wed,
Swearing, despite ourselves, eternal love.

    Now vent thy fury, having heard enough,
On him who is a traitor bitterly
Against his will yet by his will. For me,
I nowise would restrain thy righteous wrath.
Myself, like thee, perchance it solaceth.
Give me all names which those who falsely swear

Are called. It is thy silence that I fear,
Not thy reproaches; for mine own heart says,
That hath so many secret witnesses,
The more as thou dost say the less to me.

HERMIONE.

Sir, in this frank avowal I can see
That to thyself, at least, thou dost not lie;
That when thou chosest to break our solemn tie,
Thus doing a crime, thou knewest thee criminal.
But ought a conqueror to stoop, after all,
To such base codes as bid him keep his word?
Nay, falseness hath some charm for thee, my lord,
And but to boast thereof thou seekest me.
Nor oath nor duty avails aught with thee:
Thou wooest a Greek while for a Trojan fain;
Thou leavest me, again takest me, yet again
From Helen's child to Hector's widow turnest;
Now crownest the princess, now the captive; burnest
Troy for the Greeks, undoest Greece for the son
Of Hector. From a heart that is its own
Master at all times spring such deeds as these,—
A hero nowise bound by promises!
    I must perhaps call thee, to pleasure her
Thou weddest, such sweet names as perjurer
And traitor. Even now thou camest to look
Upon my pallid face, and then go mock
My sorrow in her arms. Thou wouldst I might
Follow her chariot, weeping, in the sight
Of all. But that, sir, would be too much bliss
For one day. Cannot what thou hast suffice,
That in new fields thou must acquire renown?
Hector's old helpless father smitten down

At his loved ones' feet, to die before their eyes,
While thy sword, searching in his bosom, tries
Still of his frozen blood to find some store;
Troy burning, while her streets run red with gore;
Polyxena slaughtered by thine own hand[36]
Though even the hosts of Greece, beholding, stand
Indignant:—who could e'er resist the spell
Of such brave deeds?

PYRRHUS.

I know the terrible
Lengths to which vengeance for the ravishment
Of Helen drove me. I could make complaint,
Myself, thereof to thee, her child. But I
Am willing now to let the past go by.
I thank the gods that thy indifference
Tells me that I may breathe in innocence
Love's happy sighs. My heart, I see, was prone
To put itself to pain. It should have known
Thee better—better searched itself. To be
Remorseful, was to insult thee mortally;
For one must deem oneself beloved, to deem
Oneself unfaithful. Thou hast ne'er, 'twould seem,
Desired to hold me fast. I feared to have done
A wrong to thee; I may confer a boon.
Our hearts were never fashioned to entwine.
I did my duty; thou didst follow thine.
Naught ever made thee love me—that is true.

HERMIONE.

I never loved thee? What, then, did I do,
Thou cruel one? I spurned for thee the pleas
Of all our princes, in thy provinces

Came unto thee myself, and here still am
Despite thy falseness and despite the shame
Of my Greek followers that I show such grace
To thee. I bade them speak not of the base
Wrongs that I suffered. I have secretly
Hoped the forsworn one would return to me.
I deemed that soon or late thou wouldst be true
And bring me back the heart that was my due.
I loved thee faithless; what would I have done
Hadst thou been constant? And e'en now, when thine own
Merciless lips have calmly sentenced me
To death, I question if it may not be,
O thou unfaithful, that I love thee still!
But, sir, if heaven in anger needs must will
That to another's glance the honour fall
Of winning thee, wed; I consent, withal.
But oh, at least do not compel mine eyes
To see those marriage rites! It may be, this
Is the last time that I shall speak with thee.
Wait but one day. To-morrow thou shalt be
Master. . . . Thou answerest naught. Ah, wretch, 'tis clear
Thou countest the moments lost thou spendest here
With me. Impatient to behold again
Thy Trojan love, thou art regretful when
Some one else talks with thee. Thy heart doth speak
Ever to her, within thee. Thine eyes seek
Ever but her alone. No longer here
Shall I detain thee. Escape hence. Go swear
To her the faith that thou hast sworn to me.
Go, and profane the gods' high majesty.
Those gods, those righteous gods, will not forget
That the same oaths bound thee to me of late.
Bear thou that heart which hath abandoned me

To the altar's foot. Quick; run; but dread to see
Hermione once more before thee there!

[*Exit* HERMIONE.

PHOENIX.

My lord, thou hearest her. Thou hadst best beware
Of one who in her love's mad frenzy seeks
Revenge. Her strength here is too great. The Greeks
Have common cause with her for enmity
'Gainst thee. Orestes loves her still, and he
Perhaps, when such a prize may thus be won . . .

PYRRHUS.

Andromache awaits me. Guard her son.

ACT V

The scene is the same. Enter HERMIONE, *distractedly.*

HERMIONE.

Where am I? What have I done? What ought
I to do now?[37] What fury sways me? What
Anguish devours my heart? All aimlessly
Hither and thither through this palace I
Have rushed. Alas! Is there no way I can
Know if I love or hate? Oh, the cruel man!
With what chill glance he spurned me, and no whit
Showed of compassion or even of feigned regret!
Did he appear to pity me or feel
Remorse one instant? Could a syllable
Of ruth for me be drawn from him this day?
Deaf to my groans, unmoved at my dismay,
Cared he, 'twould seem, in the slightest for my tears?
And still I mourn for him? And my weak heart cares—
Still cares—for him? Ah, bitterest crown of woe!
I tremble at the thought, e'en, of the blow
That threatens him, and on the very stroke
Of vengeance pardon him! . . . I will not revoke
The doom my wrath pronounced! Nay, let him die.
He lives no more for me. Triumphantly
He laughs, the wretch forsworn, at all my rage!
He deems its tempest will in tears assuage
Itself. He thinks that, ever feeble and
Irresolute of soul, I with one hand
Will shield him from the other's blow. He still
Doth judge me by the kindness that erewhile
I showed to him. But no! the traitor hath

Full store of other thoughts; and nowise doth
He in the temple in his triumph wis
Whether indeed his life or death it is
That she who is not present will desire.
He leaves me, the false villain, in this dire
Perplexity. No, once again say I;
No! Let Orestes act; let Pyrrhus die,
Since he should have foreseen what doth impend,
And since he made me wish it, in the end.
Wish it? In truth? 'Tis I that so decree?
He perishes because Hermione
Hath loved him, this brave prince, whose deeds of old
Gave my heart joy, however often told;
Whom I had chosen for mine within my breast
Before this fatal troth had bound us fast?
O'er such far seas, then, I pursued my path,
O'er lands so many, but to work his death?—
Murder him?—kill him? Nay, before he dies . . .

[*Enter* Cleone.

What have I done, Cleone? Oh, what is
The news thou bringest me? Where is Pyrrhus?

CLEONE.

He
Stands at the summit of felicity,
The proudest mortal and the most in love.
These eyes beheld him toward the temple move,
Where waits the wedding, like a conqueror
Leading his new prize. When he looked on her,
With glance wherein his hope and his delight
Sparkled, he seemed made drunken by the sight.[38]
Andromache, 'mid all the cries of joy,
Bears in her breast the memories of Troy

Unto the very altar. She, like one
Who is with love and hate for ever done,
Seems without plaint or gladness to submit.

HERMIONE.

And my betrayer? Does he carry it
Through to the very end? But didst thou scan
His brow, indeed, Cleone? Does he, then,
Enjoy serehe and perfect happiness?
Hath he not even one instant turned his face
Here toward the palace? Did his eyes ne'er fall
Upon thee? Tell me, did this criminal
Flush when he saw thee? Did he not confess
By his embarrassment his faithlessness,
Or doth his haughty pride remain the same?

CLEONE.

He seeth naught, madam. Safety and fair fame
Seem like thyself both vanished from his ken.
Paying no heed who followeth in his train,
Subjects or foes, he is intent alone
Upon his love's fulfilment. Round the son
Of Hector he hath marshalled all his guard,[39]
Deeming that only over him the sword
Impendeth. Phoenix hath himself the care
Of the child's safety, and hath borne him far
Away from temple and from palace both,
For this cause, to a stronghold. Pyrrhus doth
Feel, in his rapture, no anxiety
Save this.

HERMIONE.

The recreant villain! He shall die.
What did Orestes say?

CLEONE.

He with his men
Hath gone into the temple.

HERMIONE.

Is he, then,
Not ready to avenge my wrongs?

CLEONE.

I do
Not know.

HERMIONE.

Thou dost not know? What! will he, too,—
Orestes—play me false?

CLEONE.

He worships thee;
But torn by pangs of conscience inwardly,
He follows love one instant, and the next
Honour. In Pyrrhus he at once respects
The estate of king, Achilles, and withal
Pyrrhus himself. He fears lest on him fall
The wrath of Greece and of the world; but more
He fears himself, he says. As conqueror,
He gladly would have brought that hated head
To thee; the name of "murderer" instead
Alone dismays and checks him; and he now
Hath gone inside with heart uncertain how
He shall come forth, blood-guilty or as he
Who but looks on.

HERMIONE.

Oh, no, no! He will see
Their triumph without hindrance. He will guard

His deeds, that this occasion be unmarred.
I know the qualms with which he is beset:
The dastard fears death, and naught else but that.
What! without uttering a single prayer
My mother armed all Greece to fight for her?—
Made perish in her cause, in ten years filled
With conflict, twenty kings she ne'er beheld?
And I—only one traitor's death I claim;
I charge a lover to avenge my shame
And wrongs; he thus can win me, and risk naught;
I offer myself to him;—and I cannot
Gain my revenge! Come! 'tis for me alone
To procure justice for myself. Let moan
And wailing through the temple sound. Let woe
Conclude their cursèd bridal; and if so
It may be, but a moment's time let them
Be joined in marriage. Maddened as I am,
I shall not stop to choose my victim; all
Before me shall be Pyrrhus, though it befall
That 'tis Orestes' self.[40] I verily
Shall die; but I shall on mine enemy
At least take vengeance. *My* death shall not be
The only death. Some one shall die with me.

[*Enter* ORESTES.

ORESTES.

Madam, 'tis done. Thy will hath been obeyed.
Pyrrhus before the altar now hath paid
The price of falseness.

HERMIONE (*hoarsely*).
He is dead?

ORESTES.

He lies

Dying. In his own blood his perjuries
By wrathful Grecian hands are washed away.
Thus had I promised thee; and though dismay
Filled me whene'er the picture of the deed
That I must do before me rose, I sped
Unto the temple, where our men, unseen,
Crept through the crowd to the very altar, e'en.
Pyrrhus beheld me, but with countenance
Unchanged. My presence seemed but to enhance
His boldness, as if thus defying Greece
Entire, in me her envoy, would increase
The glory of his nuptials. Rapturously
Taking his diadem, he raised it high
And himself placed the circlet on the head
Of Andromache. "I give to thee," he said,
"My crown and wedlock's troth, Andromache.
Reign thou both o'er Epirus and o'er me.
I promise to thy son a father's love.
I call upon the gods to be hereof
The witness, that I to his mother swear
This thing. His enemies I now declare
Mine own. I hail him as the King of Troy!"
    Unto these words, that drew applause and joy
From his own folk, our followers replied
Only with cries of rage. On every side
The renegade beheld himself hemmed round.
No place to strike him even once I found,
Each man so vied with each at smiting him
To earth. I saw him struggling for some time,
Covered with blood, amid them, while he sought

To avoid their blows. But at the altar's foot
He finally was cut down. Then swiftly through
The press of terror-stricken folk I flew
Hither—to bear my princess from this place
Unto the port, to which our friends apace
Will come, red with the blood I promised thee.

HERMIONE (*as before*).

What is this they have done?

ORESTES.

Ah, I can see
They have betrayed thy vengeance by their zeal.
Forgive them! Thou didst wish my hand to deal
The first wound unto him, that he should know,
In dying, he for thy sake perished so.
But it was I whose ardour spurred them on.
For thee I led them, madam, and for none
Other, into the temple. Thou canst claim
Justly as thy work the deed done by them.
Thou speddest the blows . . .

HERMIONE.

Be silent, treacherous one,
And lay thy vile crime to thyself alone!
Go boast among the Greeks thy savagery.
Go; I disown it, and thou fillest me
With horror. Barbarous wretch, what hast thou wrought?
What madness hath inspired thee to cut short
A life so goodly? Were ye able, then,
To slaughter him to-day, ye cruel men,
And all your blood not rise to mutiny
For him? Nay, speak! Who hath appointed thee
The arbiter of his fate? Thou slayest him why?

For what thing done? On what authority?
Who bade thee do it?[41]

ORESTES.

O gods! What! Didst not thou
Thyself charge me to kill him, here, just now?

HERMIONE.

Ah, must thou heed a woman love-distraught?
Shouldest thou not have read mine inmost thought?
And didst thou not perceive, while I outpoured
My frenzy, that my mouth at every word
Belied my heart? Why, even if I had meant
It all, what need was thine to give consent?
Oughtest thou not to have made me say it o'er
To thee a hundred times, and then, before
Striking the blow, to have come to talk with me,
And come back yet again, or preferably
Shunned me? Why didst not leave to me the care
Of my revenge? What led thee hither, where
None wanted thee? Behold the bitter fruit
Thy love hath borne! Those ills which made pursuit
Of thee hast thou, O cruel one, brought to me!
Fatal to both alike, thine embassy
Swayed Pyrrhus to choose my rival, to his woe;—
Else should we see him yet on me bestow
His favours; he might love me,—would so feign
At least. Thou mayest depart. I shall remain
Here in Epirus. I renounce herewith
Greece, Sparta and its throne, and all my kith
And kin. Yea, dastard, 'tis enough for me
That they have bred a monstrous thing like thee!

[*She rushes out.* CLEONE *follows her.*

ORESTES.

What have I seen?—Hermione, or some
One else? And what words have I heard? For whom
Did the blood flow that I but now have shed?
If I am to believe what she hath said,
I am a treacherous murderer. Is he
Who dieth Pyrrhus, and am I verily
Orestes? Lo: I stifle reason's light
Within my breast. I do to death, in spite
Of mine unwillingness, a king whom I
Respect. I flout at once the sanctity
Of thrones, of envoys, and of humankind,
And even of altars, where my fury blind
Spareth him not. Foul villain I become,
Assassin, sacrilegious wretch.—For whom?
For an ungrateful woman, to whom I
Vowed this; who, even if Pyrrhus did not die,
No more would see me! I espouse her feud,
And when I have served her, she asks back his blood
And life from me again! She loveth him,
And I am a fierce monster! For all time
She goeth from my presence and my sight,
And for hire leaves me in her thankless flight
Every vile name I earned to pleasure her.

[*Enter* PYLADES *and Greeks, armed.*

PYLADES.

We must depart, must quit this palace, sir,
Or be resigned to issue nevermore
From it. Our men one moment hold the door.
The gathered throng pursues us furiously.
Unto the orders of Andromache
They are obedient, treating her as queen

And us as foes. She, who had ever been
Unyielding unto Pyrrhus, doth for him all
A faithful widow should,—proclaims withal
That he must be avenged; mayhap she would
Avenge Troy, too, and her first husband's blood.
Let us begone, nor wait till we have been
Cut off. We shall be joined by all our men;
And while Hermione still keeps the crowd
Standing collected round her, lo, our road
Lies open. We shall in security
Go forth.

ORESTES.

No, no, it is Hermione,
Friends, that I wish to follow. I can survive
No longer since her last decision. Leave
This place. The crime was mine, and 'tis for me
To expiate it now.

PYLADES.

Hermione,
Sir? She must be forgotten. Wouldst thou yet,
The instrument and object of her hate,
Seek for new wrongs from her amongst the dead?
And because she hath died, is there, then, need
That thou shouldst die?

ORESTES.

She hath died, sayst thou? What
Is this I hear? Ah, gods!

PYLADES.

Thou knewest it not?
We met her when we were returning here.
She had run towards the temple, as though fear

Had driven her mad, and thus on Pyrrhus came,
Borne by his soldiers, whom his bleeding frame
Stirred to avenge him. 'Twas, no doubt, that sight
Which made her frenzy mount; and from the height
Of the palace entrance we beheld her bend
O'er Pyrrhus with a dagger in her hand,
Then lift her eyes, and stab herself, and fall.[42]

ORESTES.

Thanks to the gods, mine ill fate passeth all
I had expected. Yea, I praise thee, heaven,
For thy persistence. Thou hast ever striven
Relentlessly to punish me, and so
Hast brought me to the peak and crown of woe.
Thy hate hath found its pleasure in contriving
Mine anguish. I was born to be a living
Example of thy wrath and perfectly
Serve as an instance of adversity.
So be it! I die content. Fulfilled hath been
My destiny. Where are those lovers twain?
To make my joy complete, I needs must drown
Myself alike in their blood and mine own.
I would fain look upon them both before
I die. Let us unite three hearts once more
Which naught could reconcile to amity.
But what black night is this that suddenly
Enshrouds me? Which way to win forth from it?
Why am I shuddering? What ghastly fit
Of horror grips me? Thank heaven, I see through . . .
Gods! what rivers of blood all round me flow!

PYLADES.

Alas!

ORESTES.

Ha! Pyrrhus, do I meet thee here
Again? Must I encounter everywhere
My hated rival? How hast thou escaped
Thus wounded? There—there—take the blow I kept
For thee! But what is this? Before my face
Hermione clasps him in her embrace.
She comes to snatch him from the mortal stroke
My sword would deal. Gods! what a fearful look
She casts on me! What fiends, what serpents fell
Are these she bringeth? Well, ye hags of hell,
Are your claws ready for your victim now?
For whom do these snakes hiss on each fierce brow?
For whom is meant this train that meets my sight?
Is it to bear me off into the night
Eternal that ye come? Then hasten. To
Your rage Orestes yields himself. But no:
Back with you! Let Hermione alone
Take vengeance on me. That ungrateful one,
Better than ye, can rend this frame apart.
I bring to her, to be devoured, my heart!

[*He sinks unconscious.*

PYLADES.

He swoons. Quick, friends! Time presses. Let us use
The moments which this seizure granteth us,
And save him. If he wakens here again,
Still raving, all our efforts will be vain.

[*Exeunt hurriedly, bearing the senseless body of* ORESTES

NOTES ON ANDROMAQUE

(The line-numbers are those of the French text.)

RACINE'S *Andromaque* is in situation and plot somewhat similar to the *Andromache* of Euripides but there are a number of striking differences between them. In Euripides' play, Andromache has been the concubine of Pyrrhus, her captor, and has borne him a son, Molossus; it is this child whose life is threatened. Hermione, already married to Pyrrhus, has proved barren and hence hates the bondwoman, whom she has superseded, and the son of the bondwoman. But Racine felt that the picture of Andromache as wife and mother in the *Iliad* is so beautiful and has so impressed the imagination of the world through all the ages, that one cannot satisfactorily think of her as ever having any other mate than Hector or any other child than Astyanax. He therefore represents Hector's little son as having escaped death when Troy fell, and as sharing his mother's captivity. And he represents Andromache as not forced into concubinage by Pyrrhus but sought by him in honourable marriage.

In *Andromaque,* there is no mention of Orestes' vengeance or of his consequently going mad and being pursued by the Furies. But we are told that he has been dogged by misfortune, that he has been subject to extreme melancholy, and that he has wandered in his misery far and wide over the face of the earth; and at the end of the play he does go mad and thinks himself beset by a troop of fiends who are either the Furies or else beings very much like them. His famous friendship with Pylades is preserved. Racine thus keeps him a figure vaguely in accord with the one which tradition pictures, while altering at will the events of his life.

Phoenix appears in the *Iliad,* where he is said to have been the preceptor of the youthful Achilles.

In Homer the domain of Achilles and of his son Neoptol-emus, or Pyrrhus, is Phthia in Thessaly. But Epirus is the western side of that part of the Greek peninsula of which Thessaly is the eastern; its kings claimed descent from Achilles, and the most famous of them (the great foe of early Rome) was himself named Pyrrhus. And Virgil in the *Aeneid,* in a passage (III, 292-332) which was the real germ of Racine's tragedy, represents Andromache as living in Epirus, in the city of Buthrotum, during a still later period of her life.

1 ; l. 42. To Pyrrhus who avenged him. By the destruction of Troy in vengeance for the abduction of Menelaus' wife, Helen, the mother of Hermione. In the final sack of the city, Pyrrhus played the most prominent part of all the Greek heroes.

2 ; l. 76. According to classical legend, Ulysses (or by other accounts, Pyrrhus) killed Astyanax at the time when Troy was taken.

3 ; l. 161. The same argument is used in the *Troades* of Euripides and in the *Troades* of Seneca.

4 ; l. 189. Queen Hecuba fell by lot to Ulysses, but went mad with grief before he sailed home from Troy. Cassandra, the sister of Hector, was assigned to Agamemnon and was murdered with him by his wife on his return home to Argos.

5 ; l. 234. The reference is to the anger of Achilles (the subject of the *Iliad*). He withdrew for a time from the Trojan war because his captive was taken from him by Agamemnon; and during his inaction, Hector defeated the Greeks badly.

6 ; l. 260. The language of Andromache, unlike that of Orestes, Hermione, and Pyrrhus, is always perfectly natural and without any trace of conventional preciosity. Strange that it should be so, when her thoughts, feelings, and actions, far more strikingly than theirs, are sometimes not those of

eternal human nature but of a transient, highly artificial period of society!

7; l. 280. This is an example of what has been called Andromache's "virtuous coquetry" in her dealings with Pyrrhus. To preserve an ascendancy over him for her son's sake, she plays upon his love for her with subtle turns of speech by which she herself will be in no wise committed.

Achilles had slain Andromache's father, Aëtion, and all of her seven brothers, and her husband, Hector; Pyrrhus had killed her father-in-law, Priam, as well as taken a leading part in the destruction of Troy.

8; l. 284. One thousand ships was, in round numbers, the traditional armament which Greece sent to Troy to regain Helen. Troy fell after a ten years' siege.

9; l. 315. "To boast of his carnage among her relatives and to assure her that her eyes have inflicted equal wounds on him is not the language of a hero of any race or age, but a hot-house product of the literary salons of the *Grand Siècle*." —WELLS.

10; l. 362. Another example of Andromache's "virtuous coquetry."

11; l. 456. Observe that Hermione pays not the least attention to Cleone's defence of Andromache. She cannot think or reason about the woman whom Pyrrhus loves; she can only hate her. Perhaps, too, she cannot believe that any woman exists who really does not want the love of Pyrrhus.

12; l. 492. Here and in the subsequent allusion to the Scythians Orestes refers to his adventures in Tauris (the Crimea); but as implied here, they do not accord with the Greek legend dramatized in Euripides' *Iphigenia in Tauris*.

13; l. 536. Hermione wants to be graciously encouraging to Orestes; but her words reveal the unhappy truth all too plainly to him.

14; l. 550. Hermione's flare of anger at Orestes' unfortunate reference to the disdain of Pyrrhus which wounds her,

her spiteful retaliation with words which will hurt him in turn, his outburst under this goading, her pretended indifference to Pyrrhus, followed by her betrayal of dread lest he should marry Andromache, all have a strongly comic element. Comedy is no less inherent in the scene between Pyrrhus and Phoenix later in the act, when Pyrrhus, who declares that he has put the ungrateful Andromache out of his heart, cannot stop talking about her, and especially when he wonders if she will be jealous if he weds Hermione. Again in Act III there is a comic flavour in the situation where Andromache and Pyrrhus covertly observe each other and try to overhear each other's words while they talk to their respective confidants. This mingling of comedy and tragedy, which exists in real life and which seems to us to be entirely proper and effective in drama, was condemned by the rigid theorists of the French classical period. Though in general more conventional than Racine's later plays, *Andromaque* is on this point his most daring experiment in the direction of naturalness.

15; l. 605. During the interval between Acts I and II, Pyrrhus has gone to Andromache while she was with her son, has found her more obsessed than ever with her memories of Hector, and has angrily resolved to surrender her child to the Greeks and to marry Hermione.

16; l. 615. Orestes is too thunderstruck to speak coherently in his rôle as ambassador.

17; l. 624. Observe the deliberate, wanton cruelty of Pyrrhus towards his luckless rival. Unhappy himself in the choice to which he has been driven, he wants to make Orestes suffer, too. So he asks him to witness the wedding and to give away the bride, and lays upon him the task of informing Hermione of what is planned. He knows that Orestes is not in a position to refuse to do any of these things but must endure whatever torture they involve.

18; l. 656. Her love for Hector.

19; l. 701. That is: Before announcing that you would give Astyanax to the Greeks, ought you not to have considered carefully whether you had the strength of character to do so?

20; l. 768. That is: What do I care whether Greece rejoices at the success of my efforts in her behalf, if Hermione rejoices at my disappointment in regard to her?

21; l. 772. This line and those immediately following it show that Racine did not intend that we should think of Orestes as the remorseful matricide of Greek legend.

22; l. 786. Observe how, when Orestes bids Pylades to leave him to his fate, Pylades' sense of loyalty to his friend breaks down his conscientious scruples. This is a slight touch of real characterization in the lay-figure of a confidant. But there is no evidence that Pylades hesitates, later, to help Orestes in the dastardly murder of Pyrrhus. The fact is that he holds back from the design to abduct Hermione only long enough to allow it to be discussed as much as Racine wished. He is "not a man, but an echo."

23; l. 808. Note Hermione's implied slur on the depth of Orestes' affection for her—another instance of wanton unkindliness.

24; l. 815. Hermione is still not quite certain of Pyrrhus; consequently, she wants to keep Orestes to fall back on in case of need. Her next speech is insincere with the same intent. But her real feeling towards Orestes is revealed presently in her words to Cleone, "Have we no theme, except his sighs, for cheer?"

25; l. 825. Orestes remembers just in time his promise to Pylades that he will be discreet, and checks his impulsive outburst.

26; l. 886. Hermione's heartlessness in her hour of triumph makes her subsequent fate seem the more deserved. We have already learned that it was really she who instigated the demand for the death of Astyanax. Note the venom in her mocking suggestion that Andromache has great influence over Pyrrhus and should herself appeal to him. Hermione wants the pleasure of seeing him refuse Andromache's prayer. Her hatred of the woman who was very unwillingly her rival is in no way diminished by her belief that she now need fear her no longer.

27; l. 930. Achilles dragged the corpse of Hector, tied behind his chariot, around the walls of Troy.

28; l. 934. "Virtuous coquetry" again; and similarly in the same speech, "I thought his son would be more generous still."

29; l. 944. The "monument" is not the tomb of Hector— that is at Troy—but a commemorative cenotaph which Andromache has had erected in Epirus. Such a memorial to him is mentioned by Virgil in the passage which inspired Racine's play.

30; l. 1014. That a woman who is torn between two conflicting considerations should devote a long speech to the passionate expression of one of them while totally disregarding the other, and then, at somebody's mention of that other one, should launch into an equally lengthy and equally passionate outburst about it with no further thought of the first consideration, as Racine has made his heroine do in this and her preceding speech, is stiff, naïve, and unnatural. It would seem to be another example of conventional artificiality in *Andromaque*. It is not the way that indecision is represented by other great dramatists (cf. in Euripides, Medea's debate with herself about killing her children) or by Racine in his later plays. But it is perhaps not wholly indefensible in the case of Andromache, *who is ruled by words* (see Introduction).

31; l. 1050. During the interval between Acts III and IV, Andromache has gone to Hector's monument and, on leaving it, has told Pyrrhus that she will marry him if he will swear to protect her son.

32; l. 1094. Andromache feels that she will have been unfaithful in some measure to Hector in going through the marriage ceremony with Pyrrhus, even if she kills herself immediately afterwards; but her suicide will save her from greater unfaithfulness.

33; l. 1101. It is the customary thing, in French classical tragedy, for confidants to want to die with their principals—naturally, since they have no independent existence!

34; l. 1173. Orestes has expected her to name Andromache. He recoils aghast at the suggestion that he should lift his hand against a king's consecrated head, especially when that king is the ruler of a friendly Greek State, to which he himself has come in the sacred rôle of an envoy.

35; l. 1272. The motives which bring Pyrrhus before Hermione at this time are obscure but certainly very human. Is he actuated, as she charges, by an egotistical desire to look again upon the woman who is in anguish because of her rejected love for him? Or is he driven to seek her presence by the desire to find some alleviation for the gnawings of an uneasy conscience, perhaps by confessing his fault with a frankness in which he takes pride and with a consequent improvement of his self-respect, or perhaps (as he himself suggests) by submitting, as a sort of penance, to Hermione's abusive reproaches? It is possible that each of these motives is to some extent operative within him.

The net result of the colloquy between Pyrrhus and Hermione is to intensify her resentment and to confirm her in the determination to have revenge. But when she first sees him approaching, she momentarily takes new hope and sends word to Orestes not to act further without fresh instructions from her.

36; l. 1338. After the sack and burning of Troy, during which Pyrrhus slew the aged and helpless King Priam, he sacrificed Polyxena, Priam's daughter, at the tomb of Achilles. See Euripides' drama *Hecuba*.

37; l. 1393. Between Acts IV and V, Hermione has evidently bidden Orestes to proceed with the design to kill

Pyrrhus. The hour for the latter's wedding with Andromache is at hand.

38; l. 1436. Cleone has hitherto tried to restrain Hermione
from rash acts and violent passions. Now all that she says
seems deliberately calculated to infuriate her mistress to the
utmost. It is but another case of a confidant's being a stage
property rather than a character. This time Cleone is used in
the classic rôle of "Messenger," and speaks not in a manner
which is consistent with herself, but in the way which will
affect Hermione as the author desires.

39; l. 1453. The fact that the bodyguard of Pyrrhus has
all been sent away to protect Astyanax, is essential to the
success of Orestes' attempt. Hence Racine mentions it again
and again.

40; l. 1490. That is: In my blind fury, I shall kill whoever
is in front of me, whether it is really Pyrrhus or not.

41; l. 1543. This question, one of the most astounding and
theatrically effective in all drama, has been thought by some
critics to be unnatural, even among the paroxysms of Hermione. It is paralleled, however, in Corneille's *Le Cid*,
ll. 1706 *ff.* and to some extent in Shakespeare's *King John*,
IV, ii, 205-7.

42; l. 1612. Between the exit of Hermione and the entrance
of Pylades, who thus reports her death, there are only eighteen
lines in the French text. Racine habitually, and with deliberate theory, allows too little time for the occurrence of events
off-stage in his fifth acts. See my translation of *Phèdre,*
Note 36.

BRITANNICUS

A MONG the plays of Racine, *Britannicus* occupies a somewhat anomalous position. Though of very high merit poetically, as are all his important tragedies, it is perhaps the least notable of them in this respect; and aside from one or two fine passages such as Nero's description of his first sight of Junia, its poetry is more sententious and oratorical than is customary with Racine. The love interest is less dominant in it than usual; the political interest is unusually large; its general tone is unwontedly austere and masculine; and for all these reasons it is grouped with *Mithridate* as the most Corneillian of the works of its author.

From a purely dramatic standpoint it is Racine's masterpiece. Lacking the florid appeal of the romanesque tragedies of the period, *Britannicus* is one of those rare plays in which, the characters and the situation being what they are, the outcome could be nothing else than what it is,—whereas if any factor were changed, the outcome would be changed. If Agrippina and Burrus had not been just the people they were, they would have reached an understanding and, between them, would have curbed Nero. He would not have broken from all restraint in any case, if Narcissus had not been a very Iago for infernal persuasiveness. If Junia had been more adroit, more courageous, less frank and less sweet-natured and less loving, she might have managed not to arouse Nero's jealousy or might have got Britannicus safely out of the palace, or else by defiance might have precipitated an equally tragic but somewhat different dénouement. If the Emperor— but the suppositions could be continued indefinitely.

As a single instance among many of Racine's consummate craftsmanship in this play, we may note the scene in which Nero, concealed behind a curtain, listens to Britannicus and Junia. For tension, for terror, for sheer force and effectiveness, it can hardly be matched by any similar situation in all the dramas of the world. Even that in which Orgon hides under the table and hears Tartuffe reveal his true character pales beside it, and Sheridan's much-lauded screen scene in *The School for Scandal* is utterly trivial in comparison. No wonder Voltaire called *Britannicus* "la pièce des connaisseurs"!

In naturalness and comparative freedom from convention, an immense improvement is shown over *Andromaque*. Let us take, for example, the use of confidants. In *Andromaque* there is one for each important character. In *Britannicus*, on the other hand, Albina is the only specimen of these lay figures. If some one who had never read the play, but was familiar with French classical tragedy in general, were to scan the list of its dramatis personae, he would no doubt suppose Burrus, the former tutor of Nero, to be the Emperor's confidant and Narcissus, the tutor of Britannicus, to serve in a like capacity for the young prince. But the fact is that both Nero and Britannicus confide in Narcissus, and he and Burrus are as thoroughly individualized characters, with wills and plans and purposes of their own, as any one else in the play. And there is nobody at all to whom Junia can go for counsel or sympathy,—and how poignantly effective is this very isolation of the helpless, friendless girl!

There is far less of preciosity in *Britannicus* than in *Andromaque*. Derived largely from Tacitus, it seems to catch something of the Roman historian's terse power. Whatever of Versailles and the salons does enter into this drama, as regards either language or sentiments, appears less incongruous in the setting of imperial Rome, itself complex and in some degree artificial, than in the world of Greek legend. The real Pyrrhus would forthwith have made Andromache his concubine willy-nilly; but the Nero of history, like Racine's emperor in the play, would probably have wanted Junia to dismiss the man she loved and become his wedded empress, for he later did, in fact, desire and marry Poppaea Sabina, the wife of Otho, and it was only a few years afterwards that Domitian, as Suetonius relates, took Domitia Longina from her husband and espoused her. Racine's Nero and Narcissus and the other characters in *Britannicus* still speak the jargon of gallantry now and then, but their thoughts and feelings are those of people in all ages—instead of merely those of a mannered Court society of the seventeenth century—and hence we are able to imagine the dramatis personae to be indeed the historical figures whose names they bear. The one exception is found in Britannicus himself; it apparently was next to impossible for Racine to draw an attractive picture of a young man who is in love. He succeeded in doing so after a fashion, though rather colourlessly, in the case of Xiphares in *Mithridate,* but Xiphares is older and more experienced than Britannicus and Hippolytus;—these, Racine's two most flagrant examples of the type, unfortunately are in his two best secular dramas! He meant to portray Britannicus as a high-spirited and pathetic youth; he did portray him as a *petit maître* who is at times unmanly or affected. Junia, on the other hand, is a lovely creation—of all Racine's women the least sophisticated and, unless perhaps Monime, the most appealing—with the simplicity, the directness, the sweet dignity, and the fresh, unstudied charm of young girlhood. Despite the pathos of her situation, the author somehow, by some miracle of delicate art too subtle to be analyzed, has made us feel that she was naturally of a merry disposition, as, in point of fact, his sources describe her to have been—

"festivissima omnium puellarum"—and this only adds to the piteousness of the lot which is hers. Her love for Britannicus is that of the stronger for the weaker, protective and nourished on compassion; she has cheered and comforted and mothered like an older sister the unhappy boy who loves her.

But notwithstanding the title of the play, its central figures are Nero and Agrippina. Its theme is not the death of the unfortunate prince, except in as much as that is Nero's first plunge into crime; its real object is to depict this plunge—to exhibit the royal monster in the making. And Agrippina's ambition has been the chief moulding influence in her son's life, both directly and through his reaction of antagonism against it. She is, indeed, the more impressive character of the two, for she surpasses the Emperor in force of personality, intelligence, energy, and courage; and a legitimate alternative view of *Britannicus,* according to Racine himself, is that its subject is the final defeat of her long-cherished hopes. In order that the wickedness of Nero may stand out more strikingly, the darker aspects of her nature have not been emphasized by the dramatist, but their existence is not denied and at least a glimpse of most of them is permitted. In like manner the conception of the Emperor himself is, in the main, the traditional one, but not all its phases are equally stressed; that of virtuoso, which was perhaps dominant in him, is clearly revealed only once in the play, though then at a crucial point. Racine did not attempt, as a modern author might, to show Nero to be the perverse product of corrupting environment and circumstances; he represents him as a young man fundamentally cruel, vain, and vicious, whose predisposition to evil causes him at length to break from the restraints hitherto imposed by his weakness and timidity.

The outcome of the struggle between the contending forces within him has been decided by the close of Act III, and the play really might end there. Nero has ordered the imprisonment of his rival and the detention of Agrippina under guard, and has threatened Burrus with arrest if he does not obey; the wild beast has been uncaged at last. The swiftly-ensuing murder of Britannicus might be taken for granted, as an assured sequel; its actual occurrence, even if included, could barely furnish material for one other act, at most. But inflexible convention in the age of Louis XIV required that a tragedy should have five acts. The device by which Racine triumphantly solved the difficult problem of an intervening fourth act is a supreme achievement of dramatic art. Instead of writing an obvious "filler," he contrived a succession of scenes which yield in interest and power to no other part of the play. At the end of the act the wheel has come full circle and the situation is practically the same as at the beginning of it. But in its course something more has been given us than a mere sequence of theatrically effective dialogues spiced with the excitement of real or pretended fluctuations of purpose. Racine there epitomizes and causes to pass before our eyes in brief review, as it were, all the influences, good and bad alike, to which Nero has been subjected. Agrippina with her schemes and with her claims on him, Burrus with his rectitude, Narcissus with his insidious, flattering villainy —one after the other is shown in contact with the young emperor, so that we can observe the solicitations of each and their effect upon him. It is interesting to note that Racine's problem in this act was much the same as Shakespeare's in the fourth act of *Julius Caesar,* and that Shakespeare, with his great quarrel scene between Brutus and Cassius, which alters nothing but which delineates character, met it in much the same way.

Not even a genius, however, could work two miracles in immediate succession. After having made something mag-

nificent out of nothing, Racine was unable to go on and then
make something altogether satisfying out of next to nothing.
The last act of *Britannicus* is a little flat and perfunctory. It
displays signs of abated inspiration, with several unconvinc-
ing details and with scenes which are palpably devised to
bridge the time between others of greater importance. Only
in the meeting of Agrippina and Nero after the murder, when
she charges him with it and foretells the course of crime that
he will run, does the play once more attain to those heights on
which it moved in the earlier acts. But if the conclusion does
not add to the effect of what has gone before, it at any rate
does not seriously impair it; and this drama in its entirety
ranks an impressive third in greatness among the works of
its author, surpassed only by the passion and power of *Phèdre*
and the exalted, almost flawless beauty of *Athalie*.

The advance in dramatic art which *Britannicus* exhibits
was not continued without pause, or even maintained. "In
Bérénice and *Bajazet*," observes N.-M. Bernardin, "Racine
went back completely to romanesque tragedy, from which he
had seemed to want to break away in *Britannicus*." The
reason for such a regression has, strangely, never been
pointed out. More familiar than any other author of his day
with the great tragedies of ancient Greece, Racine appears to
have been actuated, throughout his career, by two ambitions:
to write plays as nearly like those of Sophocles and Euripides
as was possible in seventeenth century France, and to write
plays that would be universally admired. *La Thébaïde* contains few pseudo-classical elements; save for Creon's love for
Antigone, it is a straightforward attempt to put the story of
the children of Oedipus as told by Seneca and the Greeks into
the form of a French tragedy; its faults are for the most part
merely those of inexperience. It enjoyed a very creditable

success for a maiden effort, but nothing like the success that Racine had hoped for. Very well, he must have said to himself, if people did not care for what *he* preferred, he would show that he could give them what *they* preferred; and he wrote the wholly romanesque *Alexandre,* which was extremely popular. He had now proved that he could win favour; perhaps he could win it also with something more nearly to his taste. In *Andromaque* he took a long stride towards naturalness and truth, and both city and Court acclaimed his daring experiment with the wildest delight. He then went still further in the same direction in *Britannicus*; but this tragedy, though it became after a few years one of the most highly esteemed of his works, was an utter failure when first presented, until it was saved by the praise which Louis XIV bestowed upon it. Two courses lay open to its author: he could continue resolutely in the vein of *Britannicus,* hoping that he might at length please the public with that sort of play, whether by more fortunate selection of subject or by educating his audiences to a better appreciation of true dramatic values, but in any event persisting in his own search for those values; or he could revert to the manner of *Andromaque,* in which case he would be certain to acquire fresh laurels. He chose the latter alternative. *Bérénice* has little less of pseudo-classical convention than has *Andromaque,* and it scored a triumph. Thereafter, Racine again made progress away from romanesque tragedy and towards a purer form of art, but this time slowly and cautiously, through *Bajazet* and *Mithridate* to an *Iphigénie* which in large part is of genuine classical inspiration, and thence, doubtless reassured by the applause that had greeted each of these dramas, to the transcendent achievement of *Phèdre.*

CHARACTERS IN THE PLAY

NERO, *Emperor of Rome, son of Agrippina.*

BRITANNICUS, *son of Claudius, the preceding Emperor, by a marriage prior to that with Agrippina.*

AGRIPPINA, *widow of Domitius Ahenobarbus (the father of Nero) and afterwards of the Emperor Claudius.*

JUNIA, *the beloved of Britannicus.*

BURRUS, *counsellor and former tutor of Nero.*

NARCISSUS, *tutor of Britannicus.*

ALBINA, *confidential friend of Agrippina.*

GUARDS.

The scene is laid in Rome, in the palace of Nero.

BRITANNICUS

ACT I

The scene represents a room in the palace of NERO. *The time is shortly after dawn. Enter* AGRIPPINA *and* ALBINA.

ALBINA.

What! must thou come, forsooth, while Nero takes
His fill of sleep, and wait until he wakes?
Shall Caesar's mother unattended roam
The palace? watch outside his door alone?
Madam, return to thine apartments.

AGRIPPINA.

Nay!

I must not for one moment go away,
Albina. I would fain await him here.
Full store have I for thought (what with the care
He causeth me) long though his rest endure.
All I foretold is but indeed too sure.
Nero declares himself against the prince
Britannicus. Nero no more restrains
His heart in its impatience. He is tired
Of being loved; he wishes to be feared.
Britannicus doth trouble him, and I feel
More and more every day that I as well
Grow irksome to him.

ALBINA.

Thou, whence he doth owe
The breath of life?—who from a state so low
Hast raised him to the throne?—who, to do thus,

Disinheriting the son of Claudius,
Hast had the fortunate Domitius[1] take
The name of Caesar? These things, madam, speak
To him in thy behalf. To Agrippina
He oweth his love.

AGRIPPINA.

He oweth it, Albina.
All things, if he is noble, must require
This of him, but if he is base, conspire
'Gainst me.

ALBINA.

If he is base, thou sayest! His whole
Conduct bespeaks a well instructed soul
Touching his duty. For three years' full sum,
What hath he said or done which unto Rome
Gives not the promise of a perfect reign?
She has thought herself, throughout that time, again
Beneath her consuls, Nero in such truth
Governs her as a father. He in youth
Has all the virtues that Augustus had
In age.

AGRIPPINA.

No, no! self-interest hath not made
My heart unjust. Lo, he beginneth where
Augustus ended, verily; but beware
Lest by the future be the past undone
And he end as Augustus had begun.[2]
Vainly would he disguise himself. I read
The tokens of Domitius' ruthless breed,
Cruel and ferocious, clearly in his face.
He joins unto the pride that marks their race

The Neros' arrogance, which he drank from me.
Always benign at first is tyranny.
Caius[3] awhile was the delight of Rome;
But presently did Rome's delight become
(When changed to frenzy his false kindliness)
Rome's horror. What care I in any case
If Nero, not more constant, some day should
Depart from virtue's path he long pursued?
Gave I the helm of State into his hands
That he should steer according as demands
The people or the Senate? Let him still
Be father of his country if he will;
But ah, let him more surely not forget
That Agrippina is his mother! Yet
How name the deed which this day's light hath shown?
He knoweth—to none their love can be unknown—
That Junia is Britannicus' beloved;
And this same Nero, whom but virtue moved,
Hath in the night had Junia carried off!
What doth he purpose? Is it hate or love
That prompts him? Seeks he only joy and sport
In injuring them; or is it not the support
That I have lent them, rather, which he now
Avengeth upon them so cruelly?

ALBINA.
Thou
Their support, madam?

AGRIPPINA.
Stop, Albina mine!
I know 'twas I myself that made incline
Their fortunes ruinward; that from the throne

Where birth should have uplifted him, alone
Through me Britannicus was headlong hurled.
Through me alone it was that from the world
Of living men, because he might not wed
Octavia, Junia's hapless brother fled—
Silanus, on whom Claudius' look was bent,
And who could from Augustus claim descent.
Nero hath all, and for reward must I
Maintain the balance 'twixt them equally,
That some day likewise may Britannicus
Maintain it 'twixt my son and me e'en thus.

ALBINA.

What plan is thine!

AGRIPPINA.

                    I fashion ere the storm
A harbour for myself. Nero will from
My power escape unless curbed by this rein.

ALBINA.

But 'gainst a son such care is surely vain!

AGRIPPINA.

I soon should fear him, when he feared not me.

ALBINA.

Groundless, perchance, is this anxiety.
But even though Nero were no longer what
He should be to thee, still his change doth not
Display itself to us, and all this is
A secret between thee and him. Nowise
Are any titles whatsoe'er conferred
On him by Rome which are not straightway shared
With thee; his lavish love begrudgeth none.

Thy name do all men honour like his own,
With scarce a word of poor Octavia said.
Thine ancestor Augustus never paid
To Livia such honours.[4] None till now,
As Nero for thy sake, would e'er allow
Laurel-decked fasces to be borne before
A woman. From his gratitude what more
Tokens desirest thou?

AGRIPPINA.

Less reverence,
Somewhat, and greater trust and confidence.
Albina, all his favours irk me when
I see my honour wax, my influence wane.
Nay, nay, the time is gone when Nero, yet
A mere youth, with a heart's true homage met
My loving heart; when he relied, in all
Affairs of State, upon me; when my call
Gathered the Senate here; and when, unseen
Though present, I, concealed behind a screen,
Of that great body was the potent will.
Assured of Rome's acceptance then but ill,
Nero was not yet drunk with empery.
That day, that bitter day, in memory
Pierces my bosom still, when he had grown
Dazzled with glory, when before his throne
From many kings, both near and far, there came
Envoys to hail him in all nations' name,
And I went, at his side to take my place.
I know not whose advice wrought my disgrace;
But Nero, soon as e'er I met his glance,
Showed his displeasure on his countenance,—
And straightway I foreboded evil thereof.

With feignèd deference masking the rebuff,
That ingrate rose, anticipating me,
And running to embrace me (lovingly,
As it were), turned my footsteps from the throne
That I had thought to seat myself upon.
The power of Agrippina, since that blow,
Gathereth speed daily toward its overthrow.
Only the shadow of it yet remains
To me, and men invoke now but the names
Of Seneca and Burrus for their aid.[5]

ALBINA.

Ah, if thy soul by this surmise be swayed,
Why dost thou let its poison gnaw thy breast?
From Caesar's lips have certainty, at least,
I pray thee.

AGRIPPINA.

Caesar now, Albina, sees
No more his mother without witnesses.
At a fixed hour, in public, I am given
Audience. His answers, and his silence even,
Are what were set for him. Two watchful-eyed
Masters are his, and eke mine, who preside,
One or the other, at each interview
Between us. But the more will I pursue
His footsteps as he shuns me. I must now
Take him at unawares. . . . Hark! hearest thou
That noise? 'Tis a door opening. Let us go
Suddenly to demand of him to know
Wherefore was this abduction, and surprise
The secrets thus, if possible it is,
Of his soul. . . .

[*Enter* BURRUS.

What! so early Burrus came
From his apartments?

Burrus.

Madam, in the name
Of the Emperor I sought thee to inform thee
As to a step which might at first alarm thee,[6]
Yet which proceeds alone from a wise care,
And of which Caesar wills that thou shouldst hear
In full.

Agrippina.

Seeing that he wills thus, go we in;
For we shall better learn of it from him.

Burrus.

Caesar hath for a time withdrawn from view.
Already, by a door known to but few,
Both consuls, madam, came ere thee.[7] But may
I be permitted to return to . . .

Agrippina.

Nay!
His privacy shall nowise be disturbed
By me. But wouldst thou that with tongue less curbed
We should together speak, both thou and I,
Frankly?

Burrus.

Always hath Burrus loathed a lie.

Agrippina.

Meanest thou to keep the Emperor long from me?
As an intruder only shall I see

His face henceforth? Thy fortunes have I, then,
So raised to put a barrier between
My son and me? Darest thou not leave him now
One moment, trusted to himself? Do thou
And Seneca in rivalry contest
As to which from his memory can best
Efface me? Gave I him to you that ye
Should make an ingrate of him or should be
Under his name the masters of the State?
Truly do I, the more I meditate,
Think less and less that thou couldst e'er presume
To reckon me your puppet: thou in whom
I could have let ambition age and die
In obscure office in some legion[8]—I
Whose ancestors before me held the throne,
Daughter, wife, sister, mother, all in one,
Unto your sovereigns.[9] What, then, seek ye for?
Think ye my voice hath made an emperor
That I might have three over me? No more
Is Nero still a child. Is not the hour
Arrived when he should reign? How long do ye
Desire that he shall fear you? Can he see
Nothing for which ye lend him not your eyes?
Does not his own ancestral stock suffice
For guides? Augustus or Tiberius
Let him choose, if he likes. Germanicus,
My father, let him copy if he can.
I do not dare with such heroic men
To rank myself, but there are qualities
That I can teach him,—at the least, what is
The furthest that his trust should e'er allow
A subject in his counsels.

BURRUS.

         I had now
Assumed the task to excuse one single deed
Of Caesar's, yet since thou desirest, instead
Of hearing that deed justified, to make
Me answerable for all his life, I take
The freedom of a soldier, who ill knows,
Madam, how one o'er verity may gloss.

     Thou hast entrusted Caesar's youth to me.
This I admit, and I perpetually
Ought to remember it. Yet did I swear
An oath to thee I would betray him, e'er,—
Would make an emperor skilled but to obey?
No. 'Tis not unto thee I need to-day
Answer for him. This is no more thy son;
This is the master of the world. Alone
Unto the Roman Empire do I owe
Account for him, which thinketh its weal or woe
Is in my hands. Ah, if he was to be
Mistaught, couldst find but Seneca and me
To lead his feet astray? Wherefore denied
Access to him were flatterers, thus to guide?
To obtain corruptors for him, didst thou have
To recall the exiled? There was many a slave
In Claudius' court—a thousand, where two men
Were all thou soughtest—who would have most fain
Been honoured with degrading him. In sooth,
They to old age would have prolonged his youth!

     Of what dost thou complain? All reverence thee.
The mother of Caesar is named even as he
In oaths. The Emperor comes no more each day,
'Tis true, the Empire at thy feet to lay,

And swell the number of thy Court. But should
He do so, madam, and can his gratitude
Only in his subserviency appear?
Shall Nero, ever humble, timid e'er,
Dare not our Caesar and Augustus be
Except in name? Shall I say all to thee
In one sole word? Rome doth not deem him wrong.
Rome, which unto three freedmen[10] was so long
Enslaved and hardly is revived again
After the yoke thus borne, from Nero's reign
Reckoneth her liberty. Nay, as of yore
It was, her virtue seems reborn. No more
Is the whole Empire now a tyrant's prey.
The people name their magistrates to-day
Upon the field of Mars. For generals, those
The soldiers trust and love, doth Caesar choose.
Thrasea in the Senate, Corbulo[11]
In the army stand yet unattaint although
Of high renown. No longer in the wild
Places, once thronged with senators exiled,
Do any, now, except informers live.[12]
What matters it if Caesar still doth give
Ear to us, if our counsels bring him naught
Save glory; if, a prosperous reign throughout,
Rome shall be free and he omnipotent?

    But Nero is already competent
To order his own course; and I obey,
Nor e'er would dream of pointing him the way.
Unto his ancestors' example he
Hath only to conform him, doubtlessly;
And to be like himself is all his need,
Would he do well. Oh, fortunate indeed,

Might his life's virtues, in unbroken chain,
Ever recall the first years of his reign!

AGRIPPINA.

Then ye dare not unto the future trust;[13]
Ye think that Nero, left without you, must
Wander astray. But thou who, satisfied
With your work thus far, hast so testified
To his great virtues, let me plainly hear
Why he hath grown to be a ravisher
And carried off the sister of the dead
Silanus. Doth he only mean to shed
Disgrace upon my father's blood, which flows
In Junia's veins? What are the charges gross
He brings against her? and she in what way
Becometh a State criminal in one day,—
She who, reared without pomp or pride till then,
Had he not had her seized, would ne'er have seen
Nero, and who would even have reckoned it
A blessing never to have met his sight?

BURRUS.

I know she is suspected of no crime;
But neither hath the Emperor at this time
Punished her. Nothing here offends her glance.
She is within a palace whose expanse
Is thronged with statues of her ancestors.
Thou knowest that the claims that would be hers
Could make a princely rebel of her spouse;
That Caesar's kindred should be joined with those
Only whom Caesar trusteth utterly;
And thou thyself wilt own that it would be
Not fitting that without his will a maid
Descended from Augustus should be wed.

Agrippina.

I understand thee. Nero through thy voice
Informs me that in vain upon my choice
Britannicus relieth; that in vain
With hope of one for whom he was most fain
I have beguiled him, thus to turn away
His eyes from his sad lot. To my dismay,
Nero desires to have it seen that more
Doth Agrippina promise than in her power
Lies to fulfil. Rome is too much imbued
With the idea of my influence, and he would
Make her, by this affront to me, discern
Her error and the world, affrighted, learn
Not to confound the Emperor and my son.
This he can do. I still dare tell him, none
The less, that he should strengthen, ere this deed,
His power, and that in driving me to the need
Of matching my authority 'gainst his
He risks his own; for in the balances
Mine may prove weightier than he doth suspect.

Burrus.

What, madam! Ever doubting his respect?
Can he not make one single step thy heart
Mistrusts not? Could he think thou takest the part
Of Junia? Could he think that thou art now
Reconciled with Britannicus? Hast thou
Become thy foes' support, to find some grounds
To complain of him? Whatso rumour sounds
Within thine ear, wilt thou for ever be
Ready to break the Empire's unity?
Wilt thou ne'er leave thy fears? Must each embrace
Be spent in explanations? Cease, oh cease

The practice of a censor's task! Take on
The indulgence of a mother toward her son.
Bear some slight coldness from him silently,—
Not warn the Court it should abandon thee.

AGRIPPINA.

Who would for Agrippina's favour care,
When Nero doth himself to all declare
My ruin? when I may come to him no more
Since Burrus dares to stay me at his door?

BURRUS.

Madam, I see 'tis time for me to be
Silent; my frankness only angers thee.
Sorrow is never just, and reasoning
Which soothes it not, sharpeneth suspicion's sting.
Here is Britannicus; I will yield place
To him, and let thee hark to his distress
And pity it—and those perchance accuse
Thereof whose counsel Caesar least did use.[14]
    [*Exit* BURRUS. *Enter* BRITANNICUS *wildly, and* NARCISSUS.

AGRIPPINA.

Nay, Prince, where rushest thou? What recklessness
Impels thee blindly 'midst thine enemies?
What dost thou seek?

BRITANNICUS.

              What do I seek? Alas,
All I have lost, madam, is in this place.
By countless cruel soldiers Junia
Saw herself shamefully dragged hither. Ah,
Gods! with what horror must her timid breast
Have been at this unwonted sight distressed!

Yes, she is snatched from me. A harsh decree
Sunders two hearts made one by misery.
Doubtless 'twas not desired that we should share
Misfortune, thus made easier to bear.

AGRIPPINA.

Enough! I too resent your injuries.
Ere now my protests have outstripped thy sighs.
But I do not pretend that bootless wrath
Acquits me of my promise or keeps faith
With thee. My meaning I have not explained;
But follow me, if thou wouldst understand,
To the house of Pallas. I shall await thee there.[15]

[*Exeunt* AGRIPPINA *and* ALBINA.

BRITANNICUS.

Shall I believe her, and for arbiter
Take her, Narcissus, 'twixt her son and me,
Trusting her speech? How seemeth it to thee?
Is she not that same Agrippina whom
Of yore my father wedded, to my doom,
And who, if sooth thou sayest, sped the pace,
Which was too slow for her, of his last days?

NARCISSUS.

It matters not. Like thee she feels outraged.
To give thee Junia, her word was pledged.
Unite your griefs; combine, your ends to gain.
This palace with your mourning rings in vain.
While ye are seen as suppliants here, who spread
But lamentation and not fear instead,
So long your wrath must all in talk be spent,
And doubtless without end will be your plaint.

BRITANNICUS.

Thou knowest, Narcissus, whether 'tis my plan
To learn yet more the wont of slavery's chain.
Thou knowest whether, by my fall o'ercome,
I have renounced the sovereignty of Rome,
Which was my right. But I am still alone.
My father's friends are only folk unknown
To me, whose zeal mine abject state hath froze;
And my youth keeps aloof from me all those
Who in their hearts renounce not loyalty.
Since a brief year's experience hath to me
Made sadly clear my fate, what do mine eyes
See round me save false friends, assiduous spies
On all my steps, who, chosen for this base part
By Nero, sell the secrets of my heart
To him? Yes, be it howsoe'er it may,
Narcissus, I am bartered every day.
My aims he doth foresee, my words doth hear.
Of what is in my breast he is aware
E'en as art thou. Seems it not to thee so,
Narcissus?

NARCISSUS.

Ah, what soul indeed thus low . . .
Thou must choose friends who can keep silent, not
A spendthrift, sir, be of each inmost thought.

BRITANNICUS.

True, but to be mistrustful is the art
Always learned latest by a generous heart,
Which hence too long 'tis easy to deceive.
Yet I believe thee—or, rather, to believe
None else but thee, I swear. My father, well

Do I recall, assured me of thy zeal.
Thou of his freedmen hast alone still been
Faithful to me. Thy vision, ever keen
To watch my courses, hath safeguarded me,
Ere this, from countless hidden reefs. Go see,
Then, if the news of this fresh storm will fan
The courage of our friends. Mark their speech. Scan
Their faces. Judge if I can without fail
Expect their succour. Observe, most of all,
Within this palace how close guard is o'er
The princess kept. Learn if no perils more
Threaten her fair head, and if I may still
Hold speech with her. I go, to seek, meanwhile,
The mother of Nero, unto Pallas' house—
He like thyself my father's freedman was—
To incite her, follow her, and, it may be,
Beyond her wish bind her to champion me.

                                   [*Exeunt severally*

ACT II

The scene is the same. NERO *is discovered with* BURRUS,
NARCISSUS, *and guards.*

NERO.

Be assured, Burrus : though unjust, yet this is
My mother, and I fain would her caprices
Quite disregard. But I intend no more
Either to disregard or to endure
The insolent minion who hath dared in her
To foster them. Pallas doth fill her ear
With poison. He corrupteth day by day
Britannicus my brother. Now will they
Hear none but him. One following their feet
Would doubtless find that even now they meet
'Neath Pallas' roof. It is too much to bear.
I needs must from them both remove him far.
For the last time, I wish and I command,
Let him depart, begone ; let not the end
Of this day find him still here in my Court
Or in Rome. Go. This order doth import
The safety of the Empire much.

[*Exit* BURRUS.

Come thou

Nearer, Narcissus.
    (*To the guards*) And do ye withdraw.

[*The soldiers retire.*

NARCISSUS.

Thank the gods, Junia in thy hands, my lord,
Hath utterly thy sway in Rome secured.

Thy foes, from height of their false hopes cast down,
To mourn their weakness have to Pallas flown.
But what do I behold? Perturbed and sad,
Thou seemest more than Britannicus dismayed.
What is this gloom mysterious that I see?
Why roams thy sombre stare bewilderedly?
Everything smiles upon thee. Fortune doth
Crown thy desires.

NERO.

Narcissus, learn the truth.
I am in love.

NARCISSUS.

Thou?

NERO.

Since but yesterday;
Henceforth for ever.[16] I love—love, say I?—nay,
I worship Junia.

NARCISSUS.

Her? Thou lov'st *her*?

NERO.

I

Last night, moved by my curiosity,
Observed her, when first brought here, to the skies
Uplifting in distress her tearful eyes,
That shone across the torches and the arms.
Most fair she was, with unadornèd charms
And simple garb of one who lately lay
In sleep. And then . . . whether her disarray
'Twas, and the shadows and the unsteady light

Of flames, the cries and silence, and the sight
Of her fierce ravishers that did enhance,
Round her, the timid sweetness of her glance,
I know not; but however it befell,
Ensorcelled by that lovely spectacle,
I fain would have addressed her, but I could
Not speak. Long dazed and motionless I stood,
And after having suffered her to pass
To her apartment, went to mine. Alas,
There was it that, alone, I vainly sought
To put her image from me. In my thought
I talked with her, whom still I saw. Indeed,
I loved the very tears I made her shed. [7]
Sometimes I craved her pardon, but too late.
I sighed to her, and even threatened. That
Is how, engrossed in my new love, I lay
With unclosed eyes and waited for the day.
But I have pictured her too favourably,
Perhaps, in fancy,—she was seen by me
To such advantage. What dost thou conceive,
Narcissus?

NARCISSUS.

Ah, my lord, can one believe
That she so long was able to conceal
Herself from Nero?

NERO.

Nay, thou knowest it well;
And be it that she charged me in her wrath
With the misfortune of her brother's death,
Or be it that her bosom's fervent pride
Her burgeoning beauty to my gaze denied,
True to her grief, shrouding herself in night,

She fled from even the fame that was her right;
And 'tis this constancy in virtue, so
New to the Court, that maketh my love grow.
Bethink thee, while there lives in Rome no dame
Who would not vaunt if she that love could claim;
Who, soon as she can trust her glances' art,
Comes not to try them upon Caesar's heart,
Chaste Junia in his palace—she alone—
Accounteth ignominious the boon
They covet, and, it may be, doth not deign
To learn if Caesar merits love, or e'en
If he himself can feel it. Tell me, doth
Britannicus love her?

NARCISSUS.

                    Canst thou in sooth
Ask this, my lord?

NERO.

                    So young as he yet is,
Knows he indeed his heart? The deadly bliss
Drained from a fond look doth he know?

NARCISSUS.

                                Love, sir,
Awaits not reason's growth. He loveth her;
Doubt it not. Taught by beauty such as hers,
His eyes ere this have learned the use of tears.
He well can to her slightest wish conform;
Perhaps already he can plead and charm.

NERO.

What! Thinkest thou he may rule within her breast?

NARCISSUS.

I know not, sire; but this I know at least:
I have seen him sometimes tear himself from hence,
Full of a wrath he would not to thy glance
Betray, complaining of an ingrate Court
That shuns him, weary of thy royal port
And his subjection, wavering between
Fear and impatience. He would hasten then
To Junia, and contented would return.

NERO.

So much the worse for him, that he could learn
To win her favour. He should have preferred
Her wrath. Narcissus, Nero can be stirred
Not without danger to feel jealousy.

NARCISSUS.

But why, my lord, hast thou anxiety?
Junia hath pitied him and shared his woe.
No tears save his she ever hath seen flow.
But when she this day, sire, with eyes unsealed,
To which thy dazzling splendour is revealed,
Sees the kings gathered, each without his crown,
About thee and amid the throng unknown,
And her own lover, hanging on thy glance,
All honoured by the looks which thou by chance
Wouldst cast on them—sees thee in such degree
Of glory come to admit her victory
With sighs;—then bid a heart already moved
To love thee, and 'tis sure thou wilt be loved.

NERO.

How much displeasure must I set my face
To meet!—what harassments!

Narcissus.

Sayst thou? Who stays
Thy will, my lord?

Nero.

All—all—Octavia
And Agrippina, Burrus, Seneca,
The whole of Rome, and three years' rectitude.
Not that a remnant of affection could
Be for Octavia found to bind me still
To her, or cause me for her youth to feel
Compassion. Long since weary of my wife,
Seldom I deign to look upon her grief.
Ah, might the blessing soon of a divorce
Release me from a yoke imposed by force!
'Twould seem e'en heaven secretly declares
'Gainst her. She hath entreated it four years
In vain. Her virtues appear not to touch
The gods. They honour with no pledge her couch,
And the Empire vainly asketh for an heir.

Narcissus.

Wherefore delayest thou to be rid of her?
The State, thy heart, everything dooms Octavia.
The great Augustus fell in love with Livia;[18]
Double divorce then joined them; and alone
To that blest severance thou owest the throne.
Tiberius, to whom marriage gave a place
Within his house, renounced before his face
His daughter. Only thou, unto this hour
Thwarting thine own desires, wilt not secure
By a divorce thy happiness.

NERO.

And dost thou
Know naught of Agrippina's wrath? E'en now,
To the confusion of my love, I see
Her in my fancy as she brings to me
Octavia and declares with blazing eyes
The sacred obligation of those ties
She knit, and, levelling reproaches rude
Against me, sets forth my ingratitude
At length. How am I to abide that dire
Meeting?

NARCISSUS.

Art thou not thine own master, sire,
And hers? Shall we for ever see thee quake
Under her sway? Live, reign for thine own sake.
Thou hast reigned for her too long. Art thou afraid?
It is not she, my lord, that thou dost dread.
Thou hast but now banished proud Pallas, whom
She hath supported.

NERO.

I, when absent from
Her sight, can give command or utter threat,
Can hear thy counsel, dare be pleased thereat;
My heart is 'gainst her stirred, and fain would I
Defy her. But (to lay bare utterly
My soul to thee) as soon as evil chance
Leads me again to stand before her glance,
Whether I yet lack courage to gainsay
Her spell who so long pointed me the way,
Or whether memory, that must recall
How much she gave me, yields her in secret all

I hold through her, my efforts naught avail;
My spirit, confounded, before hers doth quail;
And 'tis that I no longer may depend
On her, that I so shun and even offend
My mother and at times her anger stir
That she may avoid me as I would her.
    But thou art here too long, Narcissus. Go.
Britannicus may deem thee false.

NARCISSUS.

              No, no.
He trusts entirely in my loyalty.
He thinks 'tis by his hest I come to thee
To hearken here to all that doth concern
Himself, and from my mouth he hopes to learn
Thy secrets. Now, impatient to behold
Again his love, he waits but to be told
What I discover that can serve his use.

NERO.

Let it be so! Bring him this happy news:
He is to see her.

NARCISSUS.

          Banish him afar
From her, my lord.

NERO.

         For what I do, there are
Reasons, Narcissus. Thou shouldst know that dear
The joy will cost him of beholding her.
But boast how artful was thy stratagem.
Tell him that thou hast hoodwinked me for him,
And without my permission do they meet.

One cometh. It is she. Go, find thou straight
Thy master and conduct him here.

[*Exit* NARCISSUS. *A moment later* JUNIA *enters.*

(*To Junia*) Thy face
Changeth its hue. Thou seemest in distress.
Readest thou some doleful presage in mine eyes?

JUNIA.

My lord, I am not able to disguise
My error. I had thought to go unto
Octavia, not the Emperor.

NERO.

This I knew,
Madam, and could not hear without a trace
Of envy that Octavia had found grace
With thee.

JUNIA.

What, sire!

NERO.

Dost thou suppose that none
Here rightly values thee except alone
Octavia?

JUNIA.

To whom else dost thou desire
That I should sue? of whom, my lord, inquire
Touching a crime whereof I know not? Thou
Knowest, who punishest. Oh, tell me how,
I pray, have I offended!

NERO.

A small wrong
Thou thinkest it, then, to have concealed so long

Thy presence from us? What! didst thou receive
The richest gifts that heaven could bequeath
For thine adornment, but to hide them thus?
And shall the fortunate Britannicus
Serenely watch the growth, far from our sight,
Of his love and of thy beauty? From that bright
Radiance why have I been until this day
An exile in my Court? Rumour doth say,
Besides, that thou permittest him to declare
His feelings to thee, nor, that he should dare,
Takest offence; but I can nowise deem
That modest Junia thus would favour him
Without consulting me, or hath consented
To love and be loved ere I was acquainted
Therewith save by report.

JUNIA.

                    True is it, sire,
That he hath sometimes breathed his heart's desire
To me. He turned not from her in disdain
Who doth the last of a great house remain.
He may remember how in happier days
I was named his. He loves me. He obeys
Thereby the Emperor his father's will,
And thine own mother's, dare I tell thee still?
So to her wishes ever conform thine . . .

NERO.

My mother has her plans, and I have mine.
Speak we of Claudius and of her no more.
'Tis not their choice that over mine hath power.
I and none other, madam, must dispose
Of thee; I would, myself, thy husband choose.

JUNIA.

Ah, think! what union else would not disgrace
The Caesars wherefrom is derived my race?[19]

NERO.

Nay, he whom I would for thy husband name
Can join his stock to them without their shame.
Thou canst unblushingly accept his love.

JUNIA.

Who is this husband, sire, thou speakest of?

NERO.

I, madam.

JUNIA.

      Thou!

NERO.

      I would select for thee
Another, were there some one known to me
Higher than Nero. Truly have mine eyes,
To make a choice thou needest not despise,
The Court and Rome and the whole Empire scanned.
Yet the more I have sought, and seek, some hand
Meet to receive such treasure as thou art,
The clearer do I see that of thy heart
Caesar alone is worthy,—should alone
Be blessed with its possession; and to none
Save him canst thou entrust it worthily
Who is entrusted with earth's sovereignty.
Thyself, recall thy childhood. Claudius then
Destined thee for his son; but that was when
He thought to name him as the future heir
Of all his realm. This did the gods declare

Against. Not thine their purpose to oppose,
But to wed him to whom the sceptre goes!
Vain were to me their glorious gift thereof,
Unless it be not sundered from thy love;
Unless its cares are by thy charms made sweet;
Unless I may at times come to thy feet
For respite 'mid the anxious toil of days
Which men will always envy but always
Should pity, rather.
                              Let Octavia
Not trouble thee. Rome gives its preference now
Unto thee, in like manner as do I,
Rejects Octavia, bids me to untie
A knot which heaven never wished to bind.
Consider, and weigh well within thy mind
This choice, then, madam, that is just and wise
For a prince who loves thee, for thine own bright eyes
(Too long immured), and for the world to which
Thou owest thy gracious presence.

Junia.

                              At thy speech,
My lord, I stand amazed, and rightfully.
All in the course of one same day I see
Myself brought like a malefactor here,
And when before thee I have come in fear,
Scarcely relying on mine innocence,
Thou offerest me Octavia's place at once!
Yet will I dare to say that neither have I
This too-great honour nor this indignity
Merited. Canst thou, sire, wish that a maid
Who as a child her house o'erthrown surveyed,
And nursing in obscurity her grief,

To such misfortune hath conformed her life,
Should in a twinkling from the shadows' gloom
Unto a station seen of all men come,
Whereof she ne'er had borne the distant light
E'en, and which was, besides, another's right?

NERO.

I have already said to thee that I
Renounce her. Have less fear, less modesty.
Accuse me not of blindness in my choice.
I answer for thy worth; let but thy voice
Utter consent. Remember from what strain
Thy blood derives, nor do thou in disdain
Hold the substantial honours wherewith now
Caesar would clothe thee, for the glory thou
Couldst win by a refusal which may be
Repented of.

JUNIA.

The gods, my lord, can see
Mine inmost thought. With no vainglorying
I feed my pride. I know how great a thing
Thou offerest me; but the more brightly shine
Its splendours on me, the more shame is mine
And the more clearly is my guilt revealed
Of robbing her who once that prize hath held.

NERO.

Too much thou thinkest of what her interests are,
Madam, and friendship cannot go so far.
Let us have done with mystery, nor be
Deceived. The sister matters less to thee
Herein a great deal than the brother doth;
And for Britannicus . . .

JUNIA.

Yes, he in truth
Matters to me, nor have I hidden it.
Such frankness may not in a maid seem fit,
But never have my lips belied my heart.
I deemed, since from the Court I dwelt apart,
No need was mine to practise artifice.
I love Britannicus. I was plighted his
When empire was the prospect of his bride;
But those same ills that did that lot forbid,
His honours stripped from him, his palace hall
Forlorn, the flight of courtiers at his fall,
Serve only to bind Junia to him still.
All that thou seest conspireth to fulfil
Thy wishes. Calmly flows each day, each hour
Of thine, with pleasures thronged, whereof thy power
Is unto thee a never-ending source;
Or if some trouble interrupts their course,
The whole world, anxious to maintain thy bliss,
Hastens to blot out from thy memory this
Ill thing. Britannicus is quite alone.
Whatever weighs upon him, there is none
That he beholds but me that truly cares
For him, and all his joy is in my tears,
Which sometimes, sire, make him forget his woes.

NERO.

And 'tis that very happiness and those
Tears that I envy; any man save him
Would have to pay me with his life for them.
But I shall treat this prince more gently. Ere
Long, he himself shall stand before thee here.

JUNIA.

Ah, my lord, ever was I reassured,
Knowing thy virtues.[20]

NERO.

I could with a word
Have to this place forbidden him to come;
But I wish, madam, to forestall the doom
Which his resentment could bring on his head.
I fain would not destroy him. He instead
Shall from the lips he loveth learn his fate.
His life is dear to thee? Exile him straight,
Then, from thy sight, without his having cause
To think me jealous. Let him not suppose
That he is banished save alone by thee,
And whether by words or silence, let him be
Made to think from thy coldness that elsewhere
His longings and his hopes he needs must bear.

JUNIA.

I! I decree to him so harsh a doom?
My tongue hath sworn a different thing therefrom
A thousand times. Even if so far I could
Be traitor to my heart, mine eyes yet would
Forbid him to obey me.

NERO.

I, concealed
Near by, shall watch thee. Let thy love be sealed
Within the depths of thine own heart again.
No secret language shall avail thee; plain
Each glance will speak to me that seemeth mute;
And death for him will be the certain fruit
Of sign or sigh to comfort him.

JUNIA.

                              Alas!
If any wish I still may dare express,
Let me, sire, look upon him nevermore!

                                        [*Enter* NARCISSUS.

NARCISSUS.

Britannicus, my lord, is seeking for
The princess. He approacheth.[21]

NERO.

                              Straightway let
Him enter.

JUNIA.

          Sire!

NERO.

              I leave thee; and his fate
Is rather in thy hands than mine. While he
Is with thee, madam, remember that I see.

                              [NERO *retires behind a curtain.*

JUNIA.

Quick, my Narcissus, ere he cometh, run
To stay thy master. Tell him . . . Ah, undone
Am I! He is here.

                              [*Enter* BRITANNICUS.

BRITANNICUS.

              Dear madam, by what bliss
Once more do I find thee? Shall the joy of this
Meeting be mine? But even in my delight
How am I troubled! Can I have the sight
Of thee again hereafter? Must I steal
By many a ruse the happiness that till

This day thou always freely didst accord?
That fearful night! And when I waked, and heard!
Did not thy tears, thy very presence, e'en,
Disarm the insolence of those cruel men?
Where was he, all the while, who loveth thee?
What jealous deity hath denied to me
The privilege of dying at thy feet?
Ah, in the fear with which thou wast beset,
Hath thy heart cried out unto me in vain?
My princess, didst thou wish my presence then?
Thoughtest thou of the anguish I would feel
For thee? . . . Thou sayest naught. Such greeting chill
Have I? Is this the comfort I am given?
Speak; none is near. Our foe, deceived, is even
At this time busied elsewhere.²² Let us now
Waste not the moments of his absence.

JUNIA.

Thou
Art where his power extendeth everywhere.
These very walls, sir, may have ears to hear.
Caesar is never absent from this place.

BRITANNICUS.

Since when wast thou so timorous? Alas,
Thy love already endures bondage? O'er
This heart hath come what change, that ever swore
To make e'en Nero envious of our tie?
But banish empty terrors. Loyalty
Is not yet dead in every breast. The eyes
Of all seem with my wrath to sympathize.
The Emperor's mother takes our part; and Rome
Herself, that by his conduct hath become
Enangered . . .

JUNIA.

Sir, thou speakest the contrary
Of thy belief.[23] Thou hast declared to me
Often, thyself, that Rome doth sing his praise
With one united voice. Thou hast always
Had for his virtues due respect. In sooth,
Grief alone puts these words into thy mouth.

BRITANNICUS.

Thou dost surprise me, I must needs avow.
'Twas not to hear him thus extolled that now
I sought thee. Scarce can I a moment seize
To bring to thee my load of miseries,[24]
And this dear moment thou wouldst fain consume,
Madam, with good words for the foe from whom
I suffer wrong! How art thou in a day
So changed? Can even thine eyes no longer say
Aught to me? What! afraid to meet my gaze?
Is it possible that Nero hath found grace
With thee, and is it possible that I am
Disdained? If I believed it! In the name
Of the gods, shed light upon this gloom wherein
Thou hast plunged me! Speak! Do I no longer mean
Anything unto thee?

JUNIA.

I pray, sir, go.
The Emperor is at hand.[25]

BRITANNICUS.

After this blow,
Narcissus, what remaineth for me now?
[*Exit* BRITANNICUS. NERO *comes from his place of con-
cealment.*

NERO.

Madam . . .

JUNIA.

      No, sire, I cannot listen. Thou
Hast been obeyed. Permit these tears at least,
Since he will not behold them.

                       [*Exit* JUNIA.

NERO.

               So, thou seest
The fervour of their love, Narcissus. Even
Their silences revealed it. She hath given
Her heart unto my rival, 'tis too clear.
My joy shall lie in making him despair.
How charmingly doth fancy paint his grief![26]
I have already shaken his belief
In her he loveth. I shall follow her.
Britannicus waits for thee as listener
Unto his vented rage. With new surmise
Go vex him; run; and while before mine eyes
One fondly weeps for him, let him pay dear
For blessings whereof he is not aware.

                       [*Exit* NERO.

NARCISSUS (*to himself*).

Fortune, Narcissus, calls to thee again.[27]
Wilt thou not heed her voice? Let us walk, then,
Even to the end, the road she doth reveal.
Let us destroy the luckless for our weal.

ACT III

The scene is the same. NERO *is discovered with* BURRUS.

BURRUS.

Pallas will be obedient, sire.[28]

NERO.

And how
Vieweth my mother her pride's overthrow?

BURRUS.

That she is wounded sore is past all doubt,
And that ere long her anger will break out
In fierce reproaches;—nay, it thus hath done
Already, nor at helpless cries alone
Can it be stayed.

NERO.

What! Thinkest thou that she
Might go so far as to conspire 'gainst me?

BURRUS.

Ever is Agrippina to be feared.
Her ancestors are by all Rome revered
And by thy soldiers. They remember still
Germanicus, her father. She knows well
Her power; thou knowest her courage; and my dread
Of her is greater in that thou hast fed,
Thyself, her wrath and 'gainst thee armed her hand.

NERO.

I?

BURRUS.

This love, sire, that rules thee . . .

NERO.

I understand,

Burrus. There is no help for it. My own
Heart tells me more than thou canst tell me. None
The less, it needs must be that still I love.

BURRUS.

Thou fanciest so; and deeming quite enough
Some small resistance, holdest in awe an ill
Not potent at its birth. But if thy will,
Firmly resolved on duty's course, would brook
No truce made with its foe; if thou wouldst look
Upon thy years of honour hitherto;
If thou wouldst to thy memory call anew
Octavia's virtues, so unworthily
Repaid, and how her heart hath clung to thee,
Triumphing o'er thy slights; if, above all,
Thou wouldst shun Junia's presence nor let fall
During the space of several days thy glance
A single time upon her countenance—
Ah, doubt not, sire, whate'er the spell thereof,
One never loves who does not wish to love.

NERO.

Thy counsel I shall trust when 'mid alarms
Of war the ancient glory of our arms
Must be upheld, or when, more peacefully
In the assembled Senate, policy
Of State must be determined. Then shall I
Gladly on thy experience rely.
But be assured, love is a different thing,

Burrus, and I should hesitate to bring
To thy grave judgment matters such as it.
Farewell. I suffer, out of Junia's sight.

[*Exit* NERO.

BURRUS (*to himself*).

Nero at last reveals his inmost soul.
That fierceness which thou thoughtest to control
Is ready, Burrus, from its bonds to escape.
To what excesses will it rush, mayhap!
Gods! how to counsel me in this dire pass?
Seneca, who should make my burden less,
Hath business far from Rome and knows not of
This peril. But what if I could rouse the love
In Agrippina and . . .
                    Lo, there she is!
Good fortune sends her hither.

[*Enter* AGRIPPINA *and* ALBINA.

AGRIPPINA.

                    Did I miss
The mark with my suspicions, Burrus?[29] Nay,
Through thy brave teachings thou hast gained this day
For thine own name a matchless eminence.
Pallas is banished—for the crime, perchance,
Of having raised thy master to the throne.
Full well thou knowest it: never would my son
Have been adopted, save through his advice,
By Claudius, whom he swayed.
                    But worse than this:
Thou givest Octavia a rival now;
Thou freest Nero from his marriage vow,—
Fit task for the foe of flatterers, forsooth,

Chosen to curb the courses of his youth,
Himself to flatter them, and in his life
Breed scorn of mother and neglect of wife!

BURRUS.

Madam, too soon thou dost accuse me thus.
The Emperor hath done naught beyond excuse.
Deem Pallas' exile needful. Recompense
Long deserved was it for his arrogance,
And Caesar with regret did but fulfil
The secret wish of all his Court.
                           No ill
Remaineth which may not be remedied.
Octavia's tears can at their source be dried.
But calm thy rage. Thou canst far easier
By gentler means restore her lord to her.
Outcries and threats will make his heart in truth
More wayward.

AGRIPPINA.

              Oh, thou canst not stop my mouth!
Well have I seen, my silence is disdained;
And he shall not abase me whom my hand
Upraised. Not every source of strength was reft
With Pallas from me. Heaven thereof hath left
Enough for Agrippina to repay
Her fall. The son of Claudius to-day
Chafes at those crimes of which I must repent.
I shall go, never doubt it, and present
Him to the army, tell them how his young
Life was made victim, and to right that wrong
Sway them by my example. They shall see
On one side, asking for their loyalty

Again, which to his family they did swear,
The son of an Emperor, and they shall hear
The daughter of Germanicus. They shall on
The other see Ahenobarbus' son,
Supported by the tribune Burrus and
By Seneca, who, though they to this land
Were both recalled from banishment by me,
Divide now the supreme authority
Before mine eyes. Our crimes I will make known,
And by what means I led him to the throne.
To render odious your power and his,
I will avow all rumoured infamies,—
Yea, tell of exiles, murders, poisonings
Even . . .[30]

BURRUS.

                None, madam, will believe such things,
Hearing them. None will know not 'tis a ruse,
Or heed, when one in anger doth accuse
Oneself. For my part, I who first gave aid
To thy designs—I who it was that made
The army pledge their faith to him—nowise
Do I regret my honest zeal. It is
From sire to son still that the crown descends.
Claudius set aside all difference
Of rights between his child and thine when he
Adopted Nero. Rome, as she was free
To do, chose whom she wished. Selecting thus
Augustus' foster son Tiberius,
To young Agrippa though of his own blood[31]
She had denied the rank which fain he would
Have had. The Emperor cannot in his sway,
On such foundations based, be shaken to-day

By thee; and if he will but heed me still,
Madam, his goodness soon shall change thy will
To harm him. I shall to the end pursue
The work I have begun.

[*Exit* BURRUS.

ALBINA.

Madam, into
What violence thy passion leadeth thee!
May Caesar learn not of it!

AGRIPPINA.

O that he
Would show himself before me!

ALBINA.

Conceal thine ire,
In the gods' name. What! is it thy desire
To give up either for the brother's gain
Or sister's thy heart's peace? Wouldst thou constrain
The Emperor even in his loves?

AGRIPPINA.

And thou
Indeed, then, canst not see, Albina, how
They drag me down? It is to me they give
A rival. Soon, if I do not contrive
To snap those fatal bonds, my place will be
Filled and my power ended utterly.
Octavia, with her empty title decked,
Was useless to the courtiers; their respect
Observed her not. Favours and honours then
Were had of me alone, and hence all men
With suits to urge were by their interests drawn

To me. Another woman now hath won
The heart of Caesar. She will reign as wife
And empress, and the fruit of my whole life,
The splendours of the Empire, will be given
For a kind glance from her. "Will," say I? Even
Now am I shunned, forsaken. . . . I cannot,
Albina, so much as endure the thought.[32]
Though I should hasten that which heaven dooms,[33]
Nero, the ingrate . . . But his rival comes.

[*Enter* BRITANNICUS *and* NARCISSUS.

BRITANNICUS.

Our mutual foes are not invincible,
Madam, and there are bosoms that can feel
For our misfortunes. With that anger filled
Which wrong doth kindle, thy friends and mine, concealed
Hitherto, have, while we with fruitless moan
Were squandering time, made their displeasure known
Unto Narcissus. Nero hath not yet
Secured possession of the false one that
He loveth to my sister's shame. If still
Her wrongs can move thee, it is possible
To recall him to that faith which he abjured.
Of half the Senate we may be assured.
Sulla and Piso, Plautus . . .

AGRIPPINA.

What dost thou say,[34]
Prince? Sulla, Piso, Plautus! Highest are they
Of the nobles.

BRITANNICUS.

Madam, I can clearly see
That most unwelcome are my words to thee.

And that e'en now thy wrath, irresolute,
Fears to attain the goal of its pursuit.
Nay, nay, thou hast accomplished all too well
My downfall, and thou needest not dread the zeal
Of any friends for me. There now remains
None of them, for long since thou tookest the pains
To drive or win them from my side.

AGRIPPINA.

Give less
Heed, sir, to thy suspicions. Our success
And safety must on our accord depend.
I promised, and I will to the very end
Fulfil my pledge, despite thine enemies.
Let that suffice thee. Guilty Nero flees
My wrath in vain. Sooner or later he
Must hear his mother. Then severity
And gentleness shall both in turn be tried,
Which failing, with thy sister at my side
I shall on every hand make known my fears
And her distress, and rally to her tears
All hearts. Farewell. Nero I shall not leave
Anywhere unassailed. If thou wilt give
Ear to my counsel, do thou shun his sight.[35]

[*Exit* AGRIPPINA.

BRITANNICUS.

Hast thou beguiled me with vain hopes no whit,
Narcissus? On thy story can I build?

NARCISSUS.

Yea, but this mystery cannot be revealed
Unto thee in this place, my lord, or now.
Let us go forth, then. For what waitest thou?

BRITANNICUS.

For what, Narcissus, do I wait? Alas!

NARCISSUS.

Explain thyself.

BRITANNICUS.

If by thy cleverness
I might again see . . .

NARCISSUS.

Whom?

BRITANNICUS.

I blush for it,
But with less shaken spirit I then would meet
My fate.

NARCISSUS.

What! After all that I did say
To thee, thou still believest her constant?

BRITANNICUS.

Nay.

I believe her faithless, wicked, worthy of
My wrath alone; yet I do not enough
Believe it, spite of all attempts. Howe'er
She strays, my stubborn heart finds reasons for her,
Excuses her, and worships her. I would
That I could crush my disbelief and could
Hate her without a pang. Who would dream, though,
That one who seemed so noble-souled, the foe
Of a false Court from childhood, would renounce
Her fair fame in a day and plan at once
A perfidy unheard of even there?

NARCISSUS.

And who can say she did not plan to ensnare
The Emperor, all her long seclusion through?
Such beauty could not be concealed, she knew.
Perhaps she fled but to be sought the more
And to make Nero fain to triumph o'er
Her bosom's pride which none erewhile could bow.

BRITANNICUS.

I must not see her, then?

NARCISSUS.

Sir, even now
To her new lover's wooing she gives ear.

BRITANNICUS.

Well, be it so. Let us begone from here,
Narcissus.

[*Enter* JUNIA.

Nay, but whom do I behold?
'Tis she.

NARCISSUS (*to himself*).

Great gods! The Emperor must be told
Of this.[86]

[*Exit* NARCISSUS.

JUNIA.

Away, sir! Flee a wrath which I
Have kindled against thee by my constancy.
Nero is furious. I escaped from him
While yet his mother stays him for a time.
Farewell. Wrong not my love, but patient bide
Till thou with joy shalt see me justified
Some day. Within my breast shall ever dwell
Thine image. Naught can drive it thence.

BRITANNICUS.

Quite well
I understand thee, madam. Fain wouldst thou
That unto thy desires I should allow
Full scope by taking flight; that I should yield
Thus to thy new-found longings a free field.
No doubt, when thou beholdest me, some annoy
Of secret shame lingers to vex thy joy.
Well, it is time to part.

JUNIA.

My lord, without
Charging me . . .

BRITANNICUS.

Thou shouldst have at least held out
Longer. I murmur not that every one
Should choose the side that fortune smiles upon;
That thou art dazzled by an empire's throne
Which, though my sister's, thou wouldst make thine own.
But when thou hadst so long seemed unconcerned
With these things for which thou hast really yearned
Like others—no, I will again confess:
My desperate heart for that one bitterness
Was not prepared. Yet I have seen, ere now,
Injustice triumph above mine overthrow;
I have seen heaven give mine oppressors aid.
Even so, not all its wrath had been displayed,
Madam: there still remained that I should be
Forgot by thee.

JUNIA.

I would indignantly
Compel thee to repent thy lack of faith,

Were the time fit. But Nero threatens death
For thee; and in the peril in which thou art,
I am too full of cares, to wound thy heart.
Be reassured. Go, and no more complain.
Nero was listening; he had bidden me feign.

BRITANNICUS.

What! The cruel . . .

JUNIA.

Seeing, hearing everything,
He watched my face with glance unpitying,
Ready to let his vengeance on thy head
Fall, if some understanding were conveyed
To thee by any gesture.

BRITANNICUS.

Nero was
Listening to us, thou sayest? But alas!
Thine eyes might have pretended to be cold
Without deceiving me. They could have told
The name to me of him who wrought this wrong.
Is love dumb? Knoweth it but a single tongue?
From what woe could one look have rescued me!
There was need . . .

JUNIA.

There was need for me to be
Silent and save thee! Ah, how oft (if thou
Must hear of this) was I about to show
Mine anguish unto thee! How many sighs
I checked upon my lips, shunning thine eyes
The while, that mine were ever fain to seek!
With one's beloved, what torture not to speak!
To hear him groan, oneself to give him pain

When one could heal it by a glance! But then,
What tears would not that glance have caused to flow!
Ah, this thought terrified, confused me so
I felt that all too poor was my pretence.
I feared the pallor of my countenance,
And deemed my frightened eyes showed too much grief.
At every instant it was my belief
That Nero in the next would wrathfully
Upbraid me that I was so kind to thee.
Thus, trembling, with my love I vainly strove.
I wished that I might never have known love.
Alas, he read my heart and thine too well,
My lord, for his peace or for ours. Conceal
Thy person from his sight. Go, I again
Beg thee. When time permits, I will explain
In full and many things besides declare.

BRITANNICUS.

Ah, this is all too much—too much to hear:
How blest I am; how sore I wronged thee; how
Bounteous thy heart to me! And knowest thou
All thou rejectest for me? When can I
Expiate at thy feet the injury
I did thee?

[*He falls on his knees before* JUNIA.

JUNIA.

Nay, what wouldst thou? Alas, here
Is Nero now!

[*Enter* NERO. BRITANNICUS *rises.*

NERO.

Let me not interfere,
Prince, with these charming transports.
(*To Junia*) I can guess

By this display of thanks how great the grace
Thou showest him, madam: I have found him kneeling
Before thee. But he owes me, too, some feeling
Of gratitude. Here he conveniently
Can meet thee, and I keep thee here that he
May easily have interviews so sweet.

BRITANNICUS.

My joys and sorrows I can at her feet
Lay wheresoe'er her kindness doth consent;
Nor hath this place in which thou keepest her pent
Aught in its aspect to affright mine eyes.

NERO.

And hath it aught which warns thee in no wise
That I must be respected and obeyed?

BRITANNICUS.

It never saw us reared within its shade,
Me to obey thee, thee to threaten me;
Nor could it dream at our nativity
That as my master would Domitius[37]
E'er speak to me.

NERO.

Our expectations thus
Are crossed by fate. I once obeyed; in turn
'Tis thine to obey. If thou hast failed to learn
As yet that thou must let thyself be ruled,
Thou art in sooth still young and canst be schooled.

BRITANNICUS.

And who will school me?

NERO.

The whole Empire. Rome.

BRITANNICUS.

Does Rome permit thee in thy masterdom
These deeds thou doest unjustly and by force:
Imprisonment, abduction, and divorce?

NERO.

Rome never pries with curious glance too deep
Into the secrets that I choose to keep
From her. Imitate her respect.

BRITANNICUS.

                  Her thought
Hereof we know.

NERO (*fiercely*).

          At least she sayeth naught.
Imitate her in that.

BRITANNICUS.

         So Nero now
Doth curb himself no more!

NERO.

              Nero doth grow
Tired of thy talking.

BRITANNICUS.

         All men were to bless
The happiness of his reign!

NERO.

         Unhappiness
Or happiness, I care not; I am feared.

BRITANNICUS.

I ill know Junia, or thou art endeared
To her no whit by sentiments like these.

NERO.

At least, if I have not the art to please
Her, I can punish a rash rival.

BRITANNICUS.

                    Be
The peril what it may that threatens me,
Her frown alone can make me tremble.[38]

NERO.

                                Pray
To win it. That is all I have to say
To thee.

BRITANNICUS.

            Her favour is the only bliss
Which I aspire to.

NERO.

                    She hath promised this
To thee. It will be thine eternally.

BRITANNICUS.

At any rate, I do not play the spy
Upon her words. I leave her free to say
Whate'er she will of anything that may
Concern me, and I never hide somewhere
Near by, to seal her lips.

NERO.

                    Enough! Ho, there,
My guards!

                                [*Enter guards.*

JUNIA.

            What wouldst thou do? He is thy brother!
But no, alas! This is a jealous lover.

Sire, sire, a thousand ills of fortune blight
His life. Can his one happiness excite
Thine envy? Let me join again the ties
Between you. I will hide me from the eyes
Of both, and nevermore myself have sight
Of him. I will for ever heal by flight
Your fatal discord. Let me, sire, increase
The number of the vestal virgins.[39] Cease
To strive 'gainst him for my poor vows. Let none
Be troubled with them save the gods alone.

NERO.

The resolve is strange, madam, and suddenly
Conceived.
    To her apartments let her be
Led again, soldiers. Let Britannicus
Be guarded in his sister's.

    BRITANNICUS (*scornfully*).
      And 'tis thus
Nero contendeth for a woman's heart!

    JUNIA (*to* BRITANNICUS, *in a low voice*).
Prince, do not vex him. It is wisdom's part
For us to bend before this storm.

    NERO.

      Obey
My orders, guards, and make no more delay.
  [*Enter* BURRUS. BRITANNICUS *and* JUNIA *are led out.*

    BURRUS (*to himself*).
What do I see! Oh, gods!

Nero (*to himself*).

Thus the flame
Of love but burns more ardently in them.
Well do I know whose hand it was that brought
About their meeting. Agrippina sought
My presence and then talked so lengthily
Only for this vile purpose.

(*Perceiving* Burrus) Let it be
Discovered, Burrus, if my mother still
Is here within the palace. 'Tis my will
That she shall be detained, and shall be given
My guards, not hers.

Burrus.

What, sire! And without even
Hearing her? Thine own mother?

Nero.

Stop! I know
Naught, Burrus, of the things which inly thou
Dost meditate; but I for some days' time
Have found in thee, whatever wish was mine,
A censor ready to gainsay me. See
Unto my mother, now, I order thee;
Or else, if thou refusest so to do,
Others will see to her and Burrus, too![40]

ACT IV

The scene is the same. AGRIPPINA *and* BURRUS *are discovered.*

BURRUS.

Yes, madam, thou canst speak in thy defence
Unhurriedly. Caesar himself consents
To give thee audience here. If his command
Hath in the palace made thee be detained,
Perhaps his object is to talk with thee.
In any case, if I may openly
Express my thought, no more remember how
He hath offended thee. Be ready now
Rather to meet him with thine arms held out.
Justify thine own conduct, and do not
Blame his. Thou seest that 'tis to him alone
That the Court looks. Although he be thy son—
Thy handiwork—thine Emperor, too, is he.
Unto that power which he received from thee
Subject art thou, like us. As he caresses
Or threatens thee, the Court about thee presses
Or from thee stands aloof. Whenever men
Seek help of thee, it is that they may gain
His help thus. But the Emperor is here.

[*Enter* NERO.

AGRIPPINA.

Only let me be left with him![41]

[*Exit* BURRUS. *She seats herself.*
Draw near,
Nero, and take thy wonted place. I must

Prove that I do not merit thy distrust.
What crimes I am charged with, I am not aware;
All those that I have done, I will declare
To thee.
        Thou reignest. Well dost thou know how far
Thy station was from that of emperor
By birth. Mine ancestors, whom Rome hath made
Gods, would except for me have been scant aid
To thee to climb thereto. When Claudius
Had had the mother of Britannicus[42]
Put to death, and was free to wed again,
Among the many fair ones who were fain
To be his choice and of his freedmen sought
Support, was I, with but a single thought:
To lift thee to the throne with me.[43] I bent
My pride low, and for help to Pallas went.[44]
His master, daily fondled in mine arms,
Was unawares incited by the charms
Of his own niece to feel that love which I
Meant to arouse in him. But our close tie
Held Claudius back from an incestuous bed.
He dared not with his brother's daughter wed.
    The Senate was won over; a new law
Less rigorous was passed; and soon I saw
Myself the Emperor's bride, Rome at my feet.
For me 'twas much; for thee 'twas nothing yet.
I brought thee, too, into his family
With me; made thee his son-in-law; gave thee
His own child for thy wife. Silanus, who
Loved her and found himself forsaken, slew
Himself and with his life-blood stained that day.
    Still was this nothing. Seemed there then one ray
Of hope that Claudius ever might be won

To prefer his son-in-law over his son?
Again I begged the help of Pallas. He
Prevailed with Claudius, who adopted thee
And called thee "Nero" and wished even to let
Thee share the supreme power with him ere yet
He himself died. 'Twas then that every one
Saw, who recalled the past, my purpose, gone
Too far already towards accomplishment;—
Then that the ignominious imminent
Fate of Britannicus did murmurs raise
Among his father's friends. My promises
Dazzled the eyes of some of these; I sent
The most seditious into banishment,
And so was rid of them; while Claudius,
Weary of my complaints urged without truce,
Himself took from his son all those whose zeal,
Long constant to his cause, could open still
The path unto the throne for him again.
I did yet more. I chose from mine own train
Of followers those by whom I wished that he
Should have his guidance. I most carefully
Chose for thy tutors, on the other hand,
Men honoured by the voice of all the land.
Deaf to intrigue, I trusted high renown,
Called one from exile, took from the army one—
Yea, Seneca and Burrus, those same men
Who since . . . Rome praised them for their virtues then.
Meanwhile, I drained the Emperor's treasury,
Scattering his largess as it were from thee.
Pleasures and shows, appeals resistless, drew
The people's hearts to thee, and the soldiers' too,
Which burned again with old affection's fire,
Favouring in thee Germanicus, my sire.

Claudius became more feeble as time passed.
His eyes, long shut, were opened now at last.
He knew his error, and in fear let fall
Words of regret, and fain—too late—would call
His friends to him. Now were his guards, his whole
Palace, his very bed in my control.
I let his fondness for his son devour
His heart to no effect. His final hour
Was ruled by me. As if it were to spare
Him sorrow, his son's tears were by my care
Concealed from him while his life ebbed.
                                        He died.
A thousand shameful tales on every side
Were told concerning me. I stopped the spread
Of the too-prompt report that he was dead,
And even while Burrus hastened secretly
To make the army pledge itself to thee,—
While thou wast marching to the camp as I
Arranged, in Rome there rose unto the sky
From every altar of her gods the smoke
Of sacrifice, and all the anxious folk,
Obeying my deceitful orders, prayed
That he might live who was already dead.
    When the last legion's fealty was sure,
And thus thy power had been made secure,
I showed the corpse of Claudius; and then,
Amazed at what had come to pass, did men
First learn both of his death and of thy reign.
    Such is the true confession I was fain
To make to thee. Lo: these are all my crimes.
And this is their reward: for no more time's
Length than six months, while thou enjoyest the good
Things my pains won thee, showest thou gratitude;

Then, finding it a burden all too sore,
Thou choosest to acknowledge me no more!
I have seen Burrus—Seneca, too—whetting
Sharp thy suspicions and before thee setting
Lessons in thanklessness, o'erjoyed to be
Outdone in this, their own best art, by thee;
And I have seen thee take, to be thy mates,
Young Otho and Senecio, profligates
Who vilely urge thee to all base delights
To which thou dost incline;[45] and when thy slights
Make me protest and I demand of thee
The reason for such wrongs, thou answerest me
With new affronts, an ingrate's one resource
Who in no way can justify his course.

    I promised Junia's hand unto thy brother.
They were both pleased that it was thus thy mother
Decreed for them. And thou—what hast thou done?
Junia, borne to thy palace, hath become
The object of thy love all in one night.
I see Octavia, from thy heart now quite
Banished, and soon to leave perforce the bed
Where I had placed her. I see Pallas sped
To exile, and thy brother seized. Thou hast
Robbed me of mine own liberty at last.
Burrus hath laid insolent hands on me.
And when, convicted of such infamy,
Thou shouldst have sought me but in penitence,
Thou biddest me to speak in my defence!

NERO.

I always am quite well aware I owe
The throne to thee; there was no need that thou
Shouldst tire thyself with saying so to me

Again. Thou mightest without anxiety,
Madam, have trusted in my gratitude.
Therefore these doubts, these endlessly renewed
Complaints, to those who note them must appear
To show, if I may thus in private here
Speak to thee frankly, that 'twas but for thee
Thyself thou wroughtest, when seemingly for me.
"Are so great honours and such deference,"
Men ask themselves, "a trivial recompense
For that which she hath done? What crime, pray, hath
Her son committed which so stirs her wrath?
Was it but to obey her will that he
Was crowned? Is he only her deputy?"
Not that, if I could have indulged thee so,
I would not have been happy to bestow
On thee this power thou clamourest to resume;
But 'tis a master, not a mistress, Rome
Desires. Thou knowest the stir my weakness raised.
The Senate and the people, much displeased
At hearing thy mandates uttered by my breath,
Daily declared that Claudius, on his death,
Had left me not his sovereign power alone
But his docility. Thou hast been shown
Full oft our soldiers' anger when they bore
Their eagles past thee, murmuring and sore
Ashamed by such base usage to degrade
Those heroes who are still thereon displayed
In effigy.[46] No other woman would
Have held out still, when she perceived their mood;
But if thou dost not rule, there is no truce
To thy complaints. Leagued with Britannicus
Against me, thou wast fain to lend his cause

New strength by joining him and Junia. 'Twas
The hand of Pallas that hath woven all these
Intrigues. And when I make secure my peace
By taking measures, though with great regret,
Such as are necessary, rage and hate
Burst forth in thee. My rival thou will show
Unto the army, and already now
Rumour thereof unto the camp hath flown.

AGRIPPINA.

I make him Emperor, thou ungrateful one?
Canst thou believe it? What would be mine aim?
My motive what? What honours could I claim,
What rank, at *his* Court? Ah, if 'neath thy sway
I am not spared; if all my steps each day
Are dogged by mine accusers; if they dare
To assail their emperor's mother—how shall I fare
In a strange Court? They would reproach me, not
For strengthless murmurs, not for schemes begot
Only to die, but for crimes done for thee
Before thy face; and all too speedily
Would they convict me of my guilt. Nowise
Dost thou deceive me. Every artifice
Of thine is plain. Thou art ungrateful. Thou
Wert always so. Even from thy birth till now
My tender care hath ne'er wrung from thee aught
Except thy feigned affection. There was naught
That really won thee, and thy heart of stone
Should have stopped up the kindness in my own.
What misery is mine! By what ill fate
Must all my loving toil but gain me hate?
I had one only son. O gods, who hear
My voice this day, when did I lift a prayer

To you that was not uttered for his sake?[47]
Conscience, fear, danger,—nothing held me back.
I have endured thy slights, have turned aside
My gaze from all the evils prophesied
In later years to fall on me. My love
Did all it could. Thou reignest; 'tis enough.
Now, if thou wishest, with the liberty
Which thou hast robbed me of, take life from me,
If at my death the people will not rise
And tear from thee what cost me such a price.

NERO.

Nay; speak, then! What is it thou wishest of me?

AGRIPPINA.

Let my presumptuous accusers be
Punished; let the outraged Britannicus
Be pacified; let Junia freely choose
Whom she prefers for husband; let the pair
Both be released; let Pallas remain here;
Let me have access at all hours unto
Thy presence; . . .

[*Seeing* BURRUS, *as he now enters with guards.*
and let this same Burrus, who
Is listening to what we say, no more
Dare to arrest my footsteps at thy door!

NERO (*clasping her in his arms*).

Yes, I would henceforth by my gratitude
Teach every heart thy power. I bless the good
Fate that a coldness rose between us two,
For thence shall our affection kindle anew.
Whatever Pallas did, I pass it by.

I have forgotten it already. I
Shall with Britannicus make peace straightway.
As for this love which caused a breach to-day
'Twixt him and me, I name thee arbiter
And judge, to weigh our claims. Do thou go bear
These happy tidings, then, unto my brother.
   Soldiers, obey the orders of my mother.

   [*Exeunt* AGRIPPINA *and guards.* BURRUS *comes forward.*

BURRUS.

What joyful sight unto mine eyes, my lord,
This concord, these embraces, now afford!
Thou knowest if I ever lifted voice
Against her; if 'twas ever by my choice
That thy heart hath from hers been separated;
And if I have deserved to be thus hated
By her.

NERO.

         To speak quite frankly, I have been
Vexed with thee, Burrus. I had deemed ye twain
Were secretly allied. Her enmity
Once more revives my confidence in thee.
Too soon she boasts her triumph. If I clasp
My rival, 'tis to crush him in my grasp.

BURRUS

What, sire!

NERO.

           I have endured too much. His doom
Must needs deliver me for ever from
The threat of Agrippina's wrath. While he
Yet breathes, I but half-live. She wearies me

Of hearing his detested name; and I
Will suffer her not, in her audacity,
A second time to promise him my throne.

BURRUS.

Then for Britannicus she very soon
Must weep?

NERO.

Ere this day endeth, I no more
Shall fear him.

BURRUS.

And thou hast what counsellor
To move thee to this plan?

NERO.

My honour—yea,
My love, my safety, mine own life.[48]

BURRUS.

Nay, nay!
Whate'er thou sayest, never shall I believe
That thou in thine own bosom didst conceive
This horrible project.

NERO.

Burrus![49]

BURRUS.

Do I learn
Of it from thy lips? Ah, ye heavens eterne!
Without a shudder couldst thou hear of this,
Thyself? Dost realize whose blood it is
Which thou wilt shed? Is Nero weary, then,

Of reigning in all hearts? How thinkest thou men
Shall speak of thee?

NERO.

What! must I till my last
Breath be still fettered to a blameless past?
Must I regard Rome's favour, which one day,
As chance doth fall, may give or take away?
Slave to her wishes, heeding not mine own,
Am I her emperor to please her, alone?

BURRUS.

And shall it not accomplish thy desire
If thou dost make thy people happy, sire?
Thine is the choice; thou still art master. Thou
Canst be for ever virtuous, as till now.
The path is well marked out; thou canst proceed
(Naught hinders thee) from good deed to good deed.
But if by sycophants thy heart be won,
Then must thou needs from crime to crime press on,
Thy harshness with fresh cruelty sustain,
And plunge thy blood-drenched hands in blood again
And yet again. Britannicus will rouse
In death his friends, keen to espouse his cause,
And these avengers too will presently
Find champions, and yet others, when they die,
Will follow even them. Thou lightest a fire
Which never can be quenched. Feared by the entire
World, thou must fear all men, for ever strike,
For ever tremble at each turn alike,
And reckon all thy subjects as thy foes.
    Ah, but how happy was thy life in those
First years of rule! Does their experience

Teach thee to hate thy youthful innocence?
Remember what good fortune marked their days.
How peacefully they glided by, always!
What joy to think and say within thy breast:
"This moment, everywhere, my reign is blest
And I am loved. The people feel no fears
To speak my name. They never 'mid their tears
Cry it to heaven. They flee not from my face
In sullen hate, but wheresoe'er I pass,
All hearts go out to me." Thou hadst, whilere,
Delight in these things. What a change is here,
Great gods! The life of even the lowliest wight
Hath formerly been precious in thy sight.
One day the Senate urged thee, I recall,
To sign the death-warrant of a criminal.
Thou, sire, against their just severity
Didst hold out long; it seemed too cruel to thee;
And murmuring at the ills of sovereign might,
Thou saidst: "I would I knew not how to write!"

    Nay, hearken, or else death shall keep from me
The sight and sorrow of this calamity.
Never will I outlive thy honour, sire.
If thou art bent on carrying out so dire
And foul a deed, I pray thee, ere we part
    [*He falls on his knees before* NERO *and bares his breast.*
(Lo, I am ready) stab me through this heart
Which cannot to such crime consent. Or call
Those cruel ones who inspired thee. Let them all
Use me to acquaint with blood hands yet unsure.

    I see my tears have touched mine emperor.
I see him shudder at such savagery.

Delay not. Name the traitors unto me
Who dare this monstrous villainy abet.
Summon thy brother. Clasp him and forget . . .

NERO.

Ah, what is this thou askest?

BURRUS.

He hates thee not.
Nay, sire! he is traduced by some vile plot
'Gainst him. I know that he is guiltless. I
Will answer to thee for his loyalty.
I go, to speed this blessed interview.

NERO.

Bring him to my apartments. Both of you
Await me there.

[*Exit* BURRUS. *Enter* NARCISSUS.

NARCISSUS.

Sire, for this merited
And necessary death, all plans are laid.
I have the poison ready. The renowned
Locusta[50] hath employed her skill beyond
All wont for me. Before my very gaze
She killed a slave. The sword less swiftly slays
Than this new drug I have possession of
From her.

NERO.

Narcissus, thou hast done enough.
I thank thee for thy pains, and I do not
Desire thee to go any further.

NARCISSUS.

What!

Thy hatred for Britannicus grows mild,
And thou forbiddest . . . ?

NERO.

Yes, we are reconciled,
Narcissus.

NARCISSUS.

I will guard most carefully
My tongue from counter-suasion, sire. But he
Hath lately seen himself imprisoned. Long
Within his bosom he will nurse that wrong.
There are no secrets time doth not reveal.
He will yet learn some day (I know full well)
That he was to be given, by my hand,
A poison draught prepared at thy command.
May a kind heaven turn therefrom his thought,
But he might do that which thou darest not.[51]

NERO.

His heart is vouched for. I will conquer mine.

NARCISSUS.

To seal fast your accord, dost thou resign
Junia to him? Shall they be wedded?

NERO.

Thou
Urgest too much. Be it as it may, I now
Count him no more among mine enemies.

NARCISSUS.

This fulfils Agrippina's prophecies.
She hath resumed her sway o'er thee again.[52]

NERO.

How now? What hath she said? What dost thou mean?

NARCISSUS.

She hath been boasting all too openly.

NERO.

Of what?

NARCISSUS.

      That but a moment needed she
To see thee, and after all this great ado
And awesome rage a silence would ensue
Straightway; that thou wouldst be the first who fain
Would welcome peace, if she would only deign
To forget all.

NERO.

      But tell me what it is,
Narcissus, that thou wishest of me. This
Presumption would I punish willingly,
And her rash triumph very soon would be
Succeeded by regret that endeth not,
Were I to do as I should like. But what
Would all the world then say of me? Dost thou
Desire that in the steps of tyrants now
I shall set forth?—that Rome shall cancel all
Titles of honour that were mine and call
Me naught save "poisoner"? As a fratricide[53]
My deed would brand me.

NARCISSUS.

      Must thou take for guide
Men's favour? Didst thou deem their tongues will be
For ever mute? My lord, is it for thee

To lend an ear to babblings? Wilt thou lose
The memory of thine own desires?—refuse
Alone unto thyself thy trust? Nay, nay,
Thou dost not know the Roman people. They
Are much more careful of the words they speak.
Thine extreme caution maketh thy reign weak.[54]
Belief will grow among the common folk
That they are to be feared. Beneath the yoke
Long have they bowed. They love the hands that bind them.
Eager to please thee wilt thou ever find them.
Their servile ways wearied Tiberius.
Myself, when clothed with power which Claudius
Gave me together with my liberty,
Have often tried their patience utterly
By mine own acts, but could exhaust it ne'er.[55]
Fearest thou the odium of a poisoner?
Destroy the brother, cast the sister off;
Rome will invent crimes for them (yea, and proof
Thereof) however innocent they be,
With lavish sacrifices. Thou shalt see
That in the list of inauspicious days
His natal day and hers will both find place.

NERO.

Narcissus, once again I say to thee,
I will not take the course thou urgest on me.
I promised Burrus, and must needs perform
What I have promised. I will nowise arm
His rectitude against me by a breach
Of faith with him. His arguments on each
Occasion make my resolution weaken.
I cannot hear him with a heart unshaken.

NARCISSUS.

Burrus doth not believe all that he says.
His virtue shrewdly taketh care always
Of his own interest, or they àll alike,[56]
Rather, have but one object. If thou strike
This blow, they will behold their power undone.
Thou wilt be free, then, and before thy throne
These insolent masters will like us bend low,
My lord. What! dost thou verily not know
The things they dare to say? "Nero"—'tis thus
They talk—"was never born to reign. He does
Only, he speaks only as he is told
By us to do and speak. His heart is ruled
By Burrus; Seneca doth rule his mind.
His whole ambition, the one gift men find
Him master of, is aptitude to drive
A chariot in a chariot race, to strive
With rivals for some most unworthy prize,
To show himself before the Romans' eyes,
To expend upon the public stage his voice,
And to sing songs with which he would rejoice
To enrapture all, the while from time to time
His soldiers compel loud applause for him."
Hast thou no wish to force them to be dumb?

NERO.

Let us plan what to do, Narcissus. Come!
[NERO *and* NARCISSUS *go out together.*

ACT V

The scene is the same. It is now very late afternoon. BRITAN-
NICUS *and* JUNIA *are discovered.*

BRITANNICUS.

Yes, Nero doth in his apartments wait
To greet me now with clasp affectionate.
Who could have dreamed it? He hath invited there
All the Court youth. He fain with me would swear
Friendship anew 'mid festal pomp and mirth
And give our fond embraces a new birth.
His love for thee, which bred such bitter hate
Between us, he hath quenched; and of my fate
He makes thee the sole arbiter. Though I
Am banished from the station formerly
Held by my sires; though with their spoils before
Mine eyes he decks himself, yet since no more
He doth oppose my love but yields to me
The honour high of finding favour with thee
('Twould seem), I shall confess that for my part
I pardon him in secret in my heart
And yield all else to him with less regret.[57]
    Ah, shall I, then, no longer as of late
Be separated from thy loveliness,
And can I see without uneasiness
E'en at this very moment those bright eyes
Which are not changed by terrors or by sighs,—
Which unto me from throne and emperor turn!
Ah, madam! But how now! what new concern
Keeps thee from sharing in mine ecstasy?

Whence comes it now that, while thou hearest me,
Thy sad, sad eyes are raised with lingering gaze
Toward heaven? What fear affrights thee and dismays?

JUNIA.

I myself know not; but I am afraid.

BRITANNICUS.

Thou lovest me?

JUNIA.

Ah, do I not indeed
Love thee!

BRITANNICUS.

Nero no longer menaceth
Our bliss.

JUNIA.

But art thou sure of his good faith?

BRITANNICUS.

What! thou suspectest him of secret hate?

JUNIA.

He loved me, and he vowed thy death of late.
He shuns me, seeks thee. Can so great a change
Be wrought in but a moment's time? 'Tis strange.

BRITANNICUS.

Madam, the change is Agrippina's doing.
She deemed that my destruction meant her ruin
As well. Thanks to her jealousy and pride,
Our greatest foes have fought upon our side.
I trust the passions that she to my view
Displayed, trust Burrus, even trust Nero too.

I believe he, like me, will have no part
In treachery, but hates with open heart
Or else doth cease to hate.

JUNIA.

              Sir, judge not of
His heart by thine. On paths diverse ye move.
I have known him and his Court for but one day;
Yet in this Court, alas, if I dare say
That which I deem, how far is every word
From what one thinks! How little in accord
Are lips and feelings! With what alacrity
One breaks his oath here! 'Tis for thee and me
A strange abode.

BRITANNICUS.

           Be Nero's friendship true
Or false, if thou fearest him, is not he too
Afraid? No, no, he will not by a base
Crime rouse the senate and the populace
'Gainst him. What say I? He doth recognize
Well his last outrage. Even to Narcissus' eyes
His remorse showeth plainly. Ah, if thou
Hadst heard Narcissus tell, dear princess, how . . .

JUNIA.

But art thou sure Narcissus, too, is not
A traitor?

BRITANNICUS.

        Wherefore wouldst thou have me doubt
His loyalty?

JUNIA.

How do I know? It is
Thy life that is at stake. Because of this
I suspect all; I fear lest all may be
Seduced, fear Nero and the destiny
Malign which hath pursued me. Filled, despite
Myself, with dire forebodings, from my sight
Unwillingly I suffer thee to go.
Ah, if this peace in which thou joyest so
Should hide some snare against thy life designed!
If Nero, wroth because our hearts are twined
In mutual love, hath chosen night to cloak
His vengeance, and prepareth some fell stroke
While I am with thee here! If I should be
Talking e'en now for the last time with thee!
Ah, Prince!

BRITANNICUS.

Thou weepest! Oh, my princess! Is
Thy heart indeed concerned for me like this?
And when in pride of empire Nero tries
To dazzle with his regal pomp thine eyes
Here where all shun me and to him bow down,
Thou choosest my sad fortunes, not his crown!
What! in a single day and this same place,
Refuse a realm and weep before my face!
But prithee, madam, dry those precious tears.
My swift return will soon dispel thy fears.
'Twould cause mistrust if I delayed my going
Longer. Farewell. I shall, with soul o'erflowing
With love, amid youth's heedless revelry
In fancy speak with none, see none, but thee,
My princess beautiful! Farewell.

JUNIA.

Prince . . .

BRITANNICUS.

They

Expect me, madam. I must hence.

JUNIA.

But stay

At least till some one comes to fetch thee!

[*Enter* AGRIPPINA.

AGRIPPINA.

Why

Tarryest thou, Prince? Go, go immediately.
Nero hath grown impatient, and complains
Of this thine absence. Every guest restrains
His joy from utterance till he shall behold
You clasp each other. Let not a wish grow cold
That is so fit and reasonable. Away!
(*To* JUNIA) And let us, madam, seek Octavia.

BRITANNICUS.

Yea,

Go, my fair Junia, with tranquillity.
Hasten to greet my waiting sister.
(*To* AGRIPPINA) I,
As soon as e'er I can, will follow thee,
Madam, to thank thee for thine aid to me.

[*Exit* BRITANNICUS.

AGRIPPINA.

Unless I am mistaken, thou didst shed
Some tears when ye two parted. They have made
Thine eyes dim. Wilt thou tell me what distress

Hath shadowed thee? Dost thou not trust the peace
Which I have spared no labour to secure?

JUNIA.

Alas! how, madam, could I reassure
My trembling spirit after all the grief
This day hath cost me? Scarce can I believe
E'en yet this miracle. If I should still
Dread lest thy grace will meet an obstacle,
Forgive me! Change is common at a Court,
And ever doth some fear with love consort.

AGRIPPINA.

I spoke; that was enough. Now all doth wear
A different aspect. No more ground is there
For thy misgivings. I will guarantee
A pact sworn 'twixt my hands. Most solemnly
Hath Nero bound himself. Hadst thou but viewed
With what endearments he hath given renewed
Pledges to me! how many a fond embrace
Stayed me from going! his unwillingness
To take his arms from round me when we parted!
With face which showed how really kind-hearted
He is, he hastened first to talk about
The smallest personal matters. He spoke out
As a son should who comes with pride put by
Unto his mother's breast. But presently
With mien more serious, like an emperor
Who takes his mother for his counsellor,
He gave into my keeping royally
Secrets on which depends the destiny
Of nations.[58] No, it needs must be confessed
That to his honour he hath in his breast

No vestige of dark malice, and our foes
Alone it is who 'gainst us e'er dispose
His heart, abusing thus his confidence.
But now in turn at last their influence
Waneth, and Rome again shall know the power
Of Agrippina. Yea, this very hour
Men prize my favour. But we must not wait
Here until nightfall. To Octavia let
Us go at once and spend with her the rest
Of this great day which proves to be as blest
As I had earlier thought it was accurst.
    But what is this I hear—that confused burst
Of noise? What can it be?

JUNIA.

                  O gods on high,
Save, save Britannicus!

[BURRUS rushes into the room.

AGRIPPINA.

             Whither dost thou fly,
Burrus? Stay. Tell me why it is that thus . . .

BURRUS.

Madam, the deed is done. Britannicus
Lies dying.

JUNIA.

     Ah, my prince!

AGRIPPINA.

           Lies dying?

BURRUS.

                  Nay, he
Is dead e'en now.

JUNIA.

Forgive this agony
Of grief, madam. I go to succour him
Or follow him.

[*Exit* JUNIA, *hastily.*

AGRIPPINA.

Oh, what a monstrous crime,
Burrus!

BURRUS.

I never, never can survive
Such a thing, madam. I must needs now leave
The Emperor and the Court.

AGRIPPINA.

What! feared not he
To shed his brother's blood?

BURRUS.

Less openly
He compassed his design. When he set eyes
Upon Britannicus, he was quick to rise
And clasp him. Silence for a moment reigned.
Nero abruptly broke it. In his hand
He took a cup. "To crown most happily
This day, I from this goblet pour," said he,
"These drops. Ye gods to whom I now appeal
In this glad hour, be present here, and seal
Our reconcilement with your favour thus."
Next with the selfsame oath Britannicus
Pledged his good faith. The goblet, which he held
In his grasp, then was by Narcissus filled
Again, but scarcely did his lips e'en touch

The rim thereof. Sharp steel could not with such
An instant potency have wrought. The light
Was blotted from his eyes; he fell back quite
Lifeless and cold upon his couch. Judge how
Dismayed were all who looked upon him now.
Half of the guests with cries of terror fled;
But those who had at Court dwelt longer made
Their mien conform to Caesar's. All the while,
He himself on his couch reclined and still
Revealed no vestige of astonishment.
"This malady which you fear, though violent,
Attacked him oft in childhood without harm,"
He said. Narcissus fain would some alarm
Have counterfeited, but could not conceal
His treacherous joy.

            Let Nero, if he will,
Punish my boldness, but for mine own part
I left the Court and its vile folk with heart
Which grief for this foul murder doth o'erwhelm,
To mourn Britannicus, Caesar, and the realm.

               [*Enter* JUNIA, NERO, *and* NARCISSUS.[59]

AGRIPPINA (*to* BURRUS).

'Tis he. Judge now if I had in this crime
A share. Remain.

NERO (*to* JUNIA).

         Truly at such a time
Thy tears are justified. But, madam, shun
This hideous sight. I myself looked thereon
Shuddering, then turned mine eyes thence. He is dead.
Sooner or later one must needs have said
Those words to thee. 'Tis thus that destiny

Makes merry with our best-laid plans. When we
Were reconciled, lo, heaven sundered us
For ever.

JUNIA.

Sire, I loved Britannicus.
I have told thee so. If now my misery
Wins for me any pity, suffer me
To seek the bosom of Octavia
For solace in my woe.

NERO.

Fair Junia,
Go. I myself will come unto thee there
Soon. I will come, with all the tender care
Which love inspires in me, unto thee . . .

[JUNIA *rushes out.* NERO *starts to follow her.*

AGRIPPINA.

Stay,

Nero; to thee I have a word to say.
Britannicus is dead. Whence fell the blow,
I understand. The murderer I know.

NERO.

Who is it, madam?

AGRIPPINA.

Thou.

NERO.

I? Now 'tis seen
What wild suspicions thou canst entertain
Of me. No evil e'er befalls but I
Must be the guilty author of it. Why,

If one would hearken to thy words, my hand
It also was that cut short Claudius' strand
Of life.[60] Thy husband's son was dear to thee;
His death may crush thee; but I cannot be
Responsible for the calamitous
Workings of fate.

AGRIPPINA.

No, no; Britannicus
Hath died by poison. 'Twas Narcissus who
Gave it; 'twas thou who badest him so to do.

NERO.

Madam! . . . Who told thee this?

NARCISSUS (interposing).

Nay, sire, does such
An accusation wrong thee overmuch?
                    [*Turning to* AGRIPPINA.
Madam, Britannicus had secret schemes
Which rightly would have grieved thy heart. His aims
Were higher than a match with Junia. Thou
Wouldst have paid dearly for thy kindness now
To him. He was deceiving thee. With hate
Concealed, he had sworn vengeance soon or late
For all the past. Then, whether destiny
Hath served thee even though in spite of thee,
Or whether Caesar knew the plots designed
Against his life and to my care consigned
The task of thwarting them, leave to your foes
All tears. Among the number of their woes
Let them account the worst their prince's death.
But thou . . .

AGRIPPINA.

Proceed along thy chosen path,
Nero, with just such minions. Many a deed
Like this will glorify thy reign. Proceed
Along thy chosen path. Thou canst not take
The step which thou hast taken, and then draw back.
First with thy brother's blood thou hast begun.
I can foresee thy blow will fall upon
Thy mother finally. In thine inmost thought
Thou hatest me, I know; and thou wouldst not
Be bound by thine indebtedness to me.
But 'tis my will that it shall profit thee
Nothing for me to die. Nowise conceive
That thou, when I am dead, in peace shalt live.
Nay, Rome, these skies, this light to which I bore thee,
Shall everywhere and always bring before thee
My image. Like the Furies, thy remorse
Shall hound thee, and thy sole yet vain resource
To assuage its pangs will be fresh cruelty.
Thy mad rage, as thou goest on, will be
Ever augmented, so that blood, always
New-shed, will mark the course of all thy days.
But heaven, I hope, will finally become
Tired of thy crimes and in one common doom
Join thee with thine own victims. When thou hast
Bathed in their blood and mine, thou shalt at last
Have to spill thine; and generations yet
Unborn shall use for a vile epithet
Thy name to make a barbarous tyrant seem
More hateful. Lo, even this, I surely deem,
Shall be thy lot. Farewell. Thou mayst go, now.

Nero.

Narcissus, come with me.

[*Exeunt* Nero *and* Narcissus.

Agrippina.

Ah heaven, how
Unjust were my suspicions! how unjust!
I condemned Burrus and I gave my trust
Unto Narcissus! Burrus, didst thou see
The savage glance which Nero cast at me
As he went out? Yes, it is even so:
Nothing henceforth can stay him, and the blow
Predicted shall ere long descend upon
My head. He will crush thee in turn anon.

Burrus.

Alas, for my part, I had lived enough
Ere this day dawned. Would to the gods above
That with kind cruelty he had made on me
Trial of his new-found ferocity!—
That this sad murder had not given such sure
Proofs of the woes which Rome must needs endure!
'Tis not the deed itself that teacheth me
Despair, for one can see how jealousy
Might arm his hand against his brother's life.
Nay, madam; this is my real cause for grief:
Nero beheld him die, yet never turned
Pale in the least. His look, no jot concerned,
Already was the unwavering regard
That marks a tyrant from his youth grown hard
In crime. Let him complete his work and kill
A troublesome adviser who can ill
Endure him longer. To avoid his wrath,

Is far from my desire. The speediest death
Would be the dearest to me.

[ALBINA *bursts into the room.*

ALBINA.

O madam, O

Good sir, fly to the Emperor. Haste ye! Go
And rescue him from his own frenzy. He
Hath now lost Junia eternally.

AGRIPPINA.

What! Junia hath taken her own life?

ALBINA.

To lay on Caesar a perpetual grief,[61]
Although she still is living, she is dead
To him. Thou knowest how from this place she sped.
'Twas to Octavia that she feigned she went,
But down side-passages she quickly bent
Her course. I watched that flight precipitate.
She issued headlong from the palace gate,
Even as one demented, straightway spied
Augustus' statue, where it stands outside,
And thither ran. Bathing its marble feet
With tears, the while her arms clung fast to it:
"Prince, by thy knees," she said, "which I embrace,
Protect me now, the last of all thy race!
Within thy palace Rome hath just beheld
The only one of thy descendants killed
That yet remained who might have been like thee.
After his death 'tis wished that I should be
False to his memory; but that I may
Still keep the faith with him which to this day
Hath ne'er been sullied, I now dedicate

Myself unto those gods whose shrines thy great
Virtues, O Prince, have won for thee the right
To share."
           Meanwhile, astonished at the sight,
The people flocked from every side; they thronged
Around her, learned how much she had been wronged,
And pitying her distress, swore as one man
That they would shield her. To that temple, then,
They led her where from earliest days of yore
Our virgins who are chosen to serve before
The altar have preserved with faithful care
The sacred fire which burns for ever there.
Caesar beheld them go, yet dared he not
Stop them. Narcissus, who was bolder, sought
To win his master's thanks. To Junia's side
Forthwith he sprang, and with a rash hand tried,
As though he knew no fear,[62] to interpose
And stay her steps. But countless mortal blows
Punished his impious temerity,
And spattered with his traitor's blood was she.
    Dazed by these strokes of fate in one same hour,
The Emperor hath left him in the power
Of the fierce rabble round him and gone back
Into the palace, silent and with black
Looks which make all avoid him. Junia's name
Alone escapes his lips. As in a dream,
He walks; his wandering eyes' distracted glance
Is never lifted heavenward; and perchance
If night and solitude should both come now
To make more bitter his despair, and thou
Shouldst leave him still uncomforted, his grief
Will cause him soon to try to end his life.

Quick! Time is precious. He may by some quirk
Of impulse kill himself.

AGRIPPINA.

He thus would work
Justice upon himself. But let us go,
Burrus, and see how far his frantic woe
Will lead him. Let us see what change will be
Wrought by remorse in him, and whether he
To better counsel henceforth will hold fast.[63]

BURRUS.

Would to the gods this crime might be his last!

NOTES ON BRITANNICUS

(The line-numbers are those of the French text.)

THE fourth of the Roman emperors (each of whom bore the titles of "Caesar" and "Augustus") was Claudius, a grand-nephew of Augustus. Late in life he wedded Agrippina, his own niece, the daughter of the talented general Germanicus, and granddaughter of Claudius Drusus Nero, and great-granddaughter of Augustus. Claudius was a widower and Agrippina a widow, and both had offspring from their former marriages: Claudius a daughter Octavia and a son Britannicus, each by the notorious empress Messalina; Agrippina a son, named like his father Domitius Ahenobarbus. After marrying Agrippina, Claudius adopted this boy and gave him the name of Nero, by which history knows him.

Octavia and Britannicus had been plighted in youth to Silanus and Junia, respectively, who were themselves brother and sister. Silanus was a great-grandson of Augustus, and Claudius planned to make him his successor. But Agrippina was ambitious that her son should be emperor, and prevailed on Claudius to marry Octavia to him instead, whereupon Silanus killed himself; the claims of Britannicus to succeed his father were set aside and Nero was at length named heir to the throne, which he ascended upon the death of Claudius. Under the influence of upright tutors, the military tribune Burrus and the philosopher Seneca, his conduct as emperor was at first admirable.

Though there was a Junia in history, the rôle which she plays in Racine's tragedy is the invention of the dramatist. Racine takes also some liberties with chronology. He conceives Britannicus, he tells us, to be seventeen years old; as a matter of fact, the prince died at fourteen, when Nero had reigned only one year. The real Narcissus died before Britannicus.

1; l. 18. Domitius; i.e. Nero.

2; l. 34. The beginning of Augustus' reign was marked by wholesale executions of his political foes.

3; l. 40. Caius. The Emperor Caligula.

4; l. 84. See Note 18.

5; l. 114. See last sentence of second paragraph of Notes.

6; l. 130. The seizure of Junia.

7; l. 136. These lines are meant to make Agrippina feel that she is no longer on terms of special intimacy with Nero; that she is not one of the few who have access to a private entrance.

8; l. 154. Burrus was a military tribune, a rank similar to that of colonel in modern armies, when Agrippina chose him as tutor for her son.

9; l. 156. Agrippina was the sister of the Emperor Caligula, and was the wife of the Emperor Claudius, and was the mother of the Emperor Nero. Germanicus, her father, was never emperor, but he was called *Imperator* by his soldiers; and the Emperor Augustus was her forefather.

10; l. 200. The freedmen of Claudius: Pallas, Narcissus, and Callistus. They were all-powerful with their former master.

11; l. 207. Thrasea was a Stoic philosopher. On hearing of the death of Agrippina, he indignantly left the Senate. He was put to death by Nero in A.D. 66. Corbulo, an excellent and highly successful general, was one of the most honest men of his century. He, too, at length (A.D. 67) received his death-sentence from Nero.

12; l. 210. There was no official prosecutor in Rome to unearth treason and other crimes. Information as to planned or perpetrated wrong-doing was furnished by private individuals, and some of these, for rewards and favours, did a lucrative business in bringing false accusations. Nero is here

represented as having banished the professional informers as
their victims had hitherto been banished.

13; l. 221. Both Agrippina and Burrus declare (insincerely) that Nero should be trusted to govern his own course;
each of them denies (insincerely) any wish to influence him;
and neither will credit the sincerity of the other! But Agrippina seeks power for selfish reasons, and Burrus purely for
the public good.

14; l. 286. These final words of Burrus reveal that he himself had not favoured the seizure of Junia, which in loyalty
to his emperor he sought to defend.

15; l. 304. The formerly powerful freedmen of Claudius.
See Note 10.

16; l. 383. Nero is the artist-emperor. It is as an artist that
he views his love; similarly, in the long description which
follows, he paints an artist's picture of his first sight of Junia.

17; l. 402. Observe the sadistic tendency in Nero's love.
He finds joy in grief and pain.

18; l. 476. Augustus divorced Scribonia and wedded Livia,
the great-grandmother of Agrippina, after her divorce from
Tiberius Claudius Nero. The daughter of Augustus and Scribonia was Julia, who married that Tiberius who succeeded
Augustus as emperor; Tiberius divorced her (l. 480).

19; l. 568. Junia alleges whatever reasons she can think
possibly effectual to prevent Nero from marrying her to any
one but Britannicus. She is astonished at his next words; for
Nero, Britannicus, and Plautus are all that remain of the
descendants of Augustus.

20; l. 663. Junia does not flatter. Nero's reign began with
"three years' rectitude," from which he now for the first time
seriously departs.

21; l. 688. "It has been said that the sight of Narcissus
ought to reveal to Junia his treason. Let us observe that he
here simply announces Britannicus, and that, moreover,
Junia does conceive vague suspicions of Narcissus later."—

BERNARDIN. At the moment all is too hurried for her suspicions to form, and she and Britannicus never discuss in detail the rôle played by Narcissus; a comparison of their observations and impressions would have been necessary to bring the real state of affairs to light.

22; l. 710. That this impression of Britannicus is not corrected by Narcissus, would indeed have thrown suspicion on the freedman if Junia had been less terrified then or had later pondered the situation in retrospect.

23; l. 724. Junia, ever conscious of the presence of the listening Nero, interrupts Britannicus in agonized apprehension of what he will say next. At almost every breath he has been uttering words calculated to inflame Nero to jealousy or hatred.

24; l. 732. Even now, in Junia's peril as a State prisoner, Britannicus seems almost entirely egotistical in his love. He appears to care for her chiefly as some one to whom he can go, like a child, to tell his troubles with assurance of sympathy and consolings in return. He is only a youth; but a youth can be more manly, and should be if his rôle as a sympathetic character is not to be a blemish in the play.

25; l. 742. Junia, feeling that she can endure no more and can restrain her tears no longer, seizes in desperation a means to end her ordeal.

26; l. 751. Another revelation of Nero's innate love of cruelty.

27; l. 757. Narcissus had enjoyed almost unlimited power formerly as the trusted freedman of the Emperor Claudius. Now, as the facile agent of Nero's vices, he has an opportunity to gain a similar ascendancy once more.

28; l. 761. Burrus has just returned after serving Pallas with the Emperor's decree of banishment.

29; l. 809. Never, till after the final catastrophe, will Agrippina listen to Burrus. In the present instance she arrives furious at the exile of Pallas, the order for which Burrus had borne. She at once launches into a tirade of such unmeasured abuse that he is forced once more to defend, in some degree, conduct of Nero with which he is not in sympathy. Agrippina thereupon grows still more violent; it is manifestly impossible now for him to take her into his confidence, for in her hatred of him she might go and accuse him to Nero of disloyalty.

30; l. 854. This is a half-admission by Agrippina that she indeed poisoned Claudius, as it was rumoured that she did. Only in this moment of rage does she come so near to confessing her supreme crime. Cf. her words to Nero (l. 1183):

A thousand shameful tales on every side
Were told concerning me.

31 ; l. 865. The younger Agrippa was the son of the elder Agrippa and Julia, the daughter of Augustus and Scribonia. He was exiled through Livia's influence, and Tiberius was made the heir of Augustus in his place. Tiberius later put him to death.

32; l. 892. This sentence reveals the roots of Agrippina's conduct and character. Her claims that she did everything for Nero's sake are false.

33; l. 893. It has been foretold to Agrippina that Nero will kill her.

34; l. 906. In spite of Agrippina's anger against Nero, she is dismayed when she learns what powerful nobles are aligning themselves with Britannicus. Noting her instinctive recoil, the young prince feels that he cannot trust her; and he clumsily attempts to deny what he has just revealed. Agrippina thereupon chides him for his suspicions and reaffirms her support of his cause.

35; l. 926. Subsequent events show how wise was this parting bit of advice.

36; l. 956. Bernardin points out that these words of Narcissus determine for us the whole effect of the ensuing scene between Britannicus and Junia. But for them, our mood would be one of pleasure at the vindication of Junia; as it is, we await with dread, throughout, the arrival of Nero.

37; l. 1040. Britannicus calls Nero by the name which he bore when he had not yet been adopted by Claudius and had no hopes of ever being emperor.

38; l. 1062. This and the next speech of Britannicus doubtless seemed to the contemporaries of Racine appropriate words for a young gentleman of high spirit. To-day they seem, rather, a priggish young coxcomb's attitudinizing.

39; l. 1076. In reality, an adult could not become a Vestal. Racine's unfaithfulness to fact here and in the dénouement was severely criticized; but the slip is of no importance dramatically, for it would be noticed only by scholars.

40; l. 1098. Nero threatens Burrus with removal from command of the praetorian guards, and with arrest.

41; l. 1114. What heed Agrippina pays to the temperate counsels of Burrus is revealed by this exclamation and the manner in which she then seats herself and addresses Nero with maternal condescension.

42; l. 1123. Racine avoids calling the mother of Britannicus by her all-too-notorious name.

43; l. 1128. Agrippina lies. Ambition, not maternal love, was the mainspring of her conduct. See line 892, and Note 32.

44; l. 1129. Agrippina well says that she bent her pride low; for she bought the assistance of Pallas at the price of her honour.

45; l. 1206. These words suggest that Nero had already given some evidence of the sinister side of his nature. Cf. Agrippina's remarks in Act I about his heredity, and Burrus in Act III: "That fierceness *which thou thoughtest to control,*" etc.

46; l. 1248. The *eagle,* the standard of the Roman armies, was a wooden staff surmounted by an eagle and bearing, besides, images of gods and, during the empire, the images of the emperor and of other princes of the imperial family.

47; l. 1278. As a last resource, Agrippina tries pathos. (Regarding her pretence of unselfish devotion to Nero, see line 892 and Note 32 on it—also Note 43.) But the last lines of this speech show that not even in the rôle of a sorely mistreated mother can she abstain from threats!

48; l. 1324. Unable to fix on a good reason for killing Britannicus, Nero proffers several specious ones at random!

49; l. 1327. Nero's exclamation threatens displeasure at Burrus' outburst, but Burrus is too deeply moved to heed the warning.

50; l. 1392. Locusta was a very famous poisoner. It was she who was said to have aided Agrippina in poisoning Claudius.

51; l. 1408. Narcissus planned to assure himself of Nero's favour by complicity in crime; and now, if the princes are reconciled, Narcissus is lost, for the part that he has played is certain to come to light. It is life or death for him. He begins by appealing, like Burrus, to Nero's fears.

52; l. 1415. Narcissus has already tried without success to play upon Nero's fear and jealousy. Now he touches the Emperor on his most sensitive point, and the response is immediate.

53; l. 1431. Fratricide. Literally "parricide," which Racine uses in the sense of the Latin *parricidium,* which meant the murder not only of a father but of any near kinsman.

54; l. 1439. Cf. *Athalie,* ll. 1390-7.

55; l. 1448. Observe how this passage prepares for the death of Narcissus, which springs from his fearlessness of the anger of the populace.

56; l. 1463. "They all alike" means Burrus, Seneca, and Agrippina.

57; l. 1494. These words of Britannicus show how well-advised a step the seizure of Junia really was. The young prince, according to his own statements in the first act, was

wholly unreconciled to his loss of the throne, and only awaited
a fit opportunity to revolt or conspire to gain it. He was,
therefore, clearly a menace to Nero's sovereignty if not to his
life; and the Emperor, by getting possession of Junia, could
tie his hands and even, at the price of her release, make him
renounce all pretensions to power,—instead of having him
put to death as a dangerous malcontent, as by generally accepted codes he would have been quite justified in doing. It
was Nero's own sudden infatuation for his prisoner—a thing
not to be anticipated—that gave, after all, a tragic turn to
events.

To Racine and his contemporaries, however, Britannicus,
as the legitimate prince by birth, had every right to depose
Nero; and Nero, as a usurper, had not even the right of self-
defence.

58; l. 1598. The mind of a Nero could have no great ideas
or designs. But in the seventeenth century, when the doctrine
of the divine right of kings was regnant, a monarch was
popularly supposed to be a marvellous sort of person, whose
thoughts were not like those of other men; and Racine has
here momentarily lost his imaginative grip on his subject and
limply conformed with the conventional notion, which is
implicit in many plays of the period.

59; l. 1646. The translation of the next few lines follows
the original version of the play. Subsequently, Racine elimi-
nated Junia from the scene, because certain critics thought it
inartistic that she should reappear after the death of Britannicus, and the passage reads thus:

[*Enter* NERO *and* NARCISSUS.

AGRIPPINA.
'Tis he. Judge now if mine his crime.

NERO (*seeing* AGRIPPINA).
                                    Gods!

AGRIPPINA.

Stay,

Nero; to thee I have a word to say.

All modern texts of *Britannicus* accept Racine's revision in this instance as they do elsewhere in his plays; but the present translation has not done so, for the latter form cannot be reconciled with ll. 1723-4:

> Thou knowest how from this place she sped.
> 'Twas to Octavia that she feigned she went.

These lines necessitate the version used in this translation. In general, an author has every right of decision about his own works, and his preferences in variant readings ought to be respected,—but not unless he takes the trouble to make his revisions carefully enough for the final text to be intelligibly self-consistent!

60; l. 1654. It is Agrippina herself whom Nero covertly accuses of the murder of Claudius, with which rumour charged her and which she has lacked little of confessing several times in the play.

61; l. 1721. Here again Racine's imaginative grasp of his theme is loosened. Albina enters in frantic haste, imploring immediate aid for Nero. When asked what is the situation, instead of saying briefly: "Junia has escaped from the palace and found refuge with the Vestal Virgins. When Narcissus tried to stop her, the populace tore him to pieces. Nero is in despair. He may kill himself at any moment. Come quick!" she gives a leisurely, detailed account of what has happened, becoming for the time not a character but the stereotyped *Nuntius* of classical drama, who must deliver a lengthy and formal "messenger-speech"; and then when her narrative is completed, abruptly begins to clamour again for instant action!

Observe, too, the impossible number of events off-stage that are crowded into the brief space of time occupied by the dialogue between Agrippina and Burrus after the exit of Nero—only twenty-two lines in the French text. Concerning Racine's technique in this respect, see my translation of *Phèdre,* Note 36.

62 ; l. 1749. Narcissus has already expressed his contempt for the Roman populace. Cf. Note 55. The word "impious" just below is used because he laid hands on one destined for the service of Vesta.

63 ; l. 1767. Hope is renewed in the breast of the indefatigable Agrippina. She thinks that with Nero thus shaken and Narcissus dead, she may be able to regain her ascendancy.

PHÈDRE
(PHAEDRA)

P*HÈDRE* is perhaps Racine's masterpiece; it is certainly the highest achievement of French "classical" tragedy. *Athalie* is thought by many to be a greater work; but *Athalie* stands apart, representing, together with *Esther,* a unique experiment not conformable to the type established by Pierre Corneille. Of that type, *Phèdre* is the supreme example. Though less ingeniously plotted for sustained tension than *Andromaque,* and though centering its interest upon a single character, it is yet pre-eminent by virtue of the more compelling sweep and power of its passions, its finer poetry, and its loftier tone in general. It is superior also to *Britannicus,* for the same reasons.

The Greek legend of Phaedra and Hippolytus was the subject of the *Hippolytus* of Euripides, of the *Phaedra* of Seneca, and of several French dramas prior to *Phèdre.* Racine was indebted to these last for only a few minor touches. Euripides was his chief source, from which he derived the general outlines of his play and of the characters of Phaedra, Theseus, and the Nurse, and some phases of the character of Hippolytus. He followed Seneca, however, in making Phaedra herself declare her love to Hippolytus and in making the Nurse originate the slander against him, which is lent colour of truth by his loss of his sword (whereas in Euripides it is the Nurse who, unknown to Phaedra, informs Hippolytus of the Queen's passion for him, and it is Phaedra who, when the shame of this exposure and of his abusive words drives her to suicide, leaves in death a letter accusing him of having dishonoured her) ; as in Seneca, the absence of Theseus at the beginning of the play is identified with that

hero's fabled expedition to Hades, and Phaedra believes him
dead; again as in Seneca, she survives Hippolytus and in a
dying confession clears him of all blame. But Racine's bor-
rowings from his classical models are not limited to characterization and turns of plot; he at times imitates their scenes,
as to both development and language.[1]

His imitation of Euripides is closest in the dialogue between Phaedra and the Nurse at the end of the first act. Here,
as in the *Hippolytus,* the Queen enters exhausted and distraught, longing to carry her woes and her shameful secret
with her to the grave; she chafes at the oppressiveness of her
attire and vexes the Nurse with the swift changes of her
whims; she wishes dreamily that she were amid forest shades
and where chariots are racing (for that is where she would be
likely to find Hippolytus), and then starts from her reverie in
terror lest she has betrayed herself, and tries to avert suspicion from her blushes and tears. For three days she has
refused all food, says the Nurse, who now begins to plead
with her to reveal what is troubling her and desist from her
resolve to die; because her death will leave her motherless
children at the mercy of the Amazon's son, Hippolytus—and

---

[1] Passages deriving from Seneca are a portion of the scene in the second
act between Phaedra and Hippolytus (his attempt to reassure her that
Theseus is alive and her denial of the possibility of any return from the
realms of the dead, then his misunderstanding of the cause of her perturba-
tion, and her speech comparing him to Theseus at the time he slew the
Minotaur: 618-52), Phaedra's prayer to Venus to make Hippolytus love
(813-24; in Seneca the Nurse prays to Diana to bend him to the yoke of
Venus), the dialogue between Phaedra and Oenone in which the latter
protests the impossibility of winning Hippolytus and the Queen over-rides
all objections (787-90), the plan of the Nurse to defame Hippolytus
(886-9), Theseus' claim of his boon from Neptune which he had refrained
from asking for hitherto even when a captive (1069-73), the description of
the sea-monster as fire-breathing and shaped like a bull in front and like
a scaled dragon further back (1517-19, 1533-4), and the final confession of
Phaedra (1618-19, 1623-4).

at the mention of his fatal name, Phaedra cries out in protest. The Nurse, misunderstanding her reaction, is encouraged and presses the point, but without success. "It is surely not that your hands are stained with blood?"—"They are pure; would that my soul were as stainless!"—"Then what terrible thing is the matter?" Phaedra will not tell her. The old woman becomes frantic; her own death will be upon her mistress' head if her suppliant prayers are not heeded.—"But to know the truth would only make you wretched, too."—"What greater wretchedness could be mine than to lose you?"—"I shall die in any case, but more honourably if I die silent." Still beset, Phaedra at length consents to speak. But she finds much difficulty in beginning; she apostrophizes her mother, who loved so fearsomely, and her sister Ariadne, who loved and was betrayed. Again the Nurse misunderstands, thinking that she is censuring her unhappy kindred, but the Queen declares herself to be the third of her house to fall a victim to love.—"You love? Whom?"—Phaedra cannot name his name; ". . . the son of the Amazon," she manages to articulate.—"Hippolytus!"—"It was you that said it, not I!" she wails; and the Nurse is overwhelmed with horror, but later accepts the fact and counsels hope. These minute and striking correspondences between the text of the *Phèdre* and that of the *Hippolytus* occur in a scene that has no analogue in Seneca's tragedy, and the same is true of the other extended passage where the French dramatist follows Euripides in detail.

This is the scene in which Hippolytus is banished. In both plays Theseus reflects, on seeing him, that nature ought to provide signs by which one could distinguish a true man from a knave, and Hippolytus begins by asking his father to confide in him. Then Theseus launches his terrible accusation and

decrees exile to his son, with threats that if the youth ever
again sets foot within the lands he rules, he himself will slay
him as he slew so many miscreants in the past; Hippolytus in
his defence urges his blameless repute, and declares that he is
entirely chaste. He vainly proffers his oath; he asks the conditions of his exile, and is told to begone to the ends of the
earth; he asks who will receive him when charged with such
a crime, and is told to consort with those who delight in
honouring the basest of men. Finally, when Theseus threatens
immediate physical violence if he delays longer, he submits
to necessity and goes. A notable difference in handling this
scene lies in the fact that in Euripides it is before the entrance
of Hippolytus that Theseus invokes the aid of the sea-god;
in *Phèdre* his fatal prayer comes, more effectively, at the
climax of his rage.

When one great dramatist so obviously builds upon the
work of another great dramatist and so deliberately vies with
him, comparisons are inevitable. It must be clearly understood
at outset that one difference between the *Hippolytus* and
the *Phèdre* is not, as some French critics assert, that the
subject of the former is a contest between two goddesses,
between Aphrodite and Artemis, in which the human characters are but irresponsible puppets, instead of free agents as
in the play of Racine. Such an idea can spring only from the
error of taking one's notion of classical deities from Ovid
and other late writers of mythological fairy tales, and thus
quite failing to understand the real Greek concept of the
gods as somehow at once quasi-human personalities and unhu-
man physical forces. Racine's Phaedra herself says that she
perishes "by will of Venus," and that Venus has "fastened on
her prey." She builds a shrine to placate the goddess; she
cries to her for mercy and for aid. Yet all this, as every one
knows, does not mean that she is the helpless victim of a

supernatural being; nor has the Phaedra of Euripides one whit less of choice and free will than she. The shadowy figure of the Cyprian Aphrodite appears in the prologue of the *Hippolytus,* the voice of Artemis speaks from a cloud in the final scene, but all the action throughout the body of the play moves on a purely human plane and admits of rationalistic motivation. The conception of Aphrodite as "a Force of Nature or a Spirit working in the world" (against which, as an unarguable fact, it is entirely possible to speak of Hippolytus as "sinning," and which for purposes of drama is made into a person and represented in human form) is brought out by the words of the Nurse:

> She ranges with the stars of eve and morn,
> She wanders in the heaving of the sea,
> And all life lives from her.

And in the *Trojan Women* of Euripides a similar interpretation is given of the story that this goddess caused Helen to love Paris:

> thine own heart, that saw and conned
> His face, became a spirit enchanting thee.
> For all wild things that in mortality
> Have being, are Aphrodite; and the name
> She bears in heaven is born and writ of them.

Let us make no mistake about it: the *Hippolytus* of Euripides and the *Phèdre* of Racine are both human dramas.

Nor can any very important difference be established between the heroines of the two plays, though admirers of each have extolled its Phaedra at the expense of the other. There are, indeed, some points in which the characters are not identical. In destroying Hippolytus, both are actuated by desire to protect their good repute and thereby their children.

The Phaedra of Euripides combines this motive with resentment at the young man's excessive abuse of her and at his failure to comprehend the agonized struggle which she has made to preserve her purity; the Phaedra of Racine, when in a revulsion of feeling she is ready to save Hippolytus at any cost, is checked by her discovery that he loves Aricia, which fills her with jealous madness and then, in consequence, with utter horror at herself and with such confusion of soul that she is paralyzed, as it were, and incapable of action until too late. The Greek Phaedra has a sense of the essential rightness of her inmost heart in spite of all; she is less the morbid and frenetic prey of her passions—is not driven helplessly by them to do things she did not intend to do, like her French sister, and would probably not have been murderously jealous under similar circumstances, whereas the self-loathing of Racine's Phaedra is so great that she might have borne the insults of Euripides' Hippolytus meekly. The French dramatist has sought to extenuate the guilt of his heroine; to this end he has employed the false report of Theseus' death and increased the persuasiveness and forcefulness of the Nurse; yet withal he has not drawn a more appealing, more piteous, or more human character than his model. He has, however, elaborated and exploited the figure of Phaedra to a greater degree than did Euripides, and has more clearly, though not more subtly, motivated her conduct.

The point in which Racine's play departs furthest from the Greek original, is the rôle of Hippolytus, and this is also the point on which adverse criticism of *Phèdre* has been focused. Such criticism, from Boileau and Dryden down to the present day, has very imperfectly recognized what is at fault. Racine's mistake was not, as generally is declared, that he made Hippolytus in love; to do so was to create a quite legitimate variant of the story, and served the valuable purpose of giving grounds for an access of jealousy in Phaedra and in this way accounting for her failure to save Hippolytus from the fate which threatened him. The intention of the dramatist was evidently to depict a bold young huntsman, unversed in courtly ways and always hitherto absorbed in such masculine interests as horses and the chase, until the beauty and wistful charm, and perhaps also the very misfortunes, of the dispossessed princess Aricia aroused in him those feelings for which he had till then had a boy's disdainful aversion. Again and again, in references to him by various characters, his fierce pride, his unpolished manners, and his wild, free mode of life are stressed. The figure of Hippolytus, as thus conceived, is artistically valid; but his own language is entirely at variance with it. Racine clearly did not dare to put into his mouth, when he woos Aricia or at other times, the simple if not faltering speech that would alone be natural in the case of such a character. The fashionable world in seventeenth century France would never have tolerated uncourtliness in a sympathetic hero; he must express himself like a young gentleman, with all the customary phrases of gallantry; and with these the author accordingly supplied him. Between what is said of Hippolytus in the play and what he himself says, there is a hopeless incongruity; and it is therefore, and not because he is represented as being in love, that he chiefly offends us.

But he offends us also by the priggishness and fantastic absurdity of his conduct, of which we are expected to approve. "Priggishness" is only too kind a word for it when he proposes at once, on the report of Theseus' demise, to procure the throne of Athens for Aricia. He properly might have declined to accept it himself, if he thought it rightfully hers, or might even have refused to defend it for his little half-brother against her; but to set himself up as a judge of his father's legitimacy and to undertake to use the power and prestige which he had gained as Theseus' supposedly faithful son to frustrate his father's will and despoil his father's heir for a hereditary enemy as soon as the great hero-king and not unloving sire lay (he believed) helpless in death, is an ugly combination of complacent self-righteousness and disloyalty, which appears but the uglier the longer it is scrutinized. From his unfilial design he passes presently to an exaggerated squeamishness of filial scruples, and back again. The snaring promise of secrecy which prevents the Hippolytus of Euripides from refuting the charge brought against him is needed to motivate his failure to clear himself by exposing Phaedra in the French play. The only reason he has there for silence is that it would be unbecoming of him to offend his father's ear with the shameful truth; and this consideration seals his lips though at the risk of his life and though his beloved Aricia, as well as he, would gain by his speaking out. But when he goes into exile, he plans to enlist friends at Argos and Sparta and make war on his father to regain his rights and Aricia's! That is indeed to strain at the gnat and swallow the camel. The code of Racine's Hippolytus is not of one piece with the moral code of mankind in general; it is at times the sort of far-fetched, arbitrary, and purely personal code which, as Jules Lemaître has observed, is commonly had by the characters in French romanesque dramas.

But despite the blemish of the unsatisfactory figure of the prince, Racine's tragedy, taken as a whole, stands on an approximate parity with that of Euripides. It is strange indeed that two plays dealing with the same subject should be so nearly equal in greatness that the superiority of either may be plausibly argued but not convincingly established. Poetically, the *Hippolytus* doubtless bears off the palm; for though the poetry of each is almost its author's best, Euripides is a poet of loftier, lovelier strain and far more varied music than Racine. The *Hippolytus,* moreover, is full of a fresh, simple charm and a picturesque beauty which are foreign to French classical drama. And there are subtleties in the work of the great Athenian that have no parallel in *Phèdre.* One minor and one major example of them may be cited, both typical of the genius of their author.

The first of these is where Theseus, bending over the dead body of his wife, espies a tablet fastened to her hand. It contains, in reality, the slanderous charge against Hippolytus, but her husband supposes it a message about some last wish, some dying request, and observing the familiar seal upon it, says:

> Ah, see
> How her gold signet here looks up at me,
> Trustfully.

Nothing could be truer or more pathetic than this chance flash of tender, whimsical fancy crossing the mind of a grief-stricken man; it is an authentic touch of "Euripides, the human,"—one of "his touches of things common till they rose to touch the spheres." Classical French tragedy was too rhetorical and hence dealt too generally with things in the large and with obvious things to bring thus to light the intimate trivial phenomena of the heart.

Another and more impressive instance of the subtlety of the Attic dramatist is a master-stroke to which Gilbert Norwood has called attention in his volume, *Greek Tragedy.* The Phaedra of Euripides, he points out, is a noble and spirited woman. She has, it is true, a hereditary predisposition to unchastity: lawlessness is in her veins; her mother and sister both have sinned;—but though she cannot help her instincts, she can and will dispute their power over her life. Her heart is finally broken when, to the argument that the gods themselves are against her, is added proof that man is utterly unable to realize her devotion to what is pure and of good repute or the hard fight that she has made.[2] "If thy life had not been in such danger," says the Nurse, "and thou *hadst happened to be a chaste woman,* I should not thus lead thee on," and again: *"Thy duty, to be sure, forbids sin; but as things are,* be advised by me." This hideous purring is perhaps Phaedra's bitterest shame. No one can understand. Then comes the betrayal of her secret, and the intolerable endless speech of condemnation by the man whom she loves and who is hence the cause of all her suffering. No one can understand. In an agony of terrified protest she destroys him and herself —and thereby wins that appreciation for lack of which she died. For there *was* one who could understand, after all—the one who seemed the least able to understand, and whose understanding she would most have craved: the prince himself. Her suicide, her very slander which must bring about his death, opens his eyes to her real nature; it is he, the moral idealist, who can apprehend her tenacious and (as he now divines) not alien ideals; and in the shadow of his own doom he exclaims:

> Unchaste of passion, chaste of soul was she;
> But I am shamed by my cold purity.[3]

Here we have that supreme manifestation of genius, "the utterly unexpected, which we instantly accept," as in Shakespeare and a few other writers. There is nothing like this

[2] It must be confessed that she in large measure confuses in her mind actual *character* and mere *reputation,* as early civilizations like the Greek were prone to do—and as not a few people do still.

[3] The translation of the first line is Norwood's, as is much of the wording of the first part of the paragraph before it. The renderings of Murray and Way fail to bring out the significance of the Greek lines.

touch anywhere in Racine; it is quite outside his imaginative range.

On the other hand, *Phèdre* possesses a unity lacked by its rival. Though the *Hippolytus*, by intention of its author, is the "tragedy" of a young man whose persistent disregard of everything relating to sex results in his being unable to handle with intelligence and sympathetic tact a difficult, delicate situation with which he is confronted, Phaedra is the real centre of interest until her death in the middle of the play, and after that the intensity of Theseus' passions makes him as prominent as the titular hero. Racine's tragedy, however, subordinates everything to Phaedra herself; and such is the skill with which the plot is constructed to exhibit her with a maximum of sympathy and in situations requiring her to run the gamut of unrestrained and tragic emotions, and such eloquence is found for the expression of those emotions, that this drama is one of the most effective acting plays ever written, and its heroine has become the great traditional rôle of the French stage as Hamlet is of the English. Every French actress aspires to play Phaedra, as every English actor aspires to play Hamlet, yet Sarah Bernhardt said that she never undertook the part without a feeling of terror at its illimitable possibilities and her inadequacy to do justice to them.

The greatest of Racine's secular tragedies, *Phèdre* was also the last. That he at this time forsook his career as a dramatist, when he was only thirty-seven years old and in the fullness of his powers, is generally ascribed to his disgust at the tactics of his enemies, which imperilled the fortunes of the play when it was first performed, and to the Jansenist influences which had coloured his upbringing and which now regained control over him and convinced him of the sinfulness of his life and work. There should be no doubt of the importance of both these factors in shaping his decision, and they were probably paramount.[4] Yet it is reasonable to think that discouragement, too, influenced him—discouragement at his initial scant success here again, as in the case of *Britannicus*, when he departed furthest from pseudo-classical conventions. We know from the *Mémoires* of his son, Louis Racine, that he wanted to depart even further from these conventions after writing *Phèdre*,— that he planned to go back to the pattern of ancient classical tragedy and show that the love-element could be dispensed with in French drama as well as in Greek. He thought of attempting the subject of Oedipus and treating it in its essential simplicity as Sophocles had done, without introducing any factitious love-episode like Corneille before him or Voltaire after him. He did begin and almost finish a play on the story of Alcestis, which contains only conjugal love. But he may well have felt that the disappointing reception of *Phèdre* was

---

[4] Subsequent to the first publication of this book, Henry Carrington Lancaster argued in his great *History of French Dramatic Literature in the Seventeenth Century*, Part IV (Baltimore, 1940), pp. 117-126, that the sole reason Racine stopped writing plays was his appointment by Louis XIV as Royal Historiographer at this time. His theory, however, has not been generally accepted. A. B. F. Clark, whose *Jean Racine* (Cambridge, Mass.) appeared less than a year before Lancaster's discussion of the subject, and who was equally familiar with all the data concerning it, saw no reason for rejecting the traditional explanations of the dramatist's "retirement"—his treatment of which seems to me admirably judicious.

It is true that Racine long continued to take some interest in the stage and brought out editions of his dramas; but that was quite different from writing and producing plays, with the contacts thus involved with the theatrical world and all its passions and allurements. His appointment to the position of Royal Historiographer might be sufficient to account for his abandonment of dramatic composition; but it does not account for his complete departure from his old way of life and for his marriage, in the same year, with a simple, pious woman who had never read even one of his plays. Far more likely, his new duties were assigned him because the King, learning that he had resolved to sever all connections with the theatre, wanted to help him in this crisis by providing him with highly honourable, official employment and a consequent pension.

not to be wholly attributed to malicious intrigue, and that, on the contrary, its failure to be adequately appreciated at first, a failure which was common to it and to *Britannicus* and was experienced by none of his other tragedies, indicated plainly that his public would not relish such approximations to a true classicism as alone would satisfy his taste.[5] At any rate, whatever his reasons, he destroyed his nearly completed *Alceste* and wrote no plays for some twelve years. Then came a brief resumption of his old activities, in the religious dramas of *Esther* and *Athalie*—all too brief, indeed, but sufficient to prove that his genius was undiminished and to suggest poignantly how much mankind was deprived of by his retirement.

[5] A prose outline, in Racine's own handwriting, survives of the first act of an *Iphigénie en Tauride*, which prefigures a drama decidedly more romanesque than *Phèdre* or even *Iphigénie*. An appended note by his eldest child, J. B. Racine, states that this is all that survives of "several tragedies" he considered writing after *Phèdre*. If so, should we not infer from its nature that he started to repeat his former policy of recurring to what he was sure would be acceptable to his audiences—and then found he was not willing to do it again? La Grange-Chancel, however, says Racine told him that for a time he had hesitated whether to deal with the Tauris or the Aulis episode in the story of Iphigenia; if this is true, the outline was probably made just prior to *Iphigénie*.

CHARACTERS IN THE PLAY

THESEUS, *son of Aegeus and King of Athens.*

PHAEDRA, *wife of Theseus; daughter of Minos and Pasiphaë.
the King and Queen of Crete.*

HIPPOLYTUS, *son of Theseus and Antiope, the Queen of the
Amazons.*

ARICIA, *princess of the royal blood of Athens.*

OENONE, *formerly the nurse and now the chief attendant of
Phaedra.*

THERAMENES, *tutor of Hippolytus.*

ISMENE, *companion and confidante of Aricia.*

PANOPE, *one of the female attendants of Phaedra.*

GUARDS.

*The scene is laid in Troezen, a town in the Peloponnesus,
across the bay of Salamis from Athens, of which it is a
dependency.*

PHAEDRA

ACT I

The scene is the inner court of the palace of THESEUS *at Troezen.*[1] *Doorways lead from it to the apartments of* HIPPOLYTUS, ARICIA, *and the Queen, and to the exterior of the palace. Near the centre of the court is a bench.* HIPPOLYTUS *and* THERAMENES *are discovered.*

HIPPOLYTUS.

My purpose, dear Theramenes, doth stand.
I shall go hence, forsaking this fair land
Of Troezen. Racked with dreadful doubts, my soul
Groweth ashamed that I delay. A whole
Six months my father hath been absent; yet
Am I without all knowledge of his fate.
I know not even in what land he is.

THERAMENES.

And where, sir, wilt thou look for him? Ere this,
To lull thy filial anxieties,
I have made passage over both the seas
Which Corinth sunders. Even on those shores
Where the dark kingdom of the dead devours
Acheron, have I asked of Theseus.[2]
Elis I visited, and from Taenarus
Sailed to those waters which beheld the fall
Of Icarus.[3] Now what new hope, withal,
Leadeth thee on, or in what blessèd place
Expectest thou of his steps to find a trace?
Who knows? thy royal sire, it well may be,

Desireth to preserve in mystery
His absence. While we fear lest he have died,
Perchance the hero doth unharmed but hide
Some newest love, wooing some 'wildered maid . . .

HIPPOLYTUS.

Hold, my Theramenes! let respect be paid
To Theseus. From the follies of his youth
Departed, he is stayed in very truth
By no slight hindrance. Phaedra has bound fast
His sad inconstancy of heart at last;
No rival hath she dreaded this great while.

At least in seeking him I shall fulfil
Only my duty. Besides I thus shall flee
A place which I no longer dare to see.

THERAMENES.

Ah, when, my lord, didst thou begin to fear
This lovely spot thy childhood held so dear,
Whose charms I have observed thee to prefer
To Athens and the Court, their pomp and stir?
What danger, say, what sorrow dost thou shun?

HIPPOLYTUS.

All now is changed; those happy times are gone,
Since the gods wafted hither, here to be,
The daughter of Minos and Pasiphaë.[4]

THERAMENES.

I understand; and I perceive the ground
Of thy distress. Yea, to thine eyes a wound
And an affliction seemeth Phaedra here;
For scarcely had she first beheld thee, ere
With a step-mother's malice she contrived

Thine exile, as in Theseus' love she thrived.
But this her hate, upon thee fixed of old,
By now has either vanished or grown cold.
Besides, what perils counsel thee to fly
A dying woman, and one who longs to die?
For Phaedra, languishing with some disease
Which she will not reveal, aweary is
Both of herself and of the light of day.
Can she, then, work thy harm in any way?

HIPPOLYTUS.

'Tis not her futile enmity I fear.
Hippolytus avoids, by leaving here,
Another foe. I flee, I shall confess,
From young Aricia, last of all that race
Fated to plot against us.

THERAMENES.

What, my lord!
Art thou her persecutor? When the abhorred
Pallantidae[5] conspired, did ever she,
Their gentle sister, share in the perfidy?
Yet must thou hate such charming innocence?

HIPPOLYTUS.

I would not, if I hated her, fly hence.

THERAMENES.

My lord, shall I explain thy going thus?
Art thou no more the proud Hippolytus,
To ways of love for ever hostile sworn
And to the yoke thy father oft hath worn?
Can Venus, so long slighted by thy pride,
Desire that Theseus should be justified

Now, and with all the rest of humankind
Compel thee to burn incense at her shrine?
Sir, can it be thou art of love the prey?

HIPPOLYTUS.

What thing is this, my friend, thou darest to say?
Thou that since first I breathed hast known my heart,
Now wouldst thou ask of me the shameful part
Of disavowing every lofty thought
Of my disdainful soul? Is it for naught
That from the Amazon my mother's breast
I drank the pride at which thou marvellest?—
That having come to riper years, I could
Approve with reason all my habitude?

    Thyself, who served me with devoted zeal,
Wouldst oft the story of my father tell.
Thou knowest how, giving thee most eager heed,
My spirit burned at each heroic deed,
When thou didst paint him in his victories,
Taking for men the place of Hercules—
Monsters destroyed and robbers overthrown,
Procrustes, Sinnis, Sciron, Cercyon,[6]
And the bones of the Epidaurian giant now hoar,
And Crete a-reek with blood of the Minotaur.
But when of things less glorious I would hear:
Love-pledges given and taken everywhere,[7]
Helen from home in Sparta snatched amiss,
And Periboea weeping in Salamis,
And many others, whose very names are fled
Now from his memory, alike betrayed,
Too trusting, by his passion's fickle flaming;
Ariadne of her wrongs to the rocks complaining,[8]
And finally Phaedra, whom a better troth

Bound and bore hither—well thou knowest how loath
Was I to hear of these things; whence would I
Urge in thy speech a greater brevity,
Wishing that I from memory might tear
The unworthy portion of a tale so fair.

  And now must I in turn thus fettered be?
Yea, to the dust would the gods humble me,
In whom such weakness were the greater shame?
For high-heaped honours lighten Theseus' blame,
But no slain monster to this very day
Hath given me, like him, the right to stray.

  Why, even if my pride of heart were less,
Could I have chosen for my conqueress
Aricia? Whate'er my madness were,
Could I forget the eternal barrier
That stands between us twain? My father's hate
Is sealed against her. By stern laws of State
Doth he forbid that she shall ever bear
A child and to her brothers give an heir.
From such a guilty stock he dreads a shoot,
And fain would see it wither, branch and root;
Whence, till she dies, thus guarded all her days,
For her shall never torch of Hymen blaze.[9]

  Must I espouse against an angry sire
Her rights, of rashness be example dire,
And on so mad a course embark my youth?

THERAMENES.

Ah, but my lord, when comes thine hour in truth,
For all thy reasons heaven careth not.
Theseus hath oped thine eyes, that he would shut.
His ill will lights a rebel flame in thee
And lends new grace unto his enemy.

When all is said, why shun a virtuous love?
If it be sweet, this darest not thou to prove?
Wilt thou unto a barbarous prejudice
Cling always? Can one fear to walk amiss,
Following Alcides' footsteps?[10] Who so stout
Of heart that Venus hath not put to rout
And led him bound? Thyself, where wouldst thou be,
Who dost resist her, if Antiope,
Long hostile to her sway, had kept the same
Mind, nor for Theseus felt a pure love's flame?
Of what avail brave words of feigning, then?
Confess it: all is changed. Now art thou seen
But seldom, haughty and tameless as of yore,
Flying in thy chariot along the shore,
Or, master of the art which Neptune showed,[11]
Breaking unto the bit some courser proud.
Now seldom rings the forest with our cries,
But freighted with a secret fire, thine eyes
Grow dull. There cannot be a doubt. Thou art
To love enkindled. By its bitter smart,
Which thou wouldst hide, thou art consumed outright.
    Is fair Aricia pleasing in thy sight?

HIPPOLYTUS.

Theramenes, I even now depart,
And go to seek my father.

THERAMENES.

Ere thou start,

Sir, wilt thou not see Phaedra?

HIPPOLYTUS.

I have planned

E'en thus to do, since duty doth command.
Yes, I shall see her. Thou canst tell her so.

But mark!—what new calamity brings woe
To her beloved Oenone?

[*Enter* OENONE.

OENONE.

Ah, sir, when
Was there a grief like mine! Now hath the Queen
Come nearly to life's limit. Day and night
All vainly have I never left her sight,
While in mine arms she of a malady
Is dying which she still conceals from me.
Ceaseless confusion in her soul is bred;
Its anguish drives her, restless, from her bed.
She fain would see the sunlight, and her deep
Affliction biddeth me, withal, to keep
Every one from her. Lo, she comes.

HIPPOLYTUS.

Enough!
Here shall I leave her undisturbed; for loath
Am I to show her now a hated face.

[HIPPOLYTUS *and* THERAMENES *depart.* PHAEDRA *enters.*

PHAEDRA.

We shall go on no farther. In this place,
Oenone, let us stay. I cannot stand
Longer. My strength is wholly at an end.
Mine eyes are dazzled by the light of day
Which I behold again; and now give way
My trembling knees beneath me. Alas me!

[*She sinks into a seat on the bench.*

OENONE.

Almighty gods, would that our tears might be
Potent, your wrath against us to appease!

PHAEDRA.

How these vain trinkets weigh me down, and these
Veils! What officious hand these knots hath made
And all these ringlets on my forehead laid?
Everything joins to hurt me and afflict!

OENONE.

Lo, each new wish the last doth contradict.
Thou thyself, blaming thy bad moods—'twas not
A moment since—bade us to deck thee out.
Thou didst recall thy former spirit, and fain
Wouldst show thy face and see the light again.
Thou seest it, madam, and thou shrinkest away,
Hating the sunshine which thou wouldst survey.

PHAEDRA.

Ah, glorious author of a hapless race;
Thou unto whom my mother dared to trace
Her origin; who well mayest blush when thou
Beholdest me in such affliction now—
For the last time I come to look on thee,
O Sun!

OENONE.

What! Wilt thou never cease to be
Envious of death? Shall I for ever hear
This taking leave, preparing for thy bier?

PHAEDRA.

O gods! that 'neath the forest shade might I
Be sitting, thence to follow with mine eye
Through the brave dust a racing chariot
Along the course . . .

OENONE.

How sayest thou, madam? What?

PHAEDRA.

Insensate! Where am I? What have I said?
Ah, whither have my thoughts and wishes strayed?
I have lost my mind! The gods deny its use.
Oenone, look how blushes now suffuse
My face! I all too clearly let thee see
This pang and shame. Mine eyes, in spite of me,
Are filled with tears.

OENONE.

                    If blush thou must, then, oh,
Blush at that silence which still breeds thy woe!
Froward 'gainst all my care, deaf to my voice,
To end thy life—is that thy ruthless choice?
What madness cuts it off midway its course?
What spell or poison hath dried up its source?
Thrice have the shades of night o'ercast the skies
Since sleep hath visited thy weary eyes.
Thrice hath the day dispelled the night's dark cloud
Or e'er thy fainting body tasted food.
To what fell purpose dost thou let thy heart
Be tempted? Tell me by what right thou art
Against thyself so rash. Thou angerest
The gods, who gave thy life to thee; betray'st
Thy husband, unto whom thy faith is due;
Yea, and betrayest thine own children, too,
Whose necks are thus bent 'neath a cruel fate.
Think: the same day that leaves them desolate
For thee, shall to the stranger woman's son
Bring hope—to that one whom an Amazon

Of old conceived and bore within her side—
To thee and thine that foe so full of pride,
Hippolytus—

PHAEDRA.

Gods!

OENONE.

So that reproach doth gall?

PHAEDRA.

Miserable one, what name hast thou let fall!

OENONE.

Indeed with justice doth thine anger flame.
'Tis good to see thee quiver at that name.
Live, then. Let love, let duty urge thee on.
Live, nor permit the Scythian woman's son[12]
To oppress thy children with a hateful yoke,
Ruling the noblest blood of Grecian folk
And of the gods themselves. But do not wait.
Fatal is all delay. Upbuild thou straight
Thy shattered strength, while flickers yet thy flame
Of life and it may be revived again.

PHAEDRA.

I have drawn out my guilty span too long.

OENONE.

Wherefore? Art torn by some remorse? What wrong
Didst ever thou which thus doth make thee brood?
Surely thy hands have not been dipped in blood?

PHAEDRA.

Thank heaven, my hands from all such stain are free.
Would that my heart as innocent might be!

OENONE.

And what fell thought had birth and doth abide
There, that thy heart should be so terrified?

PHAEDRA.

Enough thou knowest. Spare me from the rest.
I die, to keep it locked within my breast.

OENONE.

Die, then! Thy stony silence still preserve!
To close thine eyes another hand will serve
Than mine. Though faint the light about thee shed,
I will go down before thee to the dead.
A thousand ways that lead there one may use,
Whereof the shortest, justly hurt, I choose.
Thou cruel one, when has e'er my faith deceived thee?
These arms the first, when thou wast born, received thee.
My country—children—all, I left for thee;
Am I thus paid for my fidelity?

PHAEDRA.

What shall this passion gain thee? Thou wilt shake
With horror, if my silence I should break.

OENONE.

What canst thou tell me that could horrify
More than before mine eyes to see thee die?

PHAEDRA.

When of the crime and fate which so oppress
My soul thou knowest, I shall die no less;
But I shall die the guiltier.

OENONE (*throwing herself at* PHAEDRA'S *feet*).

In the name
Of all the tears that I have wept like rain

For thee, by thy weak knees to which I cling,
Madam, resolve my doubt of this dread thing.

PHAEDRA.

It is thy will. Stand up.

OENONE (*rising*).

Speak, then. I hear.

PHAEDRA.

Ah me, what shall I say to her, and where
Shall I begin!

OENONE.

Move me no more with vain
Shrinkings.

PHAEDRA.

O wrath of Venus! Wrath our bane!
Love swept my mother along what wild ways!

OENONE.

Let us forget them. Through all future days
May silence ever hide that memory.

PHAEDRA.

Ah, Ariadne, sister mine, to thee
Also Love dealt a wound; and thou upon
That lonely strand didst perish where, time agone,
Thou wast forsaken!

OENONE.

To what leadest thou,
Madam, by this? What mortal loathing now
Prompts these reproaches against all thy kin?

PHAEDRA.

By will of Venus, of that wretched line
The last and the most miserable I die.

OENONE.

Art thou in love?

PHAEDRA.

Love's madness all have I.

OENONE.

For whom?

PHAEDRA.

Of horrors thou wilt hear the height.
I love . . . I tremble, shudder with affright
To name him! I love . . .

OENONE.

Whom?

PHAEDRA.

Thou knowest that one
I long oppressed, the son of the Amazon?

OENONE.

Hippolytus? Gods!

PHAEDRA.

'Twas thou didst name him—thou!

OENONE.

Just heaven! My blood freezeth in its flow.
O black despair! O crime! O wretched race!
O ill-starred voyage! O luckless, luckless place!
Why came we ever to thy fatal shore?

PHAEDRA.

My evil fortune dates from long before.
Unto the son of Aegeus scarce had I
Been joined in marriage, and my security
And happiness seemed sure, when Athens showed
My foe to me. I looked, and first I glowed
And then grew pale.[18] My soul at sight of him
Was shaken and distraught. Mine eyes were dim.
I could not speak. I felt through all my frame
Both heat and cold, and knew it for the flame
Of Venus, fierce and deadly and to us
Most hopeless of escape, whom she pursues.

I fondly dreamed that by assiduous vows
I could avert my doom. A sacred house
I built the goddess. To deck it, was my care.
At every hour I offered victims there
And my lost reason in their entrails sought.
For cureless love, such cures availed me naught.
Vainly my hand burned incense at the shrine;
For while my lips called on the name divine,
None but Hippolytus would I adore,
And seeing him constantly, even before
The altars, all their sacrificial flame
Rose to that god I did not dare to name.
I shunned him everywhere, but oh, my glance
Beheld him in his father's countenance;—
That was the summit of my misery.

Against myself revolting finally,
I mustered up my courage to persecute
Him whom my heart worshipped with fervour mute.
A wicked step-mother's blind prejudice
I feigned, insisting with eternal cries

Upon his exile, till, to lull my storms
Of passion, he was torn from his sire's arms.
    I breathed, Oenone, when he had gone thence;
My days flowed on in quiet and innocence;
With grief concealed, submissive to my spouse,
I reared the offspring of our fatal vows.
But ah, precautions vain! cruel destiny!
Theseus himself to Troezen carried me.
I saw anew the foe I banished; then
My wound, too recent, oped and bled again.
No more is it a longing hid away;
Venus hath wholly fastened on her prey!
    My sin fills me with horror, now. I hate
My guilty life, my love abominate.
I hoped to keep, by dying, my fair fame
And ne'er reveal so sinister a flame;
But I could not withstand thy tears nor thy
Complainings. I have told thee all, and I
Repent it not, if, seeing my death's approach,
Thou spare me now thine undeserved reproach
And leave thy futile efforts to revive
The waning spark of one who would not live.

        [*Enter* PANOPE.

PANOPE.

Madam, most willingly should I withhold
My grievous tidings, but they must be told.
Death has snatched from thee thine unconquered lord,
And this sad news all but thyself have heard.

OENONE.

What art thou saying, Panope?

PANOPE.

That the Queen,
Nursing false hope, prays unto heaven in vain
For the return of Theseus; and that from
Ships that to harbour have but lately come,
Hippolytus just now learned of his death.

PHAEDRA.

Ah, gods!

PANOPE.

The choice of Athens wavereth
Concerning the succession, madam. One
Giveth his suffrage to the Prince thy son.
Another dares, forgetful of the laws[14]
Of State, to plead the child of the alien's cause.
'Tis even said an insolent design
Is formed to place Aricia and the line
Of Pallas on the throne.
Meseemed I ought
To warn thee of the peril. To set out,
Hippolytus already is prepared;
And there is danger, if he now appeared
In the midst of all that turmoil, that he would
Capture the whole inconstant multitude.

OENONE.

Panope, 'tis enough. The Queen has heard,[15]
And will neglect thereof no weighty word.

[*Exit* PANOPE.

(*To* PHAEDRA) Mistress, I was about to cease just then
From urging thee to live; and I was fain
To follow thee to the tomb, since from thy choice
To move thee I no longer had a voice.

But now this new disaster differently
Ordains, and sets another course for thee.
Thy fortune changes, and takes another face.
Our mighty sovereign is no more. His place
Must needs be filled. To thee his death did leave
A son, to whom thou owest thyself—a slave
If thou shouldst die; if thou shouldst live, a king.
On whom dost thou expect him, sorrowing,
To lean? His tears will by no other hand
Be wiped away, but heavenward must ascend
His innocent cries, unto the gods, and stir
Against his mother their ancestral ire.

    Hence do thou live, who hast not any more
To agonize with shame as heretofore.
Thy love is now as that of other folk.
The death of Theseus those bonds hath broke
That made the crime and horror.[16] There is need
No longer for thy heart to hold in dread
Hippolytus. Thou hast the right to see
Him now without reproach. It well may be,
Since that thou hatest him is his belief,
He will supply sedition with a chief.
Then undeceive him; soften his proud thought.
These happy shores of Troezen are his lot
To rule; but as he knows, law gives thy child
The frowning ramparts that Minerva piled.[17]
You both have one same enemy. To fight
Against Aricia, must you twain unite.

PHAEDRA.

I yield me to thy counsel, to be led,
If I can struggle back, as from the dead,
And if in this grim hour love for a son
Can nerve my fainting spirit to press on.

ACT II

The scene is the same. ARICIA *and* ISMENE *are seated on the bench near the centre of the courtyard.*

ARICIA.

Hippolytus ask to see me here? He thus
Seeks me to say farewell—Hippolytus?
Is it true, Ismene? Art deceivèd not?

ISMENE.

'Tis the first change that Theseus' death has wrought.
Madam, expect on every side to see
Those hearts he checked turn swiftly now to thee.
Aricia sways her destiny at last,
And at her feet the homage will be cast
Soon of all Greece.

ARICIA.

        In sooth, Ismene, this
Is then no rumour unconfirmed? I cease
To be a slave and have not any foes?

ISMENE.

Nay, madam; thee the gods no more oppose;
And Theseus hath o'ertaken the souls now
Of all thy brothers.

ARICIA.

        Is it told us how
His days had end?

ISMENE.

Touching his death are spread
The most incredible stories. It is said
By one that while he bore off a new love,
The billows closed, his faithless head above.
'Tis even said—this everywhere they tell—
That going with Pirithoüs[18] down to hell,
He saw Cocytus[19] and the shores of night,
And living showed himself unto the sight
Of shades infernal; but from that sad place
He could not issue, nor again could pass
The strand whence one returneth nevermore.

ARICIA.

Shall I believe a man ere his last hour
Can penetrate the deep abode of death?
What lure could lead him on so dread a path?

ISMENE.

Theseus is dead,—as thou alone dost doubt.
Athens laments it; Troezen hath found it out
And hailed already Hippolytus her king.
Phaedra in this same palace, shivering
For her son's sake, imploreth counsel now
Of her distracted friends.

ARICIA.

And thinkest thou
Hippolytus, kinder than his sire to me,
Will make less grievous my captivity—
Will pity my misfortunes?

ISMENE.

I do think so.

ARICIA.

Of that cold prince what is it *thou* canst know?
What vain, light hope beguileth thee to deem
He pities me and holds me in esteem
Alone of all my sex that he disdains?
My presence he hath shunned this great while since,
And chooseth any other place instead.

ISMENE.

How he is cold, I know whate'er is said;
But I have marked this proud Hippolytus
Near thee, and I was doubly curious
At sight of him, such arrogance did fame
Ascribe him. But his look was not the same
As report hath it. At thy earliest glance
He was confused, and from thy countenance
His eyes, grown soft, had not the power to stray,
Though vainly he desired to look away.
By his high heart love's name may be abhorred;
Yet useth he love's eyes, if not the word.

ARICIA.

How gladly, dear Ismene, hear I what
Hath of foundation perchance scarce a jot!
Seems it to thee, who knowest me, that thus late
I, the sad plaything of unpitying fate,
Nourished so long with tears of bitterness,
Could wake to feel love's poignancy and stress?
The last survivor of a kingly stock,
Children of Earth,[20] I only from the shock
Of war am left. Six brothers in the flower
Of youth I lost, that bore the hopes of our
Illustrious house. The sword harvested

All; and the damp earth drank the blood thus shed
Of Erechtheus' offspring, though reluctantly.
Thou knowest how, since their death, stern laws deny
My love to any Greek, for so 'tis feared
The ashes of those brothers may be stirred
Some day and kindled by their sister's flame;
But well thou knowest, too, with what disdain
I looked upon the victor's anxious care.
Thou knowest that always I desired no share
Of love,—was thankful oft to Theseus
For his injustice, seeing that e'en thus
By happy fortune all that tyranny
Only abetted my distaste.

But I

Had never, never then beheld his son!
Not that, attracted by the eye alone,
Unworthily, for the beauty of his face
I love him, or for his renownèd grace—
Gifts with which nature chose to honour him,—
Which he himself knows not or scorns, 'twould seem.
I love, I prize more noble things than these:
His father's virtues, without his weaknesses.
I love, I will avow, that spirit proud
Which to the yoke of Venus ne'er hath bowed.
Empty were Phaedra's boast of Theseus' heart;
I am more choice, and flee the inglorious part
Of winning homage given a thousand more
And entering where on every side a door
Stands open; but to bend the neck of one
So straight and bold, to pierce a heart of stone,
To hold him captive whom the unwonted chain
Bewilders, and who struggles all in vain
Against so sweet a yoke—ah, that would please

Me well; that thrills my fancy! Hercules
Were easier than Hippolytus disarmed
By love, more often snared, and swifter charmed.
Less honour she who made him hers could claim.
(*Checking herself*) But, dear Ismene, alas, how rash I am!
Only too stoutly I shall be withstood,
And thou, mayhap, wilt hear me, in a mood
More humble, sorrow at the pride I now
Admire.

   Yet could Hippolytus, thinkest thou,
Be touched by love? Might I, through happiest chance,
Prevail . . .

ISMENE.

  Learn of himself. He comes.
   [*Enter* HIPPOLYTUS. ARICIA *and* ISMENE *rise.*

HIPPOLYTUS (*to* ARICIA).

         Ere hence,
Madam, I go, meseemed I ought to give
Thee knowledge of thy fortunes. Now doth live
My sire no longer. My well-grounded fears,
Prophetic, were too true interpreters
Of his continued absence. Death alone,
By cutting short his deeds and their renown,
Could for so great a while conceal him from
The world. At last the gods have unto doom
Delivered him, the friend of Hercules,
Companion and successor—yea, e'en these
Names which are due him, I believe thy hate,
Sparing his virtues, heareth without regret.

  My sorrow is made lighter by one thought:
From the stern guardianship that was thy lot

I can release thee. I revoke those laws
Whose rigour stirred my pity. Thou canst dispose
Both of thy heart and of thyself; and here
In Troezen, which to-day falls to my share—
The portion of Pittheus in former while,
My great-grandfather,[21] which with a single will
Hath named me for its king—do I decree
Thou art as free as I am, and more free.

ARICIA.

Make not thus great thy bounties. Their excess
O'erwhelms me. To honour me in my disgrace
With kindness all so generous, sir—why, this,
More than thou dreamest of, but only is
Again to set me 'neath those cruel laws
From which thou wouldst deliver me.

HIPPOLYTUS.

In the choice

Of a successor, Athens, not at one,
Talketh of thee, of me, and the Queen's son.

ARICIA.

Of me, my lord?

HIPPOLYTUS.

I know, for I would not

Flatter myself, one statute strict is thought
To exclude me.[22] Greece counts mine alien mother
As a reproach; yet were alone my brother
My rival, I would have a righteous cause
And could maintain it 'gainst unequal laws.
A check more just doth curb my forwardness.
I yield—nay, I restore—to thee a place,

A sceptre, which thy fathers had of yore
From that famed mortal whom the Earth once bore.
Adoption gave it unto Aegeus' hand;
And so did Theseus augment and defend
Athens, that she with joy hailed this great king
And left thy hapless brothers languishing.

 Thee Athens now recalls within her gates.
She hath enough mourned over ancient hates.
Thy blood, drunk by her furrows, hath enough
Made the fields smoke that first it sprang from off.[23]
Troezen obeys me. The domain of Crete
Affords the son of Phaedra a retreat
Of princely richness. Attica by right
Is thine. I go, and will for thee unite
All of the votes we two between us share.

ARICIA.

Amazèd and confused by what I hear,
I almost am afraid—yea, am afraid—
'Tis but a dream. Am I awake indeed?
Can I believe such purpose thine? Ah, what
God, sir, what god has given thee this thought?
How justly thy fair fame in every place
Is spread, yet how much does the truth surpass
Rumour! Thyself for me thou wouldst defraud?—
Thyself? Was it not enough thou hast ne'er allowed
Thy soul to hate me—yea, hast kept so long
From enmity—

HIPPOLYTUS.

   I? Hate thee? Howso wrong
The colours men have used to paint my pride,
Thinkest thou a monster bore me in her side?

What savage nature, what relentless wrath
Looks upon thee and never softeneth?
Could I resist the enchantment of thy spell?

ARICIA.

What? . . . my lord? . . .

HIPPOLYTUS.

                I have said too much. Oh, well
I know that to the winds my reason is cast!
But since I have begun to speak at last,
I must go on and unto thee declare
A secret that I can no longer bear
In silence. Here before thee in distress
Thou seest a prince, of most rash haughtiness
A signal instance. I who in my pride
Was rebel against love, and who defied
His captive chains—I who would oft deplore
The shipwreck of weak mortals, from the shore
Thinking always to view the storm—ah, now,
Subjected to the universal law,
Do I behold myself swept far away
From every mooring. In one moment's fray
Was my presumptuous confidence o'erthrown.
This spirit doth finally a sovereign own.
For nearly six months, shamed and in despair,
Bearing the fatal arrow everywhere
That wounds me, I have struggled against thee
Vainly, and 'gainst myself. Present, I flee;
Absent, I seek thee. Even in the deeps
Of forests doth thine image haunt my steps,
Following; and to mine eyes alike the light
Of day recalleth and the shades of night

That loveliness I shun. All things combine
To make Hippolytus, despite him, thine.
My every effort fruitless proves; in vain
I seek to find my former self again.
My bow, my javelins, my chariot,
All weary me, and I remember not
The art which Neptune gave.[24] The only noise
The woods hear is my sighings, and this voice
Mine idle coursers grow forgetful of.

    It may be that so badly told a love
Will make thee, hearing me, to blush with shame
At having won it. Crude indeed and lame
The speech that tenders thee my heart, and I
How strange a captive for how sweet a tie!
Yet thou shouldst find mine offering hence more dear.
Remember that I speak a tongue I ne'er
Have learned. Disdain not my ill-uttered plea,
Which would not have been made, except to thee.

                              [*Enter* THERAMENES.

THERAMENES.

Sir, the Queen cometh, and I before her speed.
She seeks thee.

HIPPOLYTUS.

     Me?

THERAMENES.

             Her thought I cannot read;
But one from her was asking for thee, Prince.
Phaedra would speak with thee ere thou go hence.

HIPPOLYTUS.

Phaedra? What shall I say to her, and what
Is it she doth expect . . .

ARICIA.

Sir, thou canst not
Refuse to see her. Though too sure art thou
Of her dislike, thou owest some pity now
Unto her tears.

HIPPOLYTUS.

And meanwhile thou must go!
And I shall set forth; and I do not know
Whether I have offended that divine
One I adore—whether this heart of mine,
I know not, that I gave into thy hands . . .

ARICIA.

Go, Prince, and carry out thy generous plans.
Bring Athens under my authority.
I accept all gifts thou wouldst make to me;
But in mine eyes this mighty throne of kings
Is not the dearest of thine offerings.

[ARICIA *and* ISMENE *leave the courtyard.* HIPPOLYTUS
gazes after them a moment, and then turns to
THERAMENES.

HIPPOLYTUS.

My friend, is all in readiness? . . . But anear
Draweth the Queen. Away, and make prepare
Swiftly to sail. Let give the signal. Fly,
Dispose, and here return, that so may I
From irksome converse be delivered soon.

[*Exit* THERAMENES. *Enter* PHAEDRA *and* OENONE.

PHAEDRA (*in a low voice to* OENONE).

Ah, he is there! Now all my blood doth run
Back to my heart, and seeing him, I forget
What I have come to say to him.

OENONE (*whispering to* PHAEDRA).
                              Nay, yet
Think of thy son, whose hope doth rest in thee.
    [PHAEDRA *advances to meet* HIPPOLYTUS, *and stands
      before him.*

PHAEDRA.

'Tis said, departure takes thee speedily
From us, sir. I have come to join my tears
Unto thy grief, and tell thee of my fears
Touching my son. My son no longer hath
A father, and the day that witnesseth
His mother's death cannot be distant far.
Already do a thousand foes make war
Upon his infancy. Thou, only thou,
Hast power to shield him from them. Therefore now
In secret my remorseful heart is torn
Lest I have closed against his cries forlorn
Thine ears. I tremble lest thou shouldst pursue
On him thy wrath, his mother's rightful due.

HIPPOLYTUS.

Madam, I do not have so base a thought.

PHAEDRA.

Even shouldst thou abhor me, I would not
Complain, sir. Thou hast seen me set indeed
Upon thy hurt; my heart thou couldst not read.
To win thine enmity has been my care.
Within the land that held me I nowhere
Could suffer thee. In public, secretly,
I spake against thee. I would have the sea
Between us. Even by a law proclaimed
Did I forbid thou ever shouldst be named

To me by any. If, however, by
The malice cherished should the penalty
Be measured out and meted—if 'tis hate
Alone brings forth thy hate—no woman yet
Was of compassion ever worthier,
And of thine enmity less worthy, sir.

HIPPOLYTUS.

'Tis rare a mother jealous for her own
Children forgives an earlier consort's son.
I know this well, madam. Suspicious cares
Are found the fruits a second marriage bears
Most often. Any other woman would
Have been as bitter toward me, and I should
Mayhap have suffered usage yet more ill.

PHAEDRA.

Ah, sir, that from this general law by will
Of the high gods I am exempt, I dare
Here to give oath, and that it is a care
Far different that doth rack me and devour.

HIPPOLYTUS.

Madam, 'tis not a time to vex thee more.
Perchance thy husband still beholds the day,
And heaven, seeing our tears, yet can and may
Restore him. Neptune is his guardian,
A patron deity whom ne'er in vain
My father's voice will call upon for aid.

PHAEDRA.

Not twice upon the shores that bound the dead
One gazeth, sir. Since Theseus hath seen
That gloomy strand, hope not some god again

Will give him back, for never yet its prey
Hath Acheron let slip.
                        What do I say?
He is not dead, for, lo, he lives in thee.
Always before mine eyes I think I see
My husband. I behold, I speak to him.
This heart . . .
                        I lose my way, sir. All grows dim.
My madness will find utterance, despite
Everything!

HIPPOLYTUS.

I marvel at love's might.
Theseus, though dead, is present to thine eyes,
And round thy soul for ever twineth his.

PHAEDRA.

Yes, Prince, I pine, I long for Theseus, though
In no wise for him as the world below
Saw him, light lover of so many a maid,
Who would attempt the God of Death's own bed,
But faithful, haughty, even a little grim,
Young, handsome, drawing all hearts unto him,
Such as one pictures gods or I see thee.
Thine eyes, thy carriage, and thy speech had he.
This nobly modest hue his cheek would have
When to our Crete he traversed o'er the wave,
Worthy of the vows of Minos' daughters thus.
Thyself wast where? Without Hippolytus
Why did he cull the flower of brave Greek men,
And thou, too young, wert still not able then
To embark upon the ship which presently
Set him upon our shores? or else by thee

Would have been slain the monster fierce of Crete,[25]
Despite the windings of his vast retreat.
To guide thee its uncertain mazes through,
My sister would have armed thee with the clue.
But no, in this I would have outstripped her;
Love would have made this plan at once to stir
In me. 'Tis I, Prince, I, whose help would have
Taught thee the way through that bewildering cave.
How scrupulous a care of thy dear head
Would I have taken! Never could a thread
This heart of mine that loved thee reassure!
Bride to the peril thou must needs endure,
Myself beside thee would have wished to go
Down into the Labyrinth. Yea, Phaedra so
Would have returned with thee or shared thy fate.

HIPPOLYTUS.

Gods! What is this I hear? Dost thou forget
That Theseus is my father and thy spouse?

PHAEDRA.

And wherefore dost thou judge that I could lose
The memory of it, sir? Have I thus grown
Heedless of honour?

HIPPOLYTUS.

      Madam, forgive! I own,
Blushing, that those were words of innocence
Which I mistakenly accused. Thy glance
Can I in this my shame no longer bear.
I go . . .

PHAEDRA.

     Ah, cruel, too surely didst thou hear!
I have said enough to keep thee from mistake.

Know Phaedra, then; let all her madness speak.
I love thee. Do not think that while I love,
Spotless in mine own eyes do I approve
Of what I am; nor that of the perverse
Passion that shakes my reason, I did nurse
The poison by an abject yielding.—Nay,
Of heaven's wrath the miserable prey,
More than thou loathest me do I abhor
Myself. I call the gods to witness, more!—
Those gods that in my breast have lit the flame
Fatal to all my race!—the very same
Gods that have gloried in the cruel part
Of 'wildering a weak mortal woman's heart!
      Thou thyself call to mind the past. I not
Merely avoided thee; I drove thee out.
I wanted to seem odious to thee,
Inhuman; I have sought thine enmity
The better to resist thee. All my store
Of pains hath what availed? Thou didst the more
Hate me; but I, I did not love thee less.
An added charm hadst thou in thy distress.
I have scorched in fire, have pined with many a tear.
A glance would be enough to make this clear,
If for one moment thou wouldst look at me!
Why, this confession that I make to thee,
All shameful as it is, dost think it one
Determined on? Nay, trembling for a son
I came, whose cause I did not dare betray.
That thou wouldst hate him not, I came to pray,—
Weak purpose of a heart too full of love!
Alas, thee only have I spoken of!
      Avenge thyself. Punish me for my vile
Longings. True son of the hero who erewhile

Gave life to thee, set free the universe
From one so monstrous, whom thou canst but curse.
The widow of Theseus loves Hippolytus!
Indeed, this frightful and iniquitous
Creature ought never to escape thy sword.
Here is my heart. That is the spot, abhorred,
Which thou shouldst pierce. Impatient even now
I feel it strain forward to meet thy blow
And expiate its offence. Strike thou! But should
Thou deem unworthy of thine arms this blood,
Or if thou would not stain thy hand with it,
Or if thy hate grudge me a pang so sweet,
Lend me thy sword instead. Yea, give it! . . .

[*She seizes his sword.*

OENONE.

Oh,
What wouldst thou do, madam? Great gods! But lo,
One cometh. Let us from these proofs of blame
Escape. Be quick, or certain is thy shame!
[*Exeunt* PHAEDRA *and* OENONE, *hastily,* PHAEDRA *still blindly*
clutching HIPPOLYTUS' *sword. Enter* THERAMENES.

THERAMENES.

Can this be Phaedra who doth headlong fly,—
Is hurried away, rather? Why, sir, why
These signs of woe? I see thee pale, confounded,
And swordless.

HIPPOLYTUS.

Theramenes, let us hence. Astounded
Am I. I cannot without horror even
Think of myself. Phaedra . . . but no, just heaven!

In silence and oblivion profound
Let this dread secret be for ever drowned!

THERAMENES.

If thou would sail, the vessel is prepared.
But Athens, sir, already hath declared
Her preference. Her chief men have ta'en the voice
Of all the tribes. Thy brother is their choice,
And Phaedra triumphs.

HIPPOLYTUS.
Phaedra!

THERAMENES.

By the vote
Of Athens charged, a herald comes to put
Into her hands the reins of power, sir.
Her son is King.

HIPPOLYTUS (*to himself*).
Ye gods, who fathom her,
Is it thus, then, her virtues have reward?

THERAMENES.

Meanwhile, 'tis darkly whispered now, my lord,
That Theseus liveth, and (so runs the tale)
Hath in Epirus shown himself. But well
I know, who in that very land have sought . . .

HIPPOLYTUS.

No matter: let us hear all, neglect naught.
Search we this rumour, trace it to its source;
And if it have not weight to change my course,
Forth let us go, and cost whate'er it may,
Give unto worthy hands the sceptre's sway.

[HIPPOLYTUS *and* THERAMENES *go out together.*

ACT III

The scene is the same. PHAEDRA *sits despondently.* OENONE
stands before her.

PHAEDRA.

Ah, let the honours which they bring to me[26]
Be taken elsewhere. Why thus urgently
Wouldst have me seen of any? Why dost thou
Come to beguile my wounded spirit now?
Nay, hide me, rather. Too much have I said.
My madness hath been openly displayed.
I have spoken things that none should e'er have known.
Gods! how he heard me! How that heartless one
Avoided long my meaning deviously!
How he lived only to escape from me!
And how his blushes made my shame more hot!
Why didst thou turn me from the death I sought?
Alas, when to my breast I set his sword,
Did he grow pale, snatch it, or speak a word?
That once my grasp had touched it, did suffice
To make it loathsome to his pitiless eyes;
This luckless blade would henceforth soil his hand.

OENONE.

Thus yielding thee to sorrow unrestrained,
Thou nourishest a fire which thou hast need
Now to put out. Would it not be, indeed,
Better and worthier far of Minos' race
In nobler cares to seek to find thy peace?
Defy an ingrate who recoils in hate.
Reign, and embrace the conduct of the State.

PHAEDRA.

I reign? I rule a State, and laws decree?
I, when my soul no longer ruleth me?
When I have lost all reason and all sense?
When scarce I breathe, my shame is so intense?
When I am dying?

OENONE.

Fly.

PHAEDRA.

I cannot leave him.

OENONE.

Thou canst not, and to exile thou didst drive him?

PHAEDRA.

It is too late. He knows my folly. I
Have overstepped the bounds of decency.
I have declared my shame before his face,
And hope, despite me, secretly found place
Within my breast. 'Twas thou that didst restore,
When my soul fluttered on my lips, once more
My failing strength. Thy falsely fair advice
Revived me, and set a dream before mine eyes
Of love.

OENONE.

Guilty or innocent of thy woe,
To save thee, what was there I would not do?
But if thou e'er wast angered by offence,
Canst thou forget his scorn and arrogance?
With what cruel glance and stony features set,
He left thee all but prostrate at his feet!

How odious then was that fierce pride of his!
Why at that moment hadst thou not mine eyes?

PHAEDRA.

Oenone, he may change for other moods
His pride that vexes thee. Reared in the woods,
He shares their wildness. Hippolytus, inured
To ways most rude, for the first time hath heard
The speech of love. Perhaps 'twas from surprise
He spake not, or too violent were my cries.

OENONE.

Remember, a barbarian in her womb
Bore him.

PHAEDRA.

    She none the less to love did come,
Though Scythian and barbarian.

OENONE.
              Womankind
He holds in bitter hate.

PHAEDRA.
        I shall not find
Some rival, then, preferred to me. Make end.
Thy counsels are no longer timely, friend.
Serve thou my madness, not my reason now.
    To love he doth oppose, as sayest thou,
It may be, an invulnerable heart;
Let us attack him in some weaker part.
He seemeth to be touched by empire's lure.
Athens doth beckon him, nor had he the power
To hide it. Thitherward the prows of all
His ships are turned, and floateth every sail

Free to the winds. Therefore go thou and seek
This so ambitious youth for me, and make
The crown before his dazzled eyes to shine.
I only wish the honour to be mine,
When he assumes that sacred diadem,
Of setting it upon his brow. To him
I would give o'er what I cannot maintain.
He will teach my son to rule, perchance will deign
To be a father unto him. I place
Both child and mother subject to his grace.

    Try every means to win him. Words of thine
Will find him more accessible than mine.
Urge him, weep, wail; stir him with piteous show
Of Phaedra dying; use the voice of woe;—
I sanction all. In thy hands is my fate.
Go. To decide it, thy return I wait.

                          [Exit OENONE.

    O thou who seest the shame I wither of,
Implacable Venus, have I not enough
Been humbled? Surely thou couldst know not how
To push thy cruelty any further now!
Thy triumph is perfect; all thy shafts have ta'en
Effect. If thou, unpitying one, wouldst gain
New glory, set upon an enemy
Who would be more rebellious. Lo, from thee,
Defiant of thy wrath, Hippolytus flees.
He never at thine altars bent his knees.
To his proud ears, offensive is thy name.
Avenge thyself. Our causes are the same,
Goddess. Make him feel love . . .[27]

                      [Re-enter OENONE.

But even now,
Oenone, on thy steps returnest thou?
Already? He hates me. He would hear thee not.

OENONE.

Of thy vain longings thou must crush the thought.
Recall the virtue that was thine, instead.
The King—yea, Theseus—whom men held for dead
Shall in a twinkling stand before thy face.
He hath come back—is here! The populace
Hasten, rush headlong to behold him. I
Was going forth, as badest thou, to try
And find Hippolytus, when to the cope
Of heaven itself, a thousand cries went up . . .

PHAEDRA.

My husband lives, Oenone. 'Tis enough.
I have unworthily avowed a love
That shameth him. He lives, and I would hear
No more.

OENONE.

What!

PHAEDRA.

I foretold to thee whilere
What must be; but from this thy spirit quailed.
Over my just remorse thy tears prevailed.
This morning, worthy of men's pity, I
Was dying. Thy reed I followed, and I die
Dishonoured.

OENONE

Die?

PHAEDRA.

Oh, what things have I done
This day! My husband soon will come, his son
With him—the witness of that lawless fire
Devouring me. How can I hail his sire
While yet my heart is bursting with the sighs
He would not hear; while wet still are mine eyes
With tears that he, ungrateful, did but spurn?
Will he conceal the flame with which I burn,
Jealous of Theseus' honour as he is?
Will he permit to be deceived like this
His king and father, thinkest thou? Can he
Restrain the horror that he has for me?
Why, even if he were silent, none the less
'Twould be in vain. I know my faithlessness,
Oenone, and am not like one of those
Bold women who can show unblushing brows
And taste of tranquil peace 'mid crime on crime.
I recognize my madness—all that time
It hath endured, do I remember all.
Meseemeth e'en now that every arch and wall
About us here will find a tongue to accuse me
And but await my husband to expose me.
Oh, let me perish; from such horrors let
One death deliver me! Is it so great
And sad a thing that one should cease to be?
To die affrights not those in misery.
I only dread the name I shall have left—
For my poor children what a fearful gift!
With lofty spirit should the blood of Jove
Inspire them, but whate'er the pride thereof
That rightly animates so fair a line,

A heavy burden is this guilt of mine.
I tremble lest—alas, too truly—they
Be taunted with their mother's crime some day.
I tremble lest, bound by such load as this,
Neither shall ever dare to lift his eyes.

OENONE.

'Tis beyond doubt. For both of them I grieve.
Never couldst thou a juster fear conceive.
But why expose them to such insult? Why
Against thine own self wilt thou testify?
Thus stands the case: 'tis certain to be said
That Phaedra from the husband she betrayed
Took flight, too guilty to endure his glance;
And so Hippolytus, at thy life's expense,
Shall have his words confirmed most happily.
To thine accuser, what can I reply?
Too easy will he find me to confute,
And I shall see him in his triumph gloat
Horribly and to every ear thy shame
Tell that will hearken. Ah, rather let the flame
Of heaven blast me!
                    Come; deceive me not.
Still is he dear to thee? Confess, in what
Aspect now seest thou this bold prince?

PHAEDRA.

                              He is
Become a monster frightful to mine eyes.

OENONE.

Why yield him, then, such victory? Fearest thou him?
Be thou the first to accuse him of the crime
That he may charge thee with. Who will thy word

Gainsay? All speaks against him. Lo, his sword
Left luckily in thy hand, thy present woe,
Thine olden grief, his father long ago
Warned by thy voice, his exile formerly
Sought and obtained by thee.

PHAEDRA.

Nay, how dare I
Oppress and blacken innocence?

OENONE.

My zeal
Needs but thy silence. Like thyself I feel
Some tremblings of remorse. Thou wouldst behold me
Confront a thousand deaths instead more boldly.
But since without this bitter remedy
I lose thee, and thy life is unto me
A thing beyond all else, I will speak out.
Theseus, though by my tale incensed, no doubt
Will only his son's banishment ordain.
A father, when he punishes, doth remain
Always a father, madam, and a small
Vengeance will satisfy his wrath withal.
But e'en if innocent blood must needs be shed,
Is that a price o'er heavy to be paid
To save thy threatened honour? 'Tis too dear
A treasure to be compromised. Whate'er
The law it dictates, thou canst but submit;
Indeed, when anything imperils it,
All, even right, must bow to that decree. . . .
Some one comes. I see Theseus.

PHAEDRA.

Ah, I see
Hippolytus. In his contemptuous eyes

Do I behold my doom writ plain. Devise
Whatso thou wilt. I yield myself to thee.
I can do naught in this extremity.

[*Enter* THESEUS, HIPPOLYTUS, *and* THERAMENES.

THESEUS (*to* PHAEDRA).

Fortune no longer doth my prayers refuse,
Madam, but to thine arms—

PHAEDRA.

Nay, Theseus!
Do not profane what was erewhile so sweet.
No more for thine endearments am I fit.
Thou hast been wronged. Fate did not spare, while thou
Wert absent, thine own wife. Unworthy now
To stand beside thee or to share thy bed,
Henceforth should I but seek to hide my head.

[*Exit* PHAEDRA, *with* OENONE.

THESEUS (*turning to* HIPPOLYTUS).

What does this strange reception mean, my son,
Given to thy father?

HIPPOLYTUS.

Phaedra can alone
Explain that mystery. But if aught avail
My fervent prayers, oh, suffer it that I shall
Never again behold her anywhere!
Suffer Hippolytus to disappear
For ever from the home where she doth live!

THESEUS.

Thou, my son, leave me?

HIPPOLYTUS.

Never did I strive
To see her, sir. 'Twas thou didst lead her feet
Unto these shores. 'Twas thou didst think it meet,
Setting forth, to consign to Troezen's land
Aricia and the Queen; and thy command
It was that placed their safety in my care.
But now what duties will detain me here?
Enough through idle youth in grove and wood
My darts were stained with paltry creatures' blood.
Could I not leave inglorious repose
And show my prowess against nobler foes?
Before thy years had ever matched mine own,
More than one tyrant, monster more than one,
Had felt how heavy was thine arm and strong.
Already, the glad hunter-down of wrong,
Hadst thou made safe from outrage either shore
Of isthmian soil. The traveller no more
Knew the restraint of fear; and Hercules,
On hearing of thine exploits, breathed at ease,
Expecting thee to assume his work entire.
But I, the unknown son of such a sire—
Far even behind my mother's steps I tread.
Grant that I may at last dare some brave deed.
Grant, if some monster hath escaped thee yet,
That I may bring his spoils unto thy feet,
Or that a fair death's deathless memory
May light a life ended thus worthily
And prove to all I am indeed thy son.

THESEUS.

What do I see? What horror shed upon
This place doth make my long-lost loved ones fly

Before me? If, O heaven, so feared do I
Return, so little wished for, why didst thou
This frame from out the prison ever draw?
I had one friend. To rashness led astray
By passion's heat, he sought to bear away
The tyrant of Epirus' wife.[28] Though loath
I was, I aided his design. We both
Were blinded by indignant destiny.
The king laid hold upon us suddenly,
Taking me weaponless at unawares.
I saw Pirithoüs through a mist of tears
To savage beasts by that barbarian
Flung, who doth feed to them unhappy men;
And me myself in caverns dark and deep
He shut, that neighbour on the realms where keep
The dead. But fortune, when six months were passed,
Looked on me with a favouring glance at last.
I found a way to cheat my jailors' eyes;
I purged of one of its iniquities
The world; and he himself did serve as food
For his own monsters. Yet when now with mood
Of rapture, I expected to draw near
To all that had been left me that was dear—
Nay, when (once more restored to life) my soul
Would find its joy in a fond gaze—the whole
Welcome I have is shuddering and affright:
None will embrace me; every one takes flight;
And I myself feel the same terror I
Inspire, and in the dungeons fain would lie
Of Epirus now again. Speak. Phaedra said
I have been wronged. By whom was I betrayed?
Why am I not avenged? Greece, whom my arm
So often served—hath Greece kept safe from harm

The criminal? . . . Thou dost not answer me.
My son, mine own son,—can it be that he
Shareth the counsels of mine enemies?
I shall within. I have suffered doubts, that freeze
My heart, to live too long. So, let us seek
To learn at once the crime and culprit eke.
Her cause for sorrow Phaedra must reveal.
[*He enters the Queen's apartments.* THERAMENES *withdraws.*

HIPPOLYTUS (*to himself*).

What do these words presage that so congeal
My blood? Will Phaedra, ever frenzy's prey,
Accuse and ruin herself? Gods! what will say
The King? What poison dire hath love distilled
Through all his house! I with a fire am filled
Banned by his hate. How changed he findeth me,
Now, from the son he looked on formerly!
Black bodings rise, and I would be afraid,
But innocence hath surely naught to dread.
I must away and ponder how I best
May rouse the kindness in my father's breast,
And tell him of a love which he can make
Unhappy, but which he can never shake.

ACT IV

The scene is the same. THESEUS *and* OENONE *come into the courtyard, from the entrance to* PHAEDRA'S *suite.*

THESEUS.

Ah, what things am I told? This traitor vile
Would dare his father's honour thus defile?
Fortune, how cruelly pursuest thou!
I know not where I go, nor even where now
I am. O love, O kindness ill repaid!
So bold a plan, such odious thought he had!
And that his black desires might run their course,
Dared the presumptuous villain to use force? . . .
I recognize the blade that served his need;
I armed him with it for some nobler deed. . . .
Not all the ties of blood could hold him back!
    And Phaedra did no vengeance on him take?
Would she by silence spare his guilty head?

OENONE.

Phaedra would spare his hapless sire, instead.
Shamed utterly by his mad passion's aim,
And by the thought that she had lit such flame,
Phaedra would fain have died, and all the light
Of her pure eyes would she have drowned in night.
I saw her lift her arm and ran to her.
'Twas I alone that saved her for thee, sir;
And pitying her sorrows and thy cares,
I have unwillingly explained her tears.

THESEUS.

The caitiff! He could not help turning pale.
When first he greeted me, I saw him quail
With dread. I marvelled at his joyless face.
My tenderness froze with his cold embrace.
But was this impious fire that feeds upon
His heart ere this in Athens ever shown?

OENONE.

The old complaints recall, sir, of the Queen.
His lawless love caused all her hatred then.

THESEUS.

And so in Troezen were its embers stirred
To life?

OENONE.

          I have told thee, sir, what hath occurred.
The Queen should not be left in her distress.
Let me go and beside her take my place.
                    [*Exit* OENONE. *Enter* HIPPOLYTUS.

THESEUS (*to himself*).

Ah, it is he! That noble mien! What eye,
Great gods, were not deceived like mine thereby?
Shall a profane adulterer's forehead shine
With light of holiest virtue? Shall no sign
Be given us to distinguish from the good
A foul heart?

HIPPOLYTUS.

              May I ask what lowering cloud
Hath darkened, sir, thy countenance august?[29]
Wilt thou not to my loyalty entrust
This secret?

PHAEDRA 269

THESEUS.

Villain, darest thou to come
And stand before me thus? Thou monster, whom
The thunderbolt too long hath spared! thou vile
Survivor of those robbers I erewhile
Swept from the world! After thy frenzy's flame
Of passion that is horror did not shame
Even to rage within thy father's bed,
Thou darest to show me thy detested head?

Thou dost come here steeped in thine infamy,
Nor seekest out beneath an unknown sky
Some land whereto my name hath pierced not yet!
Flee, traitor! Stay not to defy my hate
Nor tempt the wrath I scarcely can restrain.
It is enough mine everlasting stain
To have brought into the world a son so base,
Without thy death besides to bring disgrace
Upon my memory and the glory blot
Of my great deeds. Fly, and if thou wouldst not
By a swift doom descending upon thee
Be added to the miscreants formerly
Slain by this hand, take care that nevermore
The sun that lights us see thee on this shore
Presume to set thy foot. Begone, I say!
And with all speed, returning not for ay,
Set free my State from thine abhorrèd sight.

O Neptune, Neptune, if my conquering might
Hath cleansed thy coast of murderers in the past,
Remember that to grant my first request
As guerdon for that exploit didst thou swear.
Through the long anguish of the prison drear
To thine immortal power I never prayed.

I like a miser treasured up thine aid
And saved its use for some need yet more dire.
I ask it now. Avenge a wretched sire.
To all thy wrath this traitor I give o'er.
Smother his brazen-faced desires with gore.
Thy rage shall prove thy grace to Theseus.

HIPPOLYTUS.

What? Phaedra doth accuse Hippolytus
Of criminal love? 'Tis such a dizzy peak
Of horror that, confused, I cannot speak.
So many unexpected blows to-day
Stifle my voice and take my words away.

THESEUS.

Dastard, it was thy hope that Phaedra would
In timid silence all thine outrage shroud.
Thou shouldst not in thy flight have left behind
The sword which in her hands doth help to bind
Thy guilt upon thee; nay, thou shouldst have made
Thy villainy complete, taking instead
Both speech and life from her by one sure stroke.

HIPPOLYTUS.

So black a slander justly might provoke
The truth from me, and I would speak it here,
Were it not a secret touching thee most near.
Respect the filial reverence that doth close
My lips fast. I will not increase thy woes.
But look on me; think what my life hath been.
Some lesser crimes always precede great sin.
He who hath once the bounds of right transgressed
May violate the most sacred laws at last;
But even as virtue, vice hath its degrees,

And modest innocence one never sees
Pass suddenly to wanton ways and lewd.
A single day makes no man till then good
A faithless murderer, an incestuous beast.
I, nurtured at a pure, brave mother's breast,
Have never proved unworthy of that stock;
And Pittheus, famed for wisdom, undertook
My further guidance when I left her sight.
I would not paint myself in hues too bright,
Yet if in any virtue I have share,
I think, sir, that I have at least made clear
My hatred for those heinous crimes that I
Am now by some one charged with. 'Tis thereby
That all Greece knows Hippolytus, for he
Is continent even to austerity,
His mood unbending famed in every part.
The day is not more pure than is this heart.
And he with hellish flame, do folk pretend . . . ?

THESEUS.

Yes, wretch, 'tis by that pride thou art condemned.
Now I can see wherein thy coldness lies;
Phaedra alone could please thy shameless eyes.
Thy soul, indifferent to all others, would
Disdain to feel a passion chaste and good.

HIPPOLYTUS.

Nay, father, I have hidden it long enough.
My soul doth not disdain to feel chaste love.
My true offence confess I at thy feet:
I love indeed where thou forbadest it.
Aricia hath my vows and homage won.
The daughter of Pallas hath enslaved thy son.

I worship her, and, rebel 'gainst thy word,
Am but by her to sighs and ardours stirred.

THESEUS.

Thou lovest her? Gods! . . . But the deceit is plain.
This crime to justify thee dost thou feign.

HIPPOLYTUS.

I shunned her for six months, and still I love.
Trembling, I came to tell thee now thereof.
In sooth, can nothing draw thee from thine error?
To reassure thee, what great oath of terror
Availeth? Let the universe—earth, sky . . .

THESEUS.

The wicked never shrink from perjury.
Cease, cease these odious efforts to persuade,
If thy false virtue hath no other aid.

HIPPOLYTUS.

To thee it seemeth false and full of art.
Phaedra doth judge more justly, in her heart.

THESEUS.

How my wrath kindles at thy shamelessness!

HIPPOLYTUS.

For what term is mine exile? to what place?

THESEUS.

Though past the pillars of Hercules[30] thou were,
Thy faithless presence still would be too near.

HIPPOLYTUS.

Charged with the fearful crime thou dost impute,
What friends will pity me, by thee cast out?

PHAEDRA 273

THESEUS.

Go, seek thee friends whose fell opinion doth
Esteem adultery, applaud incest, both—
Traitors and ingrates, void of honour and law,
Fit to defend a knave like thee, I vow.

HIPPOLYTUS.

Always of incest and adultery
Thou speakest. I answer not. But Phaedra—she
Springs from a mother, she is of a race
(Thou knowest it well, sir) with e'en such disgrace
And horror far more stained than mine.

THESEUS.

What! all
Restraint before me thus thy rage and gall
Have lost? For the last time, get thee from my sight!
Hence, traitor! Stay not, nor thy sire incite
To have thee driven in open shame herefrom.

[*Exit* HIPPOLYTUS.

(*Gazing after him*) Thou rushest to inevitable doom.
Neptune did by the stream that chills with fear
The immortal ones an oath unto me swear,[31]
And will discharge it. A god follows thee
Of vengeance; and from him thou canst not flee.
I loved thee, and in spite of thine offence
I feel my heart torn for thee in advance;
But thou too greatly didst arouse mine ire.
Was e'er such wrong done any other sire?
Just heaven that seest the grief which drives me wild,
How could I have begot so base a child?

[*Enter* PHAEDRA.

PHAEDRA.

Sir, with good cause afraid I come to thee;
Thy dread voice hath pierced even unto me.
I fear performance followeth close thy threat.
Oh, spare thine offspring, if 'tis not too late!
I beg thee, have respect for thine own blood.
The horror of hearing it to cry aloud—
Be this not mine, nor the eternal woe
That 'twas for me a sire's hand made it flow.

THESEUS.

Nay, madam, from that stain my hand is free.
But the foul wretch hath not escaped from me!
With his destruction an immortal hand
Is charged—my right from Neptune. Thou shalt stand
Avenged.

PHAEDRA.

          Thy right from Neptune? What! can prayer
'I hine anger prayed . . .

THESEUS.

                    Thou fearest he will not hear?
Then join, as 'tis most fit, thy voice to mine.
In all its blackness paint for me his crime.
Fan thou my tardy passion to white heat.
But his full infamy thou knowest not yet.
His fury against thee hath been outpoured
Insultingly. He saith that every word
Thy tongue doth speak is false. Indeed, he saith
Aricia hath his heart, his plighted faith,
And that he loves her.

PHAEDRA.

                    What! . . . sir?

THESEUS.

This he said
Before my face; but through so slight a thread
Of artifice I well knew how to break.
Let us hope Neptune will swift vengeance take.
I shall myself again kneel at his shrine
And urge him to fulfil his pledge divine.

[*Exit* THESEUS.

PHAEDRA.

He has gone. What tidings have assailed mine ear?
In my heart wakes what yet unstifled fire?
Oh, what a thunderbolt falls on my head!
And I was flying with single thought to aid
His son! Yea, I had torn myself by force
From terrified Oenone's arms, remorse
So racked me; and who knoweth to what length
Repentance would have carried me? Even the strength
To accuse myself perchance I might have found;
And if in shame my voice had not been drowned,
Mayhap the frightful truth I should have told.
        Hippolytus can love, and yet doth hold
No love at all for me! Aricia hath
His heart! Aricia hath his plighted faith!
Ah, gods! when from my prayer that ingrate stern
With proud eye and forbidding brow did turn,
I deemed his breast, locked ever, to be charmed
Nowise, 'gainst all my sex alike was armed.
Another woman hath brought him, none the less,
To her feet; another woman hath found grace
In his cruel eyes. He owns, it even may be,
A heart enkindled very easily;

'Tis I alone that he cannot endure.
Shall the task, then, be mine to prove him pure?

[*Enter* Oenone, *hastily.*

My Oenone, knowest what I have learned just now?

OENONE.

Nay, but I come all trembling, I avow.
Pale the intent that sped thee turneth me.
I fear some rashness deadly unto thee.

PHAEDRA.

Who would have dreamed? I have a rival.

OENONE.

                                        What!

PHAEDRA.

Hippolytus loves. Yes, I can doubt it not.
This wild and tameless foe, whom deference
Irked, and to whom entreaty gave offence—
This tiger, unto whom I never spoke
Except with dread—now wears a conqueror's yoke,
Captive, subdued. Aricia found the way
Into his heart.

OENONE.

Aricia, dost thou say?

PHAEDRA.

Ah, yet untasted, unimagined grief!
To what new pangs have I prolonged my life?
All I have suffered—fears with which I strove,
My fits of passion, the madness of my love,
The anguish of remorse, the bitter shame
Of being spurned—yea, all were weak and tame

Foreshadowings of my present agonies.
They love! They love! Oh, they have dimmed mine eyes
By what device of magic? How have they met?
How long, and where? Thou knewest it. Why, why let
Me be deceived? Of their hid sighs couldst not
Thou tell me? Oft they have been seen, I wot,
Seeking each other, or talking. Did they go
Into the forest depths to hide? No, no!
Alas, to be together they were free!
The sky bore witness to the purity
Of their fond whisperings. They walked, untorn
By conscience, down love's pleasant path. Each morn
Rose clear and calm for them, who feared no curse.
But I, sad outcast from the universe,
Cowered at the dawn and fled the light of day.
To Death, alone of gods, I dared to pray.
I waited but the hour of his release.
Too closely was I watched in my distress;
Watered with weeping, nourishèd with gall,
I never dared in sweet, assuaging fall
Of the heart's flood to drown my griefs at leisure.
Trembling, I did but taste that dangerous pleasure;
And oft beneath a tranquil brow my fears
I must conceal, and cheat me of all tears.

OENONE.

What profit shall those gather from the vain
Affection which they cherish? Henceforth, again
They shall behold each other nevermore.

PHAEDRA.

Yet shall they love each other evermore.
This moment that I speak,—ah, fearful thought!—

The anger of a woman all distraught
With passion, they defy unawed. In spite
Of exile that shall part them soon, they plight
A thousand oaths to bind them yet more sure!
A triumph which insults me, can I endure?
Have pity, Oenone, on my jealous rage!
Aricia must die. We must engage
Against her hated race my husband's wrath
Once more, nor let him halt midway his path
Of vengeance. Greater than her brothers' crime
Their sister's is. This frenzy wild of mine
Compels me to intreat of him *his* aid.

  What is it with me? Where has my reason strayed?
I jealous? Theseus he to whom I turn
For help? My husband lives, and still I burn—
For whom? What heart is this to which my love
Is dedicated? Oh, every word doth move
And lift my hair with horror! My sins are heaped
Already to o'erflowing. I am steeped
At once in incest and hypocrisy.
My murderous hands, hot for avenging me,
Are fain to plunge themselves in guiltless blood.
Wretched! And still I live—still have I stood
Before the light of that most holy Sun
From whom I am derived! Our stem is one—
The sire and master of the gods', and mine.[32]
The sky, the universe are with my line
All thronged. Oh, where to hide me! I shall fly
Down to the night infernal . . .

        Yet what say I?
There, holding the dread urn, my father stands.
Destiny placed it in his pitiless hands.

Minos, below, judges the souls of men.
Ah, how his shade aghast will shudder when
He sees his child is come before his eyes,
Forced to avow so many infamies
Diverse, and even deeds unknown to hell!
What wilt thou do, O father, at this fell
And awful sight? Methinks I see the urn
Drop from thy grasp, and crash, and overturn.
Methinks I see thee search for torments new,
And executioner become unto
Thine own flesh. Spare me! Some cruel god hath all
Thy house destroyed. See in thy daughter's fall
A final stroke! Alas, never the fruit
Of that dire crime whose shame made such pursuit
Of me, my piteous heart hath tasted once!
Behold, how sorrow still unceasing hunts
Me even to my latest breath, and I
In torture end a life of misery!

OENONE.

Nay, madam, put from thee a groundless fear!
Look on thine error with not thus severe
An eye. Thou lovest. We cannot conquer fate.
A spell, as 'twere, hath drawn thee on. Is that
With us so marvellous a prodigy?
Hath love yet triumphed only over thee?
Weakness is natural to mankind, I wot.
Bow as a mortal to a mortal's lot.
'Tis o'er a yoke long borne that thou dost wail.
Why, even the gods who on Olympus dwell—
The gods, who fright us with threats loud and dire—
Have sometimes burned with that forbidden fire!

PHAEDRA.

What do I hear? Such counsel darest thou give?
'Tis thus thou even to the end wilt strive
To poison me! Wretch! So didst thou ruin me!
Thou brought'st me back to the light, whence I would flee.
Thy prayers made me forget my duty—made
Me see Hippolytus, whom I shunned, afraid.
What hast thou wrought? Why did thy wicked tongue
Blacken his life with charge of vilest wrong?
He will die, perhaps, for that! The cruel desire
May be fulfilled of an infuriate sire.
I will hear no more! Thou monster that I hate,
Begone, and leave me to my piteous fate!
May a just heaven repay thee worthily,
And may thy punishment for ever be
A terror unto all whose artful pleas
Would basely nourish, like thine, the weaknesses
Of luckless rulers, push them to the brink
Of sin to which their hearts incline, nor shrink
From making smooth for them the fatal path
Of crime. Accursed flatterers! The wrath
Of heaven can give no deadlier gift to kings.[33]

[*Exit* PHAEDRA.

OENONE.

Oh, gods! to serve her I have done all things,
Given up everything! And thus do I
Have my reward? I earned it, verily!

ACT V

The scene is the same. HIPPOLYTUS *and* ARICIA *are discovered.*

ARICIA.

What! thou art willing in this peril dire
To hold thy peace nor undeceive a sire
That loves thee? Oh, thou cruel man! if naught
Heeding my tears, thou canst endure the thought,
Without a pang, of seeing me no more,
Go, leave the sad Aricia; but before
Thou goest, security at least obtain.
Defend thy honour from so foul a stain,
And force thy father to revoke the late
Wish that he made. There still is time for that.
Why, 'tis by what caprice that thou dost yield
To her that doth accuse thee a free field?
Enlighten Theseus.

HIPPOLYTUS.

           What have I not said?
Could I disclose the shame of his own bed?
Was I with the whole story, all too true,
To dye my father's cheeks with such a hue
As doth become them not? Thyself alone
Hast fathomed that vile mystery. Unto none
Except the gods and thee is bared my heart.
I could not hide from thee—judge if thou art
Beloved, then—all that I would fain conceal
E'en from myself. But think under what seal
I told it thee. Forget my every word

If so thou canst; and of this thing abhorred
Open not thy pure lips to speak. I trust
The righteous gods, assured they will be just.
Me their own honour bids them vindicate;
And Phaedra for her crime will soon or late
Be punished, nor the shame that is her due
Can she avoid.

              I ask, as thou art true
To me, thy silence—naught besides. I grant
Unto my wrath all else without restraint.
Break from the bondage that hath been thy plight.
Dare thou to follow me, to share my flight,
And from this fatal spot profanèd tear
Thyself, where virtue breathes empoisoned air.
To cloak thy swift escape, advantage take
Of the confusion my disgrace doth make.
Doubt not the means to fly are sure; as yet
No guards watch over thee but those I set.
Mighty defenders will our cause espouse:
Lo, Argos stretches out her arms to us
And Sparta calls. Unto our friends shall we
Appeal for justice, nor supinely see
Phaedra combine thy ruin with mine own
And alike drive us from our fathers' throne,
Giving her son what she hath robbed us of.

    Seize on this chance. It offereth enough.
What fear restrains thee? Thou dost hesitate,
'Twould seem. It is thy good that doth create
Boldness in me. When I am all on fire,
Why dost thou turn to ice? Is it so dire
To follow in the steps of one who goes
To banishment?

ARICIA.

Alas, sir, heaven knows
How dear to me would such an exile be!
How gladly, joined to thee in destiny,
Could I all other mortal lot forget!
But ununited by a tie so sweet,
Can I with honour steal beside thee hence?
The strictest code holds me without offence,
I know, in winning free from Theseus' grasp.
Not as if from my parents' loving clasp
I broke, is this; and flight assuredly
Is lawful when one flees from tyranny.
But thou dost love me, sir; and my fair fame . . .

HIPPOLYTUS.

Nay, nay, most dear to me is thy good name.
A nobler purpose brings me unto thee:
'Tis with thy husband I would have thee flee.
Our evil fortunes o'er, heaven hath ordained
Our mutual vows on no one else depend.
Not always amid torches Hymen comes.
    At Troezen's gate there stands, among those tombs
Of old, where lie the princes of my race,
A temple, to all perjurers a place
Of dread. There mortals dare not falsely swear;[34]
The faithless find a prompt requital there;
Nor can a stronger curb restrain a lie
Than expectation to win death thereby.
Thither, if thou wilt trust me, we shall steal,
By solemn oath eternal love to seal.
We shall invoke the god whose shrine it is,
And ask that as a father's care be his.
The holiest names to witness I shall call—

The chaste Diana, queenly Juno—all
The gods, indeed, who know my heart; yea, these
Will guarantee my sacred promises.

ARICIA.

The King nears. Hasten, Prince; make no delay.
To mask my flight I shall a moment stay.
Go thou; and leave for me some faithful guide
To lead my timid footsteps to thy side.

[*Exit* HIPPOLYTUS. *Enter* THESEUS *and* ISMENE, *severally.*

THESEUS (*to himself*).

O gods, enlighten my perplexity![35]
Vouchsafe ye to reveal unto mine eye
The truth which now I seek for!

ARICIA (*aside to* ISMENE).

All things, dear
Ismene, touching our escape prepare.

[*Exit* ISMENE.

THESEUS (*to* ARICIA).

Thou changest colour. Confusion fills thy face,
Madam. What did Hippolytus in this place?

ARICIA.

Sir, he was bidding me a last farewell.

THESEUS (*sarcastically*).

Thine eyes could pierce his bosom's stony shell.
Thou hadst thy triumph in his earliest sigh.

ARICIA.

The truth I am not able to deny.
No share did he inherit of thy gall.
He never used me like a criminal.

THESEUS.

I understand. He vowed a deathless love.
His fickle heart be not o'er-certain of,
For he would swear the same to others, too.

ARICIA.

He, sir?

THESEUS.

Thou shouldst have made him be more true.
[*With a sudden revulsion from irony to fury and disgust.*
How couldst thou suffer such vile partnerships?

ARICIA.

And how couldst *thou* suffer the vilest lips
To blacken thy son's life that shines so fair?
Knowest thou nothing of his heart whate'er?
Dost thou distinguish guilt from innocence
Thus badly, that alone unto thy sense
By a foul mist his virtues are concealed
Which clearly to all others are revealed?
Ah, 'tis too much that thou shouldst yield him thus
To lying tongues! Forbear. Thy murderous
Wishes, repent thee of. Fear, sir; oh, fear
Lest heaven so hate thee as to grant thy prayer.
The stern gods in their wrath fulfil oft-times
Our curses, and their gifts chastise our crimes.

THESEUS.

Nay, thou wouldst cover o'er his guilt in vain.
Love blinds thee to defend the wretch, 'tis plain.
But witnesses whose word is certain proof
Are mine. Tears have I seen, the tears of truth
To flow.

ARICIA.

      Beware, sir. Thine all-conquering hands
Have freed from monsters many as the sands
The human race. But all are not yet dead;
And thou hast let one live . . . Thy son forbade
That I should speak. I know the great respect
That still he keeps for thee. It would afflict
His heart too sorely if I dared complete
What I began to say. Like him discreet
I fain would be, and from thy sight betake
Myself, lest I be wrought upon to break
My silence.

                          [*Exit* ARICIA.

THESEUS (*to himself*).

      What means this, and what can be
Hidden by words begun so frequently
And interrupted always? Do they plan
To blind mine eyes with their deceptions vain?
Do both of them conspire to torture me?
And yet, despite all my severity,
What plaintive voice deep in my bosom sounds?
A secret pity stabs me and astounds.
I will interrogate a second time
The nurse. I would learn better of this crime.
          [*He claps his hands, and two soldiers appear.*
Guards, let Oenone come, and come alone.
    [*As they approach the Queen's suite,* PANOPE *issues from it.*

PANOPE.

I know not what thing the Queen broodeth on,
But so by frenzy is she racked, I fear
All, sir. She is the image of despair.

Death's pallor is already in her face.
Oenone, driven from her in disgrace,
Hath cast herself into the waves. None knoweth
What prompted this mad act; and the deep floweth
Above her, snatched for ever from our sight.

THESEUS.

What sayest thou?

PANOPE.

Her death has calmed no whit
The Queen. Woe seemeth in her wavering soul
To mount. Sometimes, to soothe her secret dole,
She clasps her children, bathing them with hot
Tears, and then swift, all mother-love forgot,
Thrusts them in horror from her. To and fro
With doubtful step she doth at random go.
No more she knows us, so is she distraught.
Thrice she hath written, and with altered thought
Three times destroyed the letter she began.
Vouchsafe to see her, sir; and, if thou can,
Vouchsafe to succour her.

THESEUS.

O vaulted sky!
Oenone dead and Phaedra fain would die?
Recall my son! Let him come and defend
Himself. Let him speak to me. To the very end
I will hear him now; yes, I will hear him now.
Be not o'er-hasty, Neptune, to bestow
Thy fatal bounties! I would sooner these
Should ne'er be granted. To false witnesses
Perchance I hearkened, and upraised in prayer
Cruel hands to thee too quickly. What despair,

Alas, may follow what I deemed a boon!

[*Enter* THERAMENES.

Theramenes, is it thou?[36] Where is my son?
I gave him at the tenderest age to thee
In charge . . . But whence are born the tears I see?
How is it with my son?

THERAMENES.

Oh, care too late
And useless! Oh, vain love succeeding hate!
Hippolytus lives no more.

THESEUS.

Gods!

THERAMENES.

I have seen
Die the most lovable of mortal men,
And—I dare say it still, sir—from all spot
The nearest free.

THESEUS.

My son hath perished? What!
Even while I held out mine arms to him,
Did heaven, impatient, take him ere his time?
What was the blow that ravished him away
From me? what thunderbolt so quick to slay?

THERAMENES.

Scarce had we left the gates of Troezen.[37] He
Rode in his chariot, and his soldiery,
All silent like himself and sorrowing,
Were marshalled round him. They were travelling
The road unto Mycenae. Sunk in thought,
He drove the horses with slack reins, while naught

He marked. Those noble steeds, that would rejoice
Once in their ardour to obey his voice,
Now with bowed head and melancholy eye
Seemed to conform to his sad reverie.
    Just then from out the billowy deep arose
A fearful cry that shattered the repose
Of the still air, and 'neath the earth, far down,
In answer to it came a dreadful groan,
Freezing in every heart and every vein
Our blood. The coursers hear with bristling mane.
    And now upon the water's level breast
A mountainous wave uprears its foaming crest,
Rolls usward, breaks, and vomits to our sight
Amid the spray a raging thing of fright,
A monster. Direful horns of menace rise
From his huge forehead. All his body is
Covered with yellow scales. Thus he appears
At once a savage bull, a dragon fierce
Twisting in serpent folds a sinuous neck,
While his long bellowings make the shores to shake.
    Upon this horror looks aghast the sky;
Earth shudders at it; the very air thereby
Taketh infection. E'en the wave whose side
Concealed it, now recoileth terrified.
Every one flees, nor with a courage vain
Armeth himself, but in the neighbouring fane
Takes refuge. Thy Hippolytus alone,
Of his heroic sire the worthy son,
Stayeth his steeds, graspeth his javelins, sheer
Against the monster drives, and with a spear
Hurled by a sure hand, gives it a great wound
Deep in the flank.[38] Then with a mighty bound
Of pain and fury doth it roaring fall

At the horses' feet, and writhes, and shows withal
A fiery throat that covers them with flame,
And blood, and smoke. Terror lays hold on them,
And deaf for once, they heed nor voice nor rein.
Their master struggles vainly to restrain
Their flight. With bloody foam their bits are red.
    Amid the whirling tumult, it is said,
A god was seen, who did with prick and thrust
Of goad assail their sides, besmeared with dust.[39]
Fear drives them over rocks. Loud groans the nave.
The axle snaps. Hippolytus the brave
Sees fly to pieces all his broken car,
And, tangled in the reins, is hurled afar.
Forgive my grief. This cruel sight will be
An everlasting source of tears, for me.
I saw thy hapless son, I saw him, sir,
Dragged by the horses that he fed whilere.
He calls to them to stay, yet serves it none;
For his voice frightens them, and still they run;
And soon his body is one mass of wounds;
And with our cries of dole the plain resounds.
    At last their terror's headlong fury comes
To an end. They stop, hard by those ancient tombs
Where lie his royal sires in chill repose.
Thither I rush, all gasping; his guard close
Behind me follow. His blood guides us there.
The rocks are stained. The smoking briars bear,
Torn from his locks, full many a crimson strand.
I reach his side; I call him; and with hand
Outstretched to me, his dying eyes he then
Opens, which suddenly he shuts again.
"Heaven hath of a guiltless life," he said,
"Bereft me. Have thou care, when I am dead,

Dear friend, for poor Aricia, I pray;
And if my father, undeceived some day,
Should mourn his slandered son's unhappy fate,
And would my blood and spirit propitiate,
Ask him to treat his captive tenderly,
And to restore to her . . ." At this did he
Expire, and but a mangled body leave
Within mine arms, by which the gods achieve
Their anger's triumph—a woeful thing the eyes
Of his own father could not recognize.

THESEUS.

Alas, my son! Dear hope that I have torn
For ever from me! What regrets forlorn,
Ye gods inexorable that have served
My wrath too well, are now for me reserved!

THERAMENES.

Aricia at that moment timidly
Approached the spot. She came, sir, flying from thee,
To take him, before heaven, as her lord.
She nears; she sees the red and reeking sward;
She sees (for her that loved, what thing to view!)
Hippolytus, stretched without shape or hue
Of life. But she awhile cannot believe
The truth of her misfortune, nor perceive
Herein the valiant prince, her happiness.
She looks upon him, and yet none the less
She still doth ask for him; but finally
Made all too sure that form is even he,
She lifts to the gods a sad, accusing glance,
And with a sigh falleth in swooning trance,
Cold, almost lifeless, at her lover's feet.

Ismene is beside her, and all wet
Of face herself with tears, again to life
Recalleth her, or rather to her grief.
And as for me, to whom the sunshine now
Is hateful, I have come, as seest thou,
To tell thee of a hero's last request,
And, sir, to execute the sad behest
His dying breath entrusted unto me.

But I behold his mortal enemy.

[*Enter* PHAEDRA *and* PANOPE.

THESEUS (*to* PHAEDRA).

So, then! Thou hast thy triumph. My son is dead.
Alas, what reason to fear is mine! how dread
Is that suspicion which, within my breast
Pleading his cause, doth fill me with unrest
Justly! But, madam, he is lifeless. Take
Thy victim. Be for his destruction's sake
Exultant, whether wrong it was or right.
Herein for ever blinded be my sight.
Thou sayest him guilty; I will so believe.
His death affords me grounds enough to grieve
Without my searching for some ghastly truth
Which could not give him back to me, forsooth,
And which perchance would but increase my woe.
From thee and from these shores far let me go,
Fleeing the image of my mangled son.
By that dire memory harried and undone,
From the whole world I fain would banish me.
It all doth seem against my cruelty
Uprisen. The very lustre of my name
Augments my tribulation. Were my fame
Less known to men, I easier might hide.

I even so much as hate the multiplied
Honours the gods have given me, and at once
I go now to lament their deadly boons
Nor longer weary them with useless prayer.
Do what they might, their baleful gifts could ne'er
Pay me for that which they did from me take.

PHAEDRA.

No, Theseus; it is needful that we break
An unjust silence; needful thou be taught
The innocence of thy son. He was in naught
To blame.

THESEUS.

      Oh, luckless father that I am!
And on thy word, it was, I did condemn!
Cruel woman, thinkest thou 'tis enough excuse—

PHAEDRA.

Moments are precious. Hear me, Theseus.
'Tis I that on thy duteous son and chaste
Unholy and incestuous eyes have cast.
Heaven lit a fatal flame within my breast.
The vile Oenone contrived all the rest.
She feared Hippolytus, when he had learned
Of my mad passion, would of what he spurned
With horror, tell; and hence, perfidiously
Taking advantage of my weakness, she
Sped to accuse him unto thee. She hath
Herself now paid for that, and fleeing my wrath,
Found all too easy fate beneath the wave.
My thread of life the sword, ere this, would have
Cut short, but I should leave behind me then
The cry of slandered virtue. I would fain

The whole in penitence before thee spread,
Going a slower path down to the dead.
I drank—and through my burning veins now runs—
A poison Medea brought to Athens once.
Its venom hath already reached my heart,
And maketh strangely cold that dying part.
I see no longer now, save through a cloud,
The sky or husband whom my presence lewd
Does insult to; and death, that bringeth night
Upon mine eyes, doth to the day's clear light,
Which they have been defiling, now give back
Its purity . . .[40]

           [*She falls back lifeless in* PANOPE'S *arms.*

PANOPE.

She is dead, sir!

THESEUS.

                Of deeds so black
Would that the memory might with her expire!
Come, let us go, and for mine error dire,
That hath, alas, been but too clearly shown,
Mix with the blood of my unhappy son
Our tears, and clasp all that remaineth here
Of him, repenting now my frenzy's prayer
Abominate. Let us render to him dead
The honours he so well hath merited;
And better to appease, as it is right,
His outraged ghost, Aricia shall, despite
The plots of her injurious kinsmen, be,
From this day forth, a daughter unto me.

NOTES ON PHÈDRE

(The line-numbers are those of the French text.)

1. The stage-setting here supplied is that which seems to the translator the most natural one to account for the presence of the several characters in that place during the course of the play. Various settings have been used in different actual performances.

2; l. 11. For "Theseus" the trisyllabic pronunciation "The-se-us" has been adopted in this translation as more convenient metrically and justified by historical English usage ("Knowing I know thy love to Theseus"—*Midsummer Night's Dream;* "Come forth, and fear not; here's no Theseus"—*Two Noble Kinsmen*), if less current to-day than "The-seus."

3; l. 14. The seas which Corinth, or rather the isthmus of Corinth, sunders are the Ionian and the Aegean. The river Acheron is in Epirus, where it flows into the Acherusian Lake and thence was fabled to descend into Hades. The ancient Greek State of Elis was on the western coast of the Peloponnesus, the promontory of Taenarus on the southern. Icarus, the son of Daedalus, flying from Crete with his father by means of artificial wings, fell into the Aegean Sea near the coast of Asia Minor, and hence that portion of the Aegean was called the Icarian Sea.

4; l. 36. The reference to Phaedra as the daughter of Pasiphaë recalls the story of that queen's insane love for the Cretan bull, and thus at the outset associates Phaedra in our minds with monstrous and fearful passions.

5; l. 53. The Pallantidae, or sons of Pallas, were the nephews of Aegeus, King of Athens and father of Theseus. Pallas was in the direct line of descent of the Athenian royal family, to which Aegeus belonged only by adoption. The Pallantidae conspired against Theseus upon his succession to the throne, to which they themselves had been aspirants, and were put to death by him.

6; l. 80. Procrustes, Sinnis, Sciron, Cercyon, and the Epidaurian giant (Periphetes the Club-bearer) were brigands who terrorized the isthmian road between Troezen and Athens and were slain by Theseus when, as a mere lad, he first went from his grandfather's home, where he had been reared, to claim his birthright from Aegeus. It is to their extermination that Hippolytus refers in Act III when he speaks of his father's youthful exploits which he himself has not yet emulated; it was for that same work that Neptune promised Theseus the granting of three prayers (see Act IV), whereby hangs the catastrophe of the play. The Minotaur was a Cretan monster, part man and part bull, to which Minos fed an Athenian tribute of seven youths and seven maidens yearly. Theseus ended the tribute by killing the Minotaur.

7; l. 84. Among Theseus' loves Plutarch mentions Aegle, Anaxo of Troezen, the daughters of Sinnis and Cercyon, Periboea (who was later the mother of Ajax Telamon), Pheroboea, Iope the daughter of Iphicles, and also Helen, whom he carried off forcibly though she was then a child.

8; l. 89. Ariadne, the elder sister of Phaedra, having fled with Theseus after helping him to kill the Minotaur, was abandoned by him on the island of Naxos. Phaedra, unlike the other women, was joined to Theseus by the honourable bonds of marriage.

9; l. 110. Hymen. The god of marriage.

10; l. 122. Alcides. Hercules. His exploits were interspersed with numerous loves.

11; l. 131. It was Neptune who, with a blow of his trident, first created the horse for mankind. He was hence regarded as the teacher and patron god of horsemanship.

12; l. 210. The Amazons were sometimes classified loosely as Scythians.

13; l. 273. The description of the physical effects of love in Phaedra is probably derived from that fragment of Sappho which is commonly known as the "Ode to Anactoria."

14; l. 327. As the son of a barbarian mother, Hippolytus was debarred by law from inheriting the throne of Athens.

15; l. 335. Observe that Phaedra has not spoken, save for one brief cry, since Panope burst in with the news of Theseus' death.

16; l. 352. Racine, following the traditional Christian doctrine that husband and wife become "one flesh," regarded the love of Phaedra for her stepson as scarcely less incestuous than if he had been her own son. Hippolytus, by his reaction to Phaedra's avowal of love in the next act, shows that he does not share the opinion of Oenone that Theseus' death alters their relationship, nor indeed does Phaedra herself to any great extent. It will be recalled that only in the twentieth century was the English law annulled which forbade a man to marry his deceased wife's sister. Incest-horror had, of course, no place in the *Hippolytus* of Euripides or the *Phaedra* of Seneca.

17; l. 360. The frowning ramparts that Minerva piled. The ramparts of Athens, of which Athena, or Minerva, was the patron deity.

18; l. 384. Pirithoüs. In Greek legend, the king of the Lapithae and the friend and comrade of Theseus.

19; l. 385. Cocytus. The "River of Wailing." One of the rivers of Hades.

20; l. 421. The first king of Athens was Erechtheus, a son of the Earth. See Note 5.

21; l. 478. My great-grandfather. Racine has *aieul,* literally "grandfather," but the word is often used loosely in the sense of "ancestor." Pittheus, founder and king of Troezen, was the father of Aethra, the mother of Theseus.

22; l. 488. See Note 14.

23; l. 504. The fields . . . that first it sprang from off. An allusion to the descent of the royal line of Athens from the Earth itself. See Notes 5 and 20.

24; l. 550. See Note 11.

25; l. 649. The monster is the Minotaur (see Note 6). After killing him, Theseus was able to find his way out of the trackless maze of the Labyrinth by means of a clue of thread which Ariadne (see Note 8) furnished him.

26; l. 737. The honours are those which Athens sends to the mother of her newly chosen king.

27; l. 823. The dramatic irony of Phaedra's prayer that Hippolytus may feel love, when she is soon to be confounded by the news of his love for Aricia, is powerful.

28; l. 958. The story which Theseus tells of his absence explains the rumour that he had descended to the Lower World, and substantially follows Plutarch's rationalization of that legend. For it was from Epirus that the river Acheron was supposed to descend to Hades (see Note 3) and Theseus says that his deep dungeon was close to the realms of the dead. According to Plutarch, the king of Epirus was named Aidoneus like the god of the Lower World, the parallel with whom he continued by having a wife named Proserpina and a dog named Cerberus; hence the mistake arose as to the objective of the expedition of Theseus and Pirithoüs.

29; l. 1042. Hippolytus thinks that his father has learned of Phaedra's shameful love for him. He hopes Theseus will confide in him, that thus they may be drawn closer to each other with mutual aid of comfort and counsel.

30; l. 1141. The pillars of Hercules. So the ancients called the rock of Gibraltar and the mount on the African shore across the straits from it.

31; l. 1158. Not even the gods dared to break an oath sworn by the river Styx.

32; l. 1275. Phaedra's father, Minos, was the son of Zeus and Europa. For his wisdom and justice on earth, he was appointed by Zeus to be judge over the dead in Hades. In his urn were the fates of the souls who came before him. The germ of this great passage is to be found in the *Phaedra* of Seneca, but in a different connection. Racine has utterly transformed it.

33; l. 1326. Cf. Jehoiada's warning to Joash in *Athalie,* ll. 1390 *ff.*

34; l. 1395. It has been argued, and with reason, that Racine's invention of the miraculous temple, where one cannot swear falsely without promptly dying, is a blunder. Why has not Hippolytus challenged Theseus to the easy test of his innocence which it would afford, and why does not Aricia think of it in this connection either when Hippolytus tells her of it or when she talks with Theseus a few lines later?

35; l. 1411. The sight of Hippolytus and Aricia together, supporting Hippolytus' statement that he loves her, awakens in Theseus the first doubt as to his son's guilt.

36; l. 1488. There are only seventy-seven lines, in the French, between the exit of Hippolytus and the entrance of Theramenes with the news of his death under circumstances that must have required the passage of considerable time! True, some of those seventy-seven lines have been uttered by Theseus in soliloquy; and soliloquy, representing the ideas which occupy the speaker's mind, may well be considered to cover an indefinite time, like the choral songs in Greek tragedy. But disregard of the time required for events off-stage is common in Racine, who accepts a theory of Corneille that it is unobjectionable in the fifth act of a play, when the audience is impatient to see the outcome. Cf. the time allowed for the escape of Junia and death of Narcissus in Act V of *Britannicus*; for the death of Hermione in Act V of *Andromaque*; and in *Athalie* for Abner to carry Jehoiada's message to the Queen and return to the Temple with her, also for the events reported by Ishmael, and also for the execution of Athaliah.

37; l. 1498. Theramenes' long account of the death of Hippolytus has been the subject of endless controversy. Its defenders can at least maintain undeniably that such a recital has been used, as necessary or desirable, by every dramatist who has treated the subject; that Sophocles has in his *Electra* a still longer messenger-speech describing the death of Orestes, which is not even the truth but a fabrication; and that, as narrative, the passage in question is graphic and stirring. It might, perhaps, have been somewhat shortened and made less formal, with dramatic gain.

38; l. 1530. We have been prepared for Hippolytus' brave conduct against the sea-monster by his regrets that he has not yet performed any exploits like those of his father's youth, and by his eagerness to attempt some worthy deed. The valour of Hippolytus on this occasion is the invention of Racine, though Seneca had represented him as alone unterrified by the monster.

39; l. 1540. It would seem that the sides of the horses in this situation would be streaked with mud rather than with dust; but the translation follows Racine here in rhyming thus facilely rather than appositely.

40; l. 1644. Observe that Phaedra dies with the word "purity" on her lips. Her last word is fitly of that for which she has yearned in vain, and with the loss of which she has died.

ATHALIE
(ATHALIAH)

INTRODUCTION

ATHALIE is not universally admitted to be Racine's greatest play, but beyond all question it justifies a higher estimate of his genius than does any other. For it is by all means his most original work. *Phèdre,* his own favourite, may be as great or greater; but there he was indebted to Euripides both for general outline and for many effective details, and also in some measure to Seneca. *Athalie* is entirely his; no one else had ever treated the theme which he took from Second Kings and Second Chronicles. And in structure, too, it is peculiarly his own. His secular tragedies substantially adhere to the dramatic form current in his day, though they are distinguished by less intricacy of plot and by subtler and more human characterization. But in *Athalie* Racine, following the lead of his own *Esther,* achieved a fusion of French classical tragedy with that of ancient Greece, re-introducing the Chorus but, instead of keeping it continually present, bringing it on to the stage on only four occasions to punctuate with lyric interludes the otherwise uninterrupted progress of the action—for though these choral songs nominally divide the play into the customary five acts, there is really no more act-division than in a Greek tragedy.[1] And just as in a Greek tragedy, in this masterpiece every possible sort of artistic appeal—drama, poetry, spectacle, music, and dancing—is combined in one harmonious whole.

The subject of *Athalie,* taken as it is from Holy Scripture, was a happy one for Racine. His own piety, his earnest religious convictions, here found ampler scope for expression

[1] I have, accordingly, thought it best to indicate none in the translated text, for no curtain ever descends during the course of the play, from first to last, nor is there any pause in the presentation.

than was afforded in classical or oriental plays. Moreover, he was now able, since he worked along new lines, to shake off most of the trammels of prevailing literary fashion. With the complete elimination of all love-interest—an element which he doubtless considered inappropriate in a sacred theme, but an unescapable requisite in all other dramas of the period —vanishes the conventional language of gallantry that jars in his treatment of Greek legend and Roman history. Gone, too, is the stereotyped, insipid confidant. Previously, this figure had taken on life only by transcending its rôle and becoming almost or quite a major character; that is what Narcissus and Burrus do in *Britannicus,* and Oenone in *Phèdre.* But Nabal in *Athalie* has a very minor part and discharges exactly the functions of a confidant. And yet he is a real man; in the few lines that he utters, the personality of this cool, predatory, callous ruffian is somehow created and vividly revealed.

There is another respect in which *Athalie* is superior to the secular dramas of its author. One of the chief flaws of French classical tragedy in general, and one of the chief obstacles to our enjoyment of it to-day, is its lack of what we call "local colour." Though its characters bear familiar names of olden times or far-distant lands, in speech and manner they seem French courtiers of the Age of Louis XIV. Yet it is probably a mistake to suppose that the dramatists of that age were guilty of such incongruities through intent or indifference. We know that literary criticism then had a great deal to say about ascribing to historical figures the sentiments that would have been natural to them, and dealt severely with whatever was considered a failure to do so. We know that Corneille was especially interested in the re-creation of history in his plays; his admirers declared that his Romans expressed themselves better than real Romans, his Greeks better than real Greeks; and there is a modern book on "Corneille the Historian." But Corneille made Sertorius gallant and Attila in love! He really offends worse than Racine. The truth appears to be that the seventeenth century plays falsified their dramatis personae because seventeenth century playwrights could supplement the bare facts of history with but scant data concerning the lives and minds of Greeks or Romans or Asiatics, and that their most outrageous anachronisms did not annoy their critics and audiences because the critics and audiences knew no more about these things than did the authors themselves—whereas the progress of historical research and the development of the historical imagination have now made us better informed as to such matters, and hence we demand a truer picture of the past. But the Bible and Josephus, which are still our main authorities for the Old Testament period, were as familiar to Racine as they are to ourselves; the conception of ancient Hebrew civilization which is traditional with us is not greatly different from what it was then; we see that where the dramatist had some acquaintance with the distinctive features of a remote environment, he was careful to preserve them; and as there is here no violent clash between what he depicts and what we imagine, our appreciation of his masterpiece is unimpaired.

A masterpiece it truly is. No beginning could possibly be finer than its opening scenes with their slow, majestic, ascensional movement—the meeting of high priest and solitary first-come worshipper within the neglected Temple in the dusk of dawn, the story of accumulated wrongs which cry out for vengeance and of the reassuring wonders of God's might, the first rays of the sun gilding the pinnacle of the sanctuary, the dialogue between Jehoiada and Jehosheba culminating in the great prayer of each. And the so-called "second act" (what lies between the first chorus and the second) is finer still;—

containing, as it does, the Queen's dream, her interview with the child in which with diabolical cunning she besets him with all her wiles yet is baffled at every turn by his simple innocence, her sudden outburst of fury at Jehosheba when she feels herself balked, and her marvellous revelation of her inmost heart, it is the finest act that Racine ever wrote. In its central situation, the dialogue between Athaliah and little Joash, he for the first and only time in his career improved upon a Greek model which he was directly imitating. He had fallen short of his original in *Iphigénie* and perhaps equalled it in *Phèdre*; but in this breathless scene, suggested by the meeting of Creusa and her son in the *Ion* of Euripides, he immeasurably surpassed the work which had inspired his own.

Had the rest of *Athalie* maintained the standard of excellence achieved in the first two "acts," this drama would scarcely yield in greatness to any tragedy of Aeschylus or Sophocles. But the fact is that after the second chorus there is a slight falling off. The poetry is as magnificent as ever—Racine's most beautiful poetry is in this play—but the tension is somewhat relaxed, and therewith comes a certain coldness. For Athaliah herself does not appear again until the very end, and in the physical absence of this, the figure of greatest imaginative value and one of the two principals of the action, the necessary grip and intensity could be preserved only by sheer force of religious exaltation. And this Racine simply did not possess in a sufficient degree to imbue his lines with it. A sincere Christian, he was nevertheless at heart a worldling, despite his Jansenist rearing and his ill-advised attempts to renounce the world. Sainte-Beuve's famous and toolaudatory statement that *Athalie* is "as beautiful as *Oedipus the King* with the true God added" is misleading. *Athalie* and *Oedipus* are both triumphs of dramatic construction, and *Oedipus* has a certain hardness of texture which seems to bear

a kind of analogy to the coldness of *Athalie*. But the hardness
of *Oedipus,* as it were a mathematical proposition of horrible
fatality, is artistically desirable; but the coldness of *Athalie*
is certainly not desirable. Set its most eloquent and moving
passages, such as Jehoiada's address to the assembled Levites
and Azariah's answer (ll. 1326-80), beside an excerpt from
the *Choëphoroe* of Aeschylus, and it will be plain what fervour of spirit Racine lacked and his religious tragedy was in
want of.[2]

ORESTES.

O Zeus, Zeus, gaze thou on this sight!
Behold a brood bereft of its father, thine eagle,
 killed in the twisted coils of a dreadful viper.
The nestlings, orphaned, are perishing with hunger,
 for they are not grown to bear the prey
 their father brought to the eyrie.
Even so, I and she who is with me here,—
 I name Electra,—
 stand in thy sight two children fatherless,
 both suffering like banishment from home.

ELECTRA.

And if thou leave to death the brood of him
Whose altar blazed for thee, whose reverence
Was thine, all thine,—whence, in the after years,
Shall any hand like his adorn thy shrine
With sacrifice of flesh? the eaglets slain,
Thou wouldst not have a messenger to bear
Thine omens, once so clear, to mortal men;

[2] That this fervour may be shown to reveal itself in any medium of
translation, one speech is here quoted in a poetic prose rendering by Canon
Orville E. Watson, and another, its antiphonal response, in the blank verse
of Morshead, of which I have altered the last two lines.

So, if this kingly stock be withered all,
None on high festivals will fend thy shrine.
Preserve us, and raise up a mighty house
From this low state in which thou seest us now!

But the struggle that is joined in *Athalie* is at least nobly conceived and aligns against each other two champions of no petty stature. These tower up from among the other characters of the play—the gentle, anxious Jehosheba, the worthy but commonplace Abner, and Mattan the arch-villain, themselves delineated with sure and delicate strokes. Athaliah is not so wonderful a creation as Phaedra or perhaps Hermione, but of all Racine's heroines she is the grandest figure. Certain French critics have sought to establish a similarity between her and Agrippina in *Britannicus,* and have compared them to the advantage of Agrippina. Such criticism is demonstrably wrong. It really compares the mother of Nero with Athaliah solely as the latter appears in the play, when she is, as Mattan says, no longer what she has been up to that time.

No more
Is she the bold, clear-sighted queen of yore,
Her timid sex transcending—she that flew
To overwhelm astonished foes and knew
The value of an instant lost.

Mattan was certainly in a position to understand her thoroughly, and in the next breath he speaks of her as "this great soul." No one could have called Agrippina that. She was a clever, resourceful intriguer, with endless patience and carefulness in details and with no scruples whatever in the pursuit of her ends; but we have no evidence of her administrative ability in affairs of magnitude, for though she says she formerly guided Nero in his policies, she was not his only adviser and nothing of importance resulted from her domination.

Athaliah, on the other hand, could boast of a brilliantly successful reign (ll. 471-84). And though her guilt is emphasized throughout the play, and though that of Agrippina is intentionally obscured in *Britannicus,* it may reasonably be maintained that Athaliah was not only the abler but also the less wicked of the two, for she felt herself involved in an implacable vendetta with Jehovah and the house of David, in which her parents and all her brothers had been slain, and she fought to avenge them—especially her mother, whom she unquestionably loved, whereas Agrippina loved not even Nero in comparison with her ambition. Indeed, in her great speech avowing her feud with Jehovah, Athaliah is for the moment a distinctly appealing figure. After all, victory was once within her grasp and she could have preserved her life and crown, had she chosen to carry off Joash at the end of their conversation in the Temple; for Mattan was at hand with her Tyrian mercenaries and against such force the resistance of Jehoiada and the handful of Levites whom he had hastily assembled would have been vain. It is a violation of dramatic logic and fitness, and the most serious positive defect in the play, that her doom is thus, because of her failure to strike then at the child, made to depend upon the single good impulse recorded of her, instead of being wholly the fruit of her sins.

One may feel that this terrible queen would have been a match for her human foes, and may find one's sympathies, contrary to the author's intention and the proper effect of the play, inclining towards her as a splendid even though criminal combatant who is unfairly compelled to fight against God as well as against men. One might prefer to see her worsted by Jehoiada in a more equal contest of intelligence and craft, without having her mental fibre hopelessly impaired by Heaven to render certain the triumph of the high priest. But

that is a purely modern viewpoint. To Racine the real pro-
tagonist of the drama is God himself, who after suffering
this blood-stained, impious woman to live long in her iniquity,
at last majestically avenges the moral law upon her. A ration-
alist need not interpret her fall thus, and can easily, if he
chooses, explain her irresolution and imprudence, which
brought it about, as the natural consequences of old age and
of a vicious circle of shaken nerves and disquieting dreams;
but she herself declares that it is God alone who has accomplished her destruction.

It is not merely just retribution nor the protection of helpless innocence nor the restoration of the rightful heir to the
throne nor even the return of the Jews to the faith of their
fathers which are at stake. The little Joash is the last surviv-
ing descendant of David in unbroken male succession, and it is
from David's line of kings that the promised Messiah, the
Redeemer of Israel and of the world, is to be born. Again
and again in the course of the play, this fact of cosmic significance is brought to mind, more or less unmistakably, until
it receives its final confirmation and culminating emphasis
in Jehoiada's rapt vision of futurity—the New Jerusalem and
the Saviour Christ. On the fate of Joash hangs the fate of all
mankind, the vindication of God's word, the fulfilment of the
Divine purpose.

Jehoiada is no mean agent of the Lord of Hosts. "His
unswerving faith, even under the most trying circumstances,
and under conditions that would discourage and appal the
bravest spirits; his inflexible determination to proceed at all
hazards with the task he has undertaken; his profound belief
in the religion of which he is the high priest, and his assured
demeanor in the presence of the gravest danger; his fore-
sight, his magnetic influence over his followers, the boldness
of his plans, his consummate knowledge of human nature,

mark him at once as a born leader of men and a foe of the most redoubtable sort."[3] He divides with the vizier Achmet in *Bajazet* the distinction of being the most notable study of a man that Racine, pre-eminently the portrayer of women, has painted. He is not a simple figure. To Voltaire, himself engaged in relentless war with ecclesiasticism, he appeared a blood-thirsty bigot who conspires against his sovereign and murders her. Racine surely must have intended him to be regarded with entire sympathy as the stern but upright man of God, cherishing the good and ruthlessly extirpating that which is compact of evil. If so, the hand of the artist wrought more subtly than his conscious mind conceived; for Jehoiada is indeed what his creator meant him to be, but he is also what Voltaire thought him. All the qualities of the Hebrew priest of Old Testament times, if not of the typical priest of primitive civilizations in general, are to be found in him—all the steadfast faith and the fierce intolerance, the devotion to the God he worships, the desire for theocratic domination, the protective care for his people, the patience, the shrewdness, the superstition, the capacity to go into trances, the common sense, the keen knowledge of men and affairs, the skill at intrigue, the sanguinary fanaticism, the guile, the vindictiveness, the heroism. To one of us one aspect of him will show more prominently, to another of us another; and we shall each feel differently about him, as we shall each feel differently about Athaliah and as each of us views with different opinions and different sympathies the people and the problems that we encounter in real life. *Athalie* is one of those rare plays, like the *Philoctetes* of Sophocles and the *Misanthrope* of Molière, in which it is possible to side with any of

[3] The quotation is from Sumichrast's edition of the play.

the characters or with none of them; and that is to say that in such plays can be found the very stuff of life itself.

It must have been with high hopes that Racine undertook the composition of *Athalie*. He had been asked by Madame de Maintenon to devise some scenes on a religious subject to serve as a vehicle for training the school-girls at Saint-Cyr in dramatic recital, and his *Esther* had been the result. As a play, it is but a slight thing, of merit chiefly by virtue of its lyrical passages; yet its presentation was greeted with tremendous acclaim. To the poet who, because of his chagrin and his tormenting scruples, had ceased to write for the stage years before, an immense new field, a new career, seemed to be opening. It was surely no sin but rather a work of piety to compose dramas on Biblical themes, which would be performed not by corrupt actors and actresses but by carefully reared young girls. Writing no longer for the professional stage, he was now freed from the yoke of its conventions and could write as he pleased, in close imitation of his Greek masters; and the success of *Esther* gave assurance that, writing thus, he would find favour.

A cruel disappointment awaited him. In the interval since the appearance of his first sacred drama, voices had been raised in protest against the elaborate theatrical activities of the pupils of Saint-Cyr. *Esther* had succeeded only too well. It was alleged that their triumphs had turned the heads of some of the young misses and that the devout atmosphere of the school was becoming contaminated. Therefore, instead of being produced with pomp and circumstance as its predecessor had been, *Athalie,* which far more than any other work of Racine demands the support of music and sumptuous setting to secure the intended effect, was very inadequately presented and, as a result, had a cold reception. Not until

1702, eleven years afterwards, was it played with the accessories which had been designed for it; from that time its fame slowly mounted, and at length Voltaire hailed it as *"le chef-d'oeuvre de l'esprit humain."* But Racine, who was too much discouraged to make any further effort in the field of drama, had died in 1699.

Note Added in Revision. That no one before Racine had ever written a tragedy on the subject of *Athalie* is true only as regards published dramas. An *Athalia* in Latin was played in the Jesuit college of Clermont in 1658; its program, which outlines its plot (romanesque and reminiscent of *Héraclius* and other plays of Corneille), is preserved. Racine may have read the program; it is hardly possible that he read the play itself, which must have had few resemblances to *Athalie*. See R. Lebègue in the *Revue bleue*, vol. xxxiv (1936), 357-359.

RACINE'S PREFACE

AS EVERY one knows, the kingdom of Judah was made up of the two tribes of Judah and Benjamin, and the other ten tribes (which revolted against Rehoboam) composed the kingdom of Israel. As the kings of Judah were of the house of David and had in their territory the city and the Temple of Jerusalem, all the priests and all the Levites withdrew thither and remained always loyal to them; for after the Temple of Solomon was built, it was no longer permissible to sacrifice elsewhere, and all the other altars which were raised to God on the mountains (in the Scriptures called for this reason "the high places") were displeasing to him. Thus the true faith persisted only in Judah. The ten tribes, save for a very small number of individuals, were either idolaters or schismatics.

Now, these priests and Levites constituted in themselves a very numerous tribe. They were divided into groups to serve by turns in the Temple, from one sabbath to another. The priests were of the family of Aaron, and none but members of this family could perform the rite of sacrifice. The Levites were subordinate to them, and had the duties, among other things, of singing, of preparing the victims, and of guarding the Temple. The name of Levite is, however, occasionally given to all members of the tribe. Those who were on duty for the week, as well as the high priest, had their quarters in the porches or galleries with which the Temple was surrounded, and which formed part of the Temple itself. The entire edifice was called "the Holy Place"; but by this name was designated more particularly that part of the inner Temple which contained the golden candlestick, the altar of burnt

incense, and the table of the shewbread; and this part was
further distinguished from "the Holy of Holies," where the
Ark was kept and where the high priest alone had the right
to enter once a year. It was an accepted tradition that the
mountain on which the Temple was built was the very mountain where Abraham had of old offered his son Isaac in
sacrifice.

I have thought I should explain these details here that
those who do not have the history of the Old Testament at
their fingers' ends need not be impeded in reading this tragedy.
Its subject is the recognition of Joash and his establishment
on the throne, and I should, in conformity with custom, have
entitled it *Joash*; but as most people have heard it called only
by the name of Athaliah, I have not considered its presentation under another title to be desirable, and, moreover, Athaliah plays in it a very important part, and it is her death which
brings the drama to a close. The following are some of the
principal events which preceded this great action.

Joram, who as king of Judah and son of Jehoshaphat was
the seventh monarch of the house of David, wedded Athaliah,
the daughter of Ahab and Jezebel, who reigned in Israel and
were both noted, but especially Jezebel, for their bloody per-
secutions of the prophets. Athaliah, not less impious than her
mother, soon led her royal husband to idolatry, and even made
him build in Jerusalem a temple to Baal, who was the god of
the region of Tyre and Sidon, where Jezebel was born. After
Joram had seen all the princes of his family, except Ahaziah,
perish at the hands of the Arabs and the Philistines, he himself died miserably of a protracted disease which consumed
his vitals. So ominous an example did not restrain Ahaziah
from imitating the impiety of his parents. But when this
prince, after reigning only a year, went to pay a visit to the
King of Israel, the brother of Athaliah, he was involved in

the ruin of the house of Ahab and slain by the order of Jehu, whom God had consecrated by his prophets to rule over Israel and to be the minister of his vengeance. Jehu exterminated the descendants of Ahab and had Jezebel thrown from a window, so that, as Elijah had prophesied, she was eaten by dogs in the vineyard of that same Naboth whom she had formerly put to death in order to seize on his inheritance. When Athaliah learned in Jerusalem of these massacres, she attempted on her part to destroy the whole royal race of David by slaying all her grandsons, the children of Ahaziah. But fortunately Jehosheba, Ahaziah's sister and daughter of Joram (but by another mother than Athaliah), was present when the princes her nephews were being slaughtered; she succeeded in carrying off from the midst of the slain the little Joash, still a babe in arms, and placed him with his nurse in the keeping of her husband, the high priest, who concealed both in the Temple, where the child was brought up secretly until the very day when he was proclaimed king of Judah. The Book of Kings says that this was in the seventh year afterwards. But the Greek text of Chronicles, which Sulpicius Severus has followed, says that it was in the eighth year. It is this which has been my authority in making the prince nine or ten years old, so as to put him by then at an age to answer the questions which are asked him.

I believe I have made him say nothing that would be beyond the capacity of a child of such years who has intelligence and memory. But even if I have gone a little beyond that, it must be remembered that this is a quite extraordinary child, reared in the Temple by a high priest, who, regarding him as the one hope of his nation, had early instructed him in all the duties of religion and royalty. Nor was it with the children of the Jews as with the majority of our children; they were taught the sacred writings not only as soon as they had begun to use their minds, but, to employ the phrase of St. Paul, from babyhood. Every Jew was obliged to copy once in his life, with his own hand, the entire book of the Law. The kings were even obliged to write it out twice, and were enjoined to keep it continually before their eyes. . . .

As the age of Zechariah, the son of the high priest, is nowhere indicated, we may suppose him, if we wish, two or three years older than Joash.

I have followed the explanation of some very able commentators, who prove by the text of the Bible itself that all those soldiers whom Jehoiada, or Joad as he is called by Josephus, made assume the arms consecrated to God by David, were priests and Levites, as well as were the five captains who commanded them. In fact, these expositors say, everything had to be holy in so holy an enterprise, and no unconsecrated person could have been employed in it. Its object was not merely to keep the sceptre in the house of David, but also to preserve the line of that great king's descendants, from whom the Messiah was to be born. "For this Messiah so often promised as a descendant of Abraham was to be also a descendant of David and of all the kings of Judah." Hence comes it that the eminent and learned prelate [Bossuet] from whom I have quoted these words calls Joash the precious survivor of the house of David. Josephus speaks of him in the same terms. And the Bible says expressly that God did not exterminate all the family of Joram, because he wished to preserve for David the lamp which he had promised him. And this lamp—what was it but the light which was to be revealed one day to the nations?

History in no way specifies the day on which Joash was proclaimed king. Some critics would have it that this day was a feast day. I have chosen that of Pentecost, which was one of the three great feasts of the Jews. It commemorated the giving of the Law on Mount Sinaï, and at it, moreover, the first fruits of the new harvest were offered to God; hence it was also called "the Feast of the First Fruits." I reflected that these circumstances would furnish me some variety for the songs of the Chorus.

This Chorus is composed of young girls of the tribe of Levi, and I put at their head a maiden whom I make the sister of Zechariah. It is she who brings the Chorus to her mother. She sings with it, speaks for it, and in short discharges the functions of that personage of the ancient Chorus who was called its Leader. I have also tried to imitate the ancients in the continuity of action according to which their stage was never left empty, the intervals between the acts being marked only by the hymns and the moralizing of the Chorus, which were connected with what took place.

I shall be judged, perhaps, a trifle presumptuous for having dared to introduce on the stage an inspired prophet of God, who foretells the future. But I have been careful to put into his mouth only expressions taken from the prophets themselves. Though the Bible does not say in so many words that Jehoiada possessed the spirit of prophecy, as it says of his son, it represents him as a man full of the spirit of God. And, besides, does it not appear from the Gospel narrative that he had the power of prophecy by virtue of his high priest's office? I imagine, therefore, that he sees in spirit the fatal change of Joash, who after thirty years of an eminently pious reign abandoned himself to the evil counsels of flatterers and stained his hands with the murder of Zechariah, the son and successor of Jehoiada. This murder, committed in the Temple, was one of the chief causes of the wrath of God against the Jews, and of all the misfortunes which overtook them thereafter. It has even been claimed that from that day the oracles of God were given no more from the sanctuary. This it was which led me to make Jehoiada foretell both the destruction of the Temple and the fall of Jerusalem. But as the prophets customarily joined consolations with threatenings, and as, moreover, the business in hand was to set on the throne one of the ancestors of the Messiah, I have embraced the opportunity to introduce a half-glimpsed vision of the coming of this Comforter, for whom sighed all the righteous ones of old. This scene, which is a species of episode, brings the music in very naturally in accordance with the custom that many prophets had of falling into their holy transports to the accompaniment of musical instruments;—witness the group of prophets who went to meet Saul with harps and lyres borne before them; and witness Elisha himself, who, when consulted by the King of Judah and the King of Israel in regard to the future, said, as Jehoiada here does: "Bring me a minstrel." In addition, this prophesying greatly augments the anxious uncertainty of the scene, by the consternation and conflicting emotions which it evokes in the Chorus and the chief actors.

CHARACTERS IN THE PLAY

JOASH, *King of Judah; son of Ahaziah.*

ATHALIAH, *widow of Joram and grandmother of Joash; daughter of Ahab and Jezebel, the King and Queen of Israel.*

JEHOIADA, *the high priest.*

JEHOSHEBA, *wife of Jehoiada; aunt of Joash and half-sister of Ahaziah, being Joram's daughter but not Athaliah's.*

ZECHARIAH, *son of Jehoiada and Jehosheba.*

ABNER, *one of the chief captains of the kings of Judah.*

AZARIAH, ISHMAEL, *and the three other chiefs of the priests and Levites.*

MATTAN, *an apostate priest, now chief priest of Baal.*

NABAL, *confidential friend of Mattan.*

HAGAR, *a female attendant of Athaliah.*

Priests and Levites.

Attendants of Athaliah.

Nurse of Joash.

Chorus of young maidens of the Tribe of Levi, with their Leader, SALOME, *the sister of Zechariah.*

ATHALIAH

The scene is in the Temple at Jerusalem, in a room in the
apartments of the high priest. A few steps at the back of
the room lead up to a curtained doorway. There is also
a doorway on each side of the room. It is the dusk of
early dawn; during the scene it gradually grows brighter.
ABNER *enters from one side and looks about him. After a*
moment the curtains at the back are parted by the
entrance of JEHOIADA, *who descends the steps and comes*
forward. A gesture of surprise escapes him when he
recognizes his visitor.

ABNER.

Yea, it is I. Unto his shrine I come
To pay my homage to the Eternal One.
I come, as ancient usage biddeth me,
To observe the sacred anniversary
Of the Law's gift upon Mount Sinaï.
How changed are all things now! In years gone by,
As soon as the trumpet blast proclaimed this day,
The Temple, decked throughout with garlands gay,
Was thronged with folk in every portico;
And marshalled in due order, they would go
Unto the altar, bearing in their hands
The new fruits of the fields. As He commands,
They gave their firstlings to the Lord above.
For the sacrifice, there were not priests enough.
     The hardihood of one sole woman stays
This concourse now, and turneth those fair days
To evil days and dark. The band is small
Of faithful worshippers who can recall

Some memory of that former time. The rest
Are too forgetful of their God, or haste
Even unto Baal's altars, where they learn
To share in his foul mysteries and spurn
The name of Him to whom their fathers prayed.
I will hide naught from thee; it is my dread
Lest Athaliah shall free herself at last
From that enforced respect which in the past
Hath bound her, tear thee from God's House, and take
Her vengeance upon thee.

JEHOIADA (*calmly*).
                            Why doth this black
Presage assail thee now?

ABNER.
                    Thinkest thou to be
Holy and righteous with impunity?
Long hath she hated that rare steadfastness,
Jehoiada, which maketh thy mitre blaze
With glory,—long hath called thy pious zeal
Sedition and revolt. She hates thy leal
Helpmate Jehosheba for her stainless life.
If thou art one of Aaron's line,[1] thy wife
Is sister unto our last king, deceased.
Mattan, too—Mattan—that apostate priest,
E'en worse than Athaliah, all the while
Goads her on—Mattan, the deserter vile
Of the Lord's altars, persecutor fierce
Of all things good! 'Tis not enough he wears
Upon his brow a sacerdotal crown,
And once a Levite, now to Baal bows down
In base idolatry; it marreth his joy

To see this Temple; fain would he destroy
The God whom he abandoned. Means are none
By which he hath not sought thy ruin. One
Time he doth pity thee—praise thee, even, another.
He feigns affection for thee, so to cover
The blackness of his gall;—now to the Queen
Paints thee as dangerous; now, having seen
That quite insatiate is her thirst for gold,
Pretendeth certain treasures were of old
Amassed by David in a place which thou
Knowest alone.[2]

        And then, for two days now
This haughty Athaliah has appeared
Shrouded in sombreness. 'Tis to be feared.
I watched her yesterday, and saw her eyes
Look glowering on this sacred edifice
As though it hid, armed for her punishment,
The Lord's avenger in its vast extent.
Trust me: the more I think, the less I doubt
Her wrath against thee will right soon break out.
The daughter of Jezebel, who feeds on blood,
E'en in his Temple will assail our God.

JEHOIADA.

He who can tame the waves of the wild sea
Can thwart the plottings of iniquity.
Obedient to his will, which I revere,
I fear God, Abner, and naught else I fear.
And yet I thank thee for thy kindly pains,
My friend, that thus thou keepest in my defence
Thine eyes alert. I see the secret smart
Wherewith wrong galls thee, and that still at heart
Thou art an Israelite. Praise Heaven for that!

But this inactive virtue, this pent hate—
Do they content thee? Is it faith, or no,
That never wakes to deeds? Eight years ago
An impious foreign woman seized the throne
Of David, slew the children of her son,
Bathing, foul murderess, in our princes' blood
Unpunished, and stretched even against God
Her traitor's hands;—and thou, the single stay
Of this same tottering State—thou from the day
Of the good King Jehoshaphat upbred
In camps, and under his son Joram head
Over our armies—thou who once did stand
The sole hope of our terror-stricken land
When Ahaziah's sudden death dismayed
His soldiers, and from Jehu's sight they fled—
"I fear God," sayst thou; "I perceive his truth."
Hear how God answers thee out of my mouth!
    "Zeal for my Law thou claimest?—what skills it thee?
Thinkest thou with empty words to honour me?
From all thine offerings I have what fruits?
Need I the blood of heifers and of goats?
The blood of thy kings cries out, and is not heard.
Let every pact with evil be abjured.
Stamp out the crimes amid my people; then
Shalt thou bring sacrifice to me again."

ABNER.

Ah, what can *I* do 'mid a folk thus bowed?
Benjamin is powerless; Judah is cowed.
The day that quenched their line of kings—that same
Day quenched their ancient boldness, all its flame.
"Even God," they say, "hath from us turned his face.
So jealous once for the honour of our race,

He sees, unmoved, its splendour overcast,
And his compassion is outworn at last.
No longer countless marvels doth he work
For us, to frighten men. The holy Ark
Is mute, and gives no further oracles."

JEHOIADA.

What time was e'er so rich in miracles?
When by more acts did God show forth his might?
Must your eyes, then, be always without sight,
Ungrateful people? Always on your ear
Shall wonders strike, and yet your hearts not hear?
Must I, O Abner, I the sequence trace
For thee of prodigies wrought in our days—
The famous woes of Israel's tyrant kings,
And how the Lord fulfilled his threatenings;
The wicked Ahab's death, who with his blood
That field which he by murder gained bedewed;[3]
Jezebel near the fatal soil of it
Slain, a queen trampled beneath horses' feet;
The dogs that lapped that cruel woman's gore
And her accursed body rent and tore;
The troop of lying prophets put to shame;
The altar whereon fell from heaven the flame;
Elijah ruling nature with his voice;
The sky closed by him and become of brass,
And the earth three years unwet by rain or dew;
Elisha's words raising the dead anew?
Recognize, Abner, by these shining signs
A God the same to-day and at all times.
He can reveal his glory at his will,
And in his thoughts his people ever dwell.

ABNER.

But where, now, are those honours that of old
Were promised David and again foretold
To Solomon his son? We hoped, ah me,
That from his loins a numerous progeny
Of kings should issue, and o'er every land
And every tribe One born of them extend
His power, make all war and discord cease,
And at his feet behold earth's monarchies.

JEHOIADA.

Why of God's promise doth thy heart despair?

ABNER.

This prince, this son of David—we shall where
Seek him? Can Heaven itself revive this tree
That to the root is withered utterly?
Even the babe did Athaliah slay
In his cradle. When eight years have passed away,
Shall the dead rise again out of the tomb?
Ah, had her rage miscarried! had but some
One drop been left us of our royal blood . . .

JEHOIADA.

Say on! What wouldst thou do?

ABNER.

                              Oh, joyous would
This day then be! How gladly would I go
To hail my sovereign! Canst thou doubt that so
Our eager people would upon their knees . . .
                          [*Checking himself.*
But why beguile my heart with thoughts like these?
Sad heir of kings that ruled victorious once,

Was Ahaziah left, he and his sons.
By Jehu's shafts I saw the father slain,
And thou his children slaughtered by the Queen.

JEHOIADA.

I say no more; but when the orb of day
Hath finished the third portion of his way,
When the third hour⁴ calls to prayer, return
Unto the Temple, should thy zeal yet burn;
And God, perchance, by blessings then conferred,
May show to thee how changeless stands his word
And never fails. Go; I must needs prepare
Myself for this great day. E'en now 'tis here:
The dawn gleams white upon the Temple roof.

ABNER.

What is this secret that I know not of?
        [JEHOIADA *does not answer. A pause. Enter* JEHOSHEBA.
Jehosheba doth bend her steps toward thee.
I shall depart, and join the company
Of faithful ones who hearken to the call
To keep with solemn pomp this festival.

                                [*Exit* ABNER.

JEHOIADA.

Princess, the time is ripe. Now is there need
To speak. Thy happy theft cannot be hid
Further. The insults of God's enemies
Have branded false too long his promises,
Turning our silence 'gainst him.
                        What say I?
Success hath spurred their fury on, till thy
Wicked stepmother fain would burn to Baal
Idolatrous incense in this hallowed pale.

Let us show him thou savedst, the young king.
Reared in the Temple 'neath God's sheltering wing,
He will be brave like all his race; and sage
Is he already, far beyond his age.
I shall, ere I his destiny explain,
Present him to the Lord, by whom kings reign;
Then, gathering priests and Levites, shall declare
At once to them he is their sovereign's heir.

JEHOSHEBA.

His name and rank—are they yet known to him?

JEHOIADA.

He answereth still but to Eliakim,
And thinks himself some child his mother left,
To whom I in my pity have vouchsafed
To be a father.

JEHOSHEBA.

Woe is me! Of yore
I saved him from what peril, and once more
He falls into what peril!

JEHOIADA.

How! So quick
To be dismayed and in thy faith grown weak?

JEHOSHEBA.

I yield to thy wise counsels, good my lord.
E'en from that hour I snatched him from the sword,
His fate have I entrusted to thy care.
Holding the violence of my love in fear,
I shun his very presence all I may,
Lest, seeing him, this troubled heart betray
My secret with some burst of grief. Methought

That truly these three days and nights I ought
To dedicate to tears and prayers entire.
Yet might I be permitted to inquire
This morn of thee what friends thou hast at hand
For thy support? Abner?—will he defend
Our cause, brave Abner? Hath he given his word
To stand beside his king?

JEHOIADA.

                    Although assured
Is Abner's faith beyond all questioning,
As yet he knows not that we have a king.

JEHOSHEBA.

But to whose care confidest thou Joash? To
Ammon or Obediah, as their due?
My father's kindnesses to them of old . . .

JEHOIADA.

To the evil Athaliah they have sold
Themselves.

JEHOSHEBA.

          Against her minions thou hast, then,
Whom to oppose?

JEHOIADA.

          Have I not told thee plain?
Our priests. Our Levites.

JEHOSHEBA.

                    Well I know that here,
Secretly gathered by thy prescient care,
Their numbers are redoubled; and that between
Their love for thee and horror for the Queen
They have been wrought till they with oaths are sealed

To David's heir, who is to be revealed
To them. But howso bright their ardour flame,
Can these alone uphold their sovereign's claim?
For such a task can zeal of theirs avail?
Hast thou a doubt that, soon as first the tale
Is whispered that a son of Ahaziah
Is hidden here, at once will Athaliah
Gather her savage foreign cohorts,[5] straight
Surround the Temple, and break down its gate?
Against them will thy holy ministers
Suffice then, who have only uttered prayers,
With their pure hands uplifted to the Lord
And lamentations for our sins outpoured,
And shed but sacrificial victims' blood?
E'en in their arms may Joash, pierced . . .

JEHOIADA.

                                    And God
Countest thou as naught, who fights in our defence?—
God, who protects the orphan's innocence
And doth in weakness best reveal his power?—
God, who hates tyrants; who in Jezreel swore
He would destroy Ahab and Jezebel;[6]
Who in their daughter's husband Joram still,
And even in Joram's son, pursued their race
With anger?—God, whose vengeful arm always,
Though for a time withheld, is poised to fall
Upon their brood?

JEHOSHEBA.

                    And 'tis because on all
These kings the same stern justice hath been done,

That now I fear for my sad brother's son.
Who knoweth if this child was for their sin
Not doomed at birth, like all that impious line;
Or if God, setting him from such a race
Apart, for David's sake will show him grace?

    Ah me, the dreadful vision of his state
When Heaven gave him to me, rises yet
Each moment to affright my soul! All strewed
The chamber was with princes in their blood.
Fell Athaliah, a dagger in her hand,
Running her course of murders unrestrained,
Urged her fierce soldiery to slay and slay.
Mine eyes saw Joash, left for dead; to-day
I picture in my thought his nurse again,
Who had thrown herself before the steel in vain
To save him, and who held his bleeding form
Clasped to her breast. I took him, and my warm
Tears did revive him, falling on his face;
And whether still in fright or for caress,
I felt his little arms now cling to me.

    O mighty God, let my love never be
Fatal to him! The last, the precious seed
Is he of faithful David. He was bred
Within thy House, in reverence for thy Law.
No father save thyself he knoweth. If now
In danger, at the moment to attack
A queen so terrible, my faith is weak
And cowardly,—if flesh and blood, dismayed
For him, too many tears this day have shed,—
Preserve the heir of thy rich promises!
Punish but me for my faint-heartedness!

JEHOIADA (*more gently*).

Thy tears, Jehosheba, are not a sin;
But 'tis God's will that we should trust in him.
Never doth he, in blindness of his ire,
Visit the impiety of any sire
Upon the son that fears him. All who still
Among the Hebrews remain loyal will
To-day come to him to renew their vows.
Deep as their reverence is for David's house,
Jezebel's daughter hath their hate no less.
Joash will touch them with his modest grace,
Wherein doth shine his glorious ancestry;
And God, with secret voice, our aid shall be,
There in his Temple, making their hearts burn.
Two kings idolatrous have each in turn
Defied him. We must to the throne upraise
A king who shall recall in after days
That to the estate his father held, the Lord
Hath him by efforts of his priests restored,
Hath snatched him from the oblivion of the tomb,
And David's lamp relit, when quenched in gloom.
　　Great God, if thy foreknowledge seeth him base
And fated to abandon David's ways,
Let him be like as fruit plucked ere its hour
Or nipped by hostile blast while yet in flower;
But if, to thy commands obedient,
He is to prove a useful instrument
For thy designs, grant that we may restore
The sceptre to the lawful heir once more!
Give his great foes into my feeble hands.
Confound a cruel queen in all her plans.
Deign to bestow on Mattan and on her,

O God, a spirit rash and prone to err,
Whereby are monarchs utterly undone.[7]
   The hour calleth me. Farewell. Thy son
And daughter bring the maids of holiest race.
[*Enter* ZECHARIAH, SALOME, *and the Chorus, young maid-
   ens of the Tribe of Levi, with garlands of flowers. Exit*
   JEHOIADA.

JEHOSHEBA.

Dear Zechariah, stay not; go apace;
Accompany thy venerable sire.

[*Exit* ZECHARIAH.

Daughters of Levi, whom the Lord doth fire
With faithful zeal for him, young though you be;
Who come so oft to share my sighs with me—
Children, mine only joy amid long griefs!
These crowns of flowers, and in your hands these wreaths,
Our stately festivals of old became.
But in this time of sorrows and of shame
What offering is more fit than tear on tear?

[*A trumpet sounds.*

   But lo, e'en now, the sacred trump I hear,
And entrance to the Temple will be soon
Vouchsafed us. I must go prepare, anon
In the procession mine own place to take.
Sing, meanwhile; praise the Lord ye come to seek.

[*Exit* JEHOSHEBA.

CHORUS.[8]

All the Chorus.

Full of his majesty are the heavens and the earth!
Let us bow to this God, and invoke him all our days!
His dominion precedeth the time of time's birth.
   Sing loud, tell abroad his bounties' praise!

A Single Voice.

The wicked might is nothing worth
Of them that fain would of his worship make a dearth.
His Name shall fail not, nor our lays;
But day shall unto day his sovereign power set forth.
Full of his majesty are the heavens and the earth!
Sing loud, tell abroad his bounties' praise!

All the Chorus.

Full of his majesty are the heavens and the earth.
Sing loud, tell abroad his bounties' praise!

A Single Voice.

He makes the flowers assume their lovely hue,
And the fruits to be shaped and swell;
He metes to them with measure due
Both the heat of the day and night's coolness as well;
And manifold the fields return us revenue.

Another.

He commandeth the sun upon nature to shine;
Also the light is a gift of his grace;
But his pure Law and divine
Is the greatest bequest he has made to our race.

Another.

O mount of Sinaï, preserve the memory
For ever of that day, most hallowed and renowned,
When, on thy summit fiery-crowned,
God, in thick clouds concealed and girt with darkness round,
Made shine a bright ray of his glory to our eyes.
Tell us wherefore these fires' and lightnings' flare,
These dense torrents of smoke and this noise in the air,
These thunders and trumpetings.

The order of this world came he to overthrow?
     To shake, though 'stablished long ago,
     Its foundations with quiverings?

Another.

He had come to reveal unto Israel's seed
The living light of his sacred hest.
     He had come to demand due meed
Of love for ever from his people blest.

All the Chorus.

     O his Law, the delight thereof!
     O justice, O kindness supreme!
How great reason, what sweetness extreme
To pledge to this God both one's faith and one's love!

A Single Voice.

From slavery's yoke he delivered our race;[9]
He fed the people manna in the wilderness;
He gave to them his Law; he gave himself to them.
     For such good gifts he but our love doth claim.

The Chorus.

     O justice, O kindness supreme!

The Same Voice.

He cleft for them the waters of the sea,—
From driest rocks made springs gush forth abundantly;
He gave to them his Law; he gave himself to them.
     For such good gifts he but our love doth claim.

The Chorus.

     O his Law, the delight thereof!
How great reason, what sweetness extreme
To pledge to this God both one's faith and one's love!

Another Voice, alone.

Ye who know naught save only a servile fear,
Ungrateful, have ye for so kind a God no zeal?
Does this indeed so difficult appear,
And grievous, love for him to feel?
The slave doth hold his tyrant lord in dread,
But children their devotion owe instead.
Ye would this God should make your cup with good o'er-run,
Yet love ye give him none.

All the Chorus.

O his Law, the delight thereof!
O justice, O kindness supreme!
How great reason, what sweetness extreme
To pledge to this God both one's faith and one's love!

———

[*Enter* JEHOSHEBA.

JEHOSHEBA.

Enough, my daughters; sing no more. Now nears
Our time for joining in the public prayers.
Let us begone, to stand before the Lord
In our own turn and to this day accord
Its proper rites. . . .

[ZECHARIAH, *greatly agitated, bursts into their midst.*

But what is this? My son,
What brings thee back? And whither dost thou run
Thus pale and breathless?

ZECHARIAH.

Oh, my mother!

JEHOSHEBA.

Yes?

Speak out!

ZECHARIAH.

The Temple is profaned!

JEHOSHEBA.

Alas,

How?

ZECHARIAH.

And the altar of the Lord forsaken.

JEHOSHEBA.

Tell me all, quickly. With what fear is shaken
My heart!

ZECHARIAH.

Already, e'en as the Law bids,
Father, as high priest, to the God who feeds
Mankind had offered up the first baked food
Of the new harvest; and now, stained with blood,
His hands again hold out the gift he brings,
The smoking entrails of peace-offerings.
Like me beside him young Eliakim,
Clad in a linen stole, assisted him,
While the priests on the altar and the crowd
Sprinkled the blood of sacrifice.

A loud
Tumult was heard. The people in surprise
Turned thitherward at once their thoughts and eyes.
A woman—can one name her and yet be
Sinless?—a woman—'twas Athaliah, she
Herself!

JEHOSHEBA.

Ye heavens!

ZECHARIAH.

She enters, bold and proud,
The courts reserved for men, with head unbowed,
And even prepares to pass the sacred bound
Which none save Levites e'er may go beyond.
The throng on every side in terror flies.
My father—ah, what wrath blazed from his eyes!
Moses to Pharaoh seemed less dire of mien.
"Begone from this dread spot," he said, "O Queen,
Forbidden thy sex and thy impiety!
Comest thou to defy the majesty
Of the living God?" She gave him a fierce glance,
And oped her lips—for blasphemy, perchance—
But whether now the Angel of the Lord
Appeared before her with a flaming sword,
I know not; yet her tongue froze instantly
Within her mouth, and her audacity
Was to confusion turned. She never dared
To shift her frightened gaze, and, it appeared,
Was most of all stunned by Eliakim.

JEHOSHEBA.

Eliakim? What! she hath looked on *him*?

ZECHARIAH.

We both alike gazed at this cruel queen,
And equal horror seized our hearts. But then
The priests around us closed, and made us go
Thence. Of what more befell, I do not know.
I sped to tell thee of this evil stour.

JEHOSHEBA.

Oh, they have come, have come, 'tis all too sure,
To snatch him from our arms! Yea, he it is

She seeks at the very altar. Perhaps by this
Moment the object of so many tears . . .
Remember David, Lord, who seest my fears!

SALOME.

For what or whom is it thy tears are shed?

ZECHARIAH.

Can it be that danger threateneth the head
Of Eliakim?

SALOME.

          Can he have won the wrath
Of Athaliah?

ZECHARIAH.

        In a child that hath
No stay nor father, what is there to fear?

JEHOSHEBA.

Ah, she comes! Quick! she must not find us here.
   [*Exeunt* JEHOSHEBA, ZECHARIAH, SALOME, *and the*
     Chorus. Enter ATHALIAH, ABNER, HAGAR, *and the*
     retinue of the Queen.

HAGAR.

Madam, why linger in this place, where all
Things thou beholdest but offend and gall?
Leave to its priests this shrine they make their home.
Flee all the tumult. When to thy palace come,
For thy vexed heart thou canst again win peace.

ATHALIAH.

No, I cannot. Thou seest my distress
And weakness. Go, fetch Mattan here in haste.

I shall be fortunate if I can taste
Through aid of him this peace I seek and ne'er
Can find.

> [*Exit* HAGAR. ATHALIAH *presently seats herself.*

ABNER.

Forgive me, madam, if I dare
Defend Jehoiada. His fiery zeal
Ought not to have surprised thee. Our God's will
Is changeless. He himself hath traced for us
The manner of his altar and his House.
The sacrifice he unto Aaron's sons
Entrusted; and their place and work at once
Assigned the Levites; and especially
Forbade that any other deity
Might share with him worship and offerings.

Canst thou, the wife and mother of our kings,
Be still among us such a foreigner
As not to know our laws? Must this day . . . Here
Thy Mattan is. With him, then, leave I thee.[10]

> [*Enter* MATTAN *and* HAGAR.

ATHALIAH.

Thy presence is yet needful unto me,
Abner. The rash presumption we shall pass
O'er of Jehoiada, and all the mass
Of those vain superstitions which would bar
Your Temple unto alien folk. A far
More urgent matter now my heart alarms.
I know that, reared from childhood amid arms,
Noble of soul is Abner, and doth pay
His debt to both his God and sovereign. Stay.

MATTAN.

Great Queen, is this a fitting place for thee?
What terror chills and what anxiety
Shakes thee? Among thy foes what seekest thou?
Darest thou approach this cursed Temple? Now
Doth thy strong hate no longer persevere?

ATHALIAH.

Each of you lend me an attentive ear.
    I would not call to mind the past, nor would
I give account unto you for the blood
That I have shed. What I have done was what,
O Abner, seemed to me the things I ought
To do. I take not for my judge this folk.
Whate'er of me their insolence hath spoke,
Heaven itself hath vindicated me.
My power, established so triumphantly,
Spreads Athaliah's fame to both the seas.[11]
Through me Jerusalem is lapped in peace.
Jordan the roving Arab doth no more
Behold; nor the Philistine, as of yore
Under your kings, with endless raids lay waste
Its banks. The Syrian monarch hath addressed
Me as the queen his sister. And e'en he
Who overthrew my house so traitorously,
And meant to visit upon me as well
The doom that on its other members fell,
Jehu, fierce Jehu, in Samaria quails,
Whom a strong neighbour everywhere assails,
That I have roused against this murderer.
Therefore am I left sovereign mistress here.
    I tasted undisturbed the fruits of all
My statecraft, when a care most sharp to gall

Came to me some days since to check the stream
Of my good fortune. A dream (why should a dream
Trouble me?) all my heart with fear imbues.
I shun it ever, yet it still pursues.

'Twas in the depths of night's dark mystery.
My mother Jezebel appeared to me,
Richly adorned, as on the day she died.
Misfortune had abated not her pride.
She even wore that borrowed brightness still
That she would spread upon her face erewhile
To cover o'er the ravages of time.

"Tremble," she said, "O worthy daughter mine!
The Jews' cruel God against thee doth prevail.
I grieve for thee, that thou must fall as well
As I, my child, into his fearful hands."

These words of horror ending, as one bends
Above a bed, her shadow seemed to stoop
Towards me; and I stretched out mine arms with hope
To clasp her, but I found only a dire
Mass of bones, mangled flesh, and limbs with mire
Befouled, and tattered rags all soaked in gore,
Which the devouring dogs contended o'er.[12]

ABNER.

Great God!

ATHALIAH.

Then, after being thus dismayed,
I saw the vision of a young boy, clad
In a bright robe such as one seeth worn
By Jewish priests. My spirit was reborn
At sight of him; but when, forgetting care,
His sweet charm and his noble, modest air
I was admiring, suddenly I felt

A murderous blade, which to the very hilt
The traitor buried in my heart. To you
Perhaps from chance appeareth to ensue
This strange conjunction of things so diverse.
I myself, ashamed sometimes of my fears,
Have deemed they were from brain-sick vapours sprung.
But now my soul, while still that memory clung,
Hath twice in sleep the same cruel vision seen.
Twice before my sad eyes hath risen again
The same child, who would always pierce my breast.
Worn with such horrors hounding me, at last
I went forth to seek aid of Baal through prayer
Before his shrine, hoping for comfort there.
Yet how are mortal spirits ruled by dread!
Into the Temple of the Jews instead
An impulse drove my steps. Thoughts I conceived
Of pacifying their God; for I believed
Gifts would allay his anger, and he could,
Whoe'er he be, grow kindlier thus of mood.
Baal's pontiff, pardon thou my cowardice!
    I entered. Halted was the sacrifice;
The people fled; the high priest wrathfully
Came towards me. Then, while yet he spake to me,
That very child (O terror, O surprise!)
I saw, who threatens me, just as mine eyes
In fearful dreams beheld him—the same mien
And the same linen stole, his carriage, look, e'en
His every feature: 'twas himself I viewed.
I have seen him! By the high priest's side he stood,
But soon was removed thence, to disappear.
That is the thing which makes me tarry here;
And touching it, with both of you I fain

Would speak in consultation. What doth mean,
Mattan, a wonder so incredible?

MATTAN.

This dream, this likeness seem to me most fell.

ATHALIAH.

Abner, thou sawest the boy whom I describe.
Who is he? Of what blood, and of what tribe?

ABNER.

Two children serve before the altar. One
Of these twain is Jehoiada's own son
Born of his wife Jehosheba. To me
The other is unknown.

MATTAN.

            Why should there be
Debate? 'Tis needful both should be secured.
That Jehoiada stands high in my regard,
Thou knowest well;—that, ever moderate,
I have not sought to avenge me for his hate;
That in my counsel justice reigns alone.
But would he, though a child were e'en his own,
One moment wish to let the guilty live?

ABNER.

And what crime, thinkest thou, can a child contrive?

MATTAN.

Heaven made us see a dagger in his hand;
And Heaven is wise, nor warnings vain doth send.
What needest thou more?

ABNER.

So, trusting in a dream,
Wouldst have us bathe in a child's blood? Not e'en
Knowest thou what sire he is begotten of,
Nor who he is.

MATTAN.

We fear him. 'Tis enough.
If he is born of noble parentage,
His ruin should for such a heritage
Be all the speedier. If an obscure lot
Is fortune's gift to him, it matters what
That without nicety base blood should flow?
With monarchs too is justice to be slow?
Their safety on prompt measures oft depends.
Our vexing scruples must not bind their hands.
As soon as they suspect one, he hath ceased
To be innocent.

ABNER.

How, Mattan! From a priest
Such words? I, reared in war 'midst carnage dire
And the relentless agent of the ire
Of kings, 'tis I who utter here my plea
For the unfortunate; and as for thee
That owest a father's breast to such as these
And shouldst in times of wrath turn hearts to peace—
For thee that hidest hate 'neath seeming zeal—
Blood is shed all too slowly for thy will!

Thou badest me speak my mind without deceit,
Madam. This thing thou fearest—what is it?
A dream, a weak child whom thine anxious eyes
Perchance mistakenly could recognize.

ATHALIAH.

I fain would think so, Abner. It may be
That I was wrong and that too thoroughly
My thoughts have with a vision light and vain
Been filled. I must behold this child again
And closer,—must at leisure scan his face.
Let both the boys be brought me to this place.

ABNER.

I fear . . .

ATHALIAH.

Shall my commands be disobeyed?
To excuse such conduct what could there be said?
'Twould wake suspicions wild and dread in me.
Then bid Jehosheba, I order thee,
Or else Jehoiada to bring them in.
I can, when there is need, speak as a queen.
Thy priests, I tell thee candidly, have great
Occasion, Abner, to congratulate
Themselves on Athaliah's grace. I know
How far the licence of their talk doth go
Touching my deeds and 'gainst my governance;
Yet still they live, and still their Temple stands.
But soon my clemency must end, I feel.
Let Jehoiada restrain his savage zeal
Nor with a second insult anger me.
Go!

[*Exit* ABNER.

MATTAN.

I at last can freely speak with thee!
I can set all the truth before thee. Queen,
There is some dire thing growing up within

This Temple. Wait not for the storm to break.
With the high priest ere sunrise Abner spake.
Thou knowest the love he hath for his kings' race.
What if Jehoiada should in their place
Now wish to substitute the child with whom
Heaven threatens thee—his son, perhaps, or some
Other . . .

ATHALIAH.

　　　　Yes, yes, thou openest mine eyes.
I see light in this counsel of the skies.
But fain would I be free from every doubt.
A child is little apt to mask his thought.
One word doth oft reveal designs most dim.
Let me, dear Mattan, see him, question him.
Go thou, meanwhile, and raising no alarm,
Order that all my Tyrians shall arm.[13]

　　　[*Exit* MATTAN. *Enter* ABNER, JEHOSHEBA, JOASH,
　　　ZECHARIAH, *two Levites, and the Chorus.*

JEHOSHEBA (*to the Levites*).

Ye ministers of God, let your eyes ne'er
Leave these so precious children and so dear.

ABNER.

Princess, be reassured. I will protect
Them 'gainst all peril.

ATHALIAH (*to herself*).

　　　　The closer I inspect
His face, ah Heaven! and the more I mark . . .
'Tis he! With horror all again grows dark.
(*Aloud*) Wife of Jehoiada, is this thy son?

JEHOSHEBA.

Who, madam? This one, meanest thou?

ATHALIAH.

                    This one.

JEHOSHEBA.

I am not his mother. This is my son.

ATHALIAH (*to* JOASH).

                    And thou?
Who is thy father? Little child, speak now
And answer me.

JEHOSHEBA.

          Heaven hath till this day . . .

ATHALIAH.

Why in his stead seekest *thou* to answer? Nay,
It is for *him* to speak.

JEHOSHEBA.

          From one so young
What canst thou hope to learn?

ATHALIAH.

                    His artless tongue
Will utter nothing but the simple truth
Unaltered; ever innocent is youth.
Hence let him freely of himself explain
All that concerns him.

JEHOSHEBA (*aside*).

          Deign, O great God, deign
To put thy wisdom in the mouth of him!

ATHALIAH (*again addressing* JOASH).

What is thy name?

JOASH.

I am named Eliakim.

ATHALIAH.

Thy father?

JOASH.

I am an orphan, so they say,
Given into God's hands from my life's first day.
I never knew my parents.

ATHALIAH.

Thou hast no

Parents?

JOASH.

They abandoned me.

ATHALIAH.

How long ago?

JOASH.

When I was born.

ATHALIAH (*coaxingly*).

At least thou knowest thy

Country?

JOASH.

This Temple is my country. I
Have had no other.

ATHALIAH.

It was in what spot
That thou wast found?

JOASH.

Amid cruel wolves about
To eat me up.[14]

ATHALIAH.

Who placed thee here within
This Temple first?

JOASH.

An unknown woman. Then
She did not tell her name, and later she
Was never seen.

ATHALIAH.

But in thine infancy
Whose hands were diligent on thine account?

JOASH.

Hath the Lord ever let his children want?
He gives its food to every little bird.
His bounty on all nature is conferred.
Daily I pray; and with a father's care
He feeds me from the sacred offerings here.

ATHALIAH (*to herself*).

Fresh wonder now disturbs me and dismays!
The sweetness of his voice, his youth, his grace
Insensibly make my hostility
Become . . . Do I feel pity? Can it be?

ABNER.

This, madam, is the foe thou dreadest, then!
The falseness of thy boding dream is plain,
If the compassion which doth seem to pierce
Thy heart, be not that stab which roused thy fears.

ATHALIAH (*to* JEHOSHEBA *and the children*).
Ye are going?

JEHOSHEBA.
He has told thee everything.
His presence might at length prove wearying.

ATHALIAH.
Nay. Come back.
    (*To* JOASH) Child, what tasks each day are thine?[15]

JOASH.
I worship God; I am taught to read within
His Book, and have begun now with my hand
To write it; and I hear his Law explained.

ATHALIAH.
And what does this Law say?

JOASH.
               That God doth claim
Our love; that blasphemy against his Name
He soon or late avenges; that he defends
The orphan; that he humbles arrogance
And punishes the murderer.

ATHALIAH.
           I see.
But all the other people who like thee
Dwell here within these walls—what are the ways
In which they occupy themselves?

JOASH.
              They praise,
They bless God.

ATHALIAH.

But does he wish that folk should pray
And worship him throughout the livelong day?

JOASH.

In his Temple are all worldly doings banned.

ATHALIAH.

What are thy pleasures, then?

JOASH.

Sometimes I stand
At the altar, and give the incense and the salt
To the high priest. I hear our songs exalt
God's infinite glory, and I see the rare
Pomp of the ceremonies.

ATHALIAH.

What! is there
Naught happier in the life which thou hast led?
I grieve that a child's lot should be so sad.
Come! live within my palace; thou shalt see
My splendour.

JOASH.

I? I should lose the memory
Of all God's blessings!

ATHALIAH.

I would in no way
Constrain thee to forget him.

JOASH.

Thou dost not pray
To him.

ATHALIAH.

But thou couldst pray to him.

JOASH.

I would,

However, see invoked another god.

ATHALIAH.

I have my god to serve; thou wilt serve thine.
They are, both, powerful gods.

JOASH.

Thou must fear mine.

He is the one God, madam; thine is naught.

ATHALIAH (*trying another tack*).

With me thou shalt be compassed round about
By thronging pleasures.

JOASH.

The prosperity

Of the wicked, like a torrent, soon runs dry.

ATHALIAH.

Those wicked, who are they?

JEHOSHEBA.

Ah, madam, he

Is but a child. Forgive . . .

ATHALIAH (*to* JEHOSHEBA, *with ominous sweetness*).

I like to see

The way in which ye have instructed him.
Listen; thou pleasest me, Eliakim.
Thou art indeed no common child, 'tis clear.
Thou seest, I am a queen and have no heir.

Then cast aside this garb; forsake this vile
Service. In all my riches 'tis my will
To have thee share. Make trial from this day
Of what I promise thee. At table, yea,
Everywhere, seated at my side 'shalt thou
Be treated as mine own son: this I vow.

JOASH.

Thy son!

ATHALIAH.

Yes. . . . Thou art silent.

JOASH.

I should leave
What father! And to . . .

ATHALIAH.

Speak!

JOASH.

To what mother cleave!

ATHALIAH (*turning upon* JEHOSHEBA).
He has learned his lesson well; in all that he
Has said, I recognize the work of thee
And of Jehoiada. It is thus, then,
Poisoning the minds of guileless youths, ye twain
Employ the peace in which I leave you still.
Frenzy and hate ye breed in them, the while.
Ye make a horror of my very name.

JEHOSHEBA.

Can our sad history be concealed from them?
There is none but knows it, and in all that scath
Thou thyself gloriest.

ATHALIAH.

Yea, my righteous wrath,
Proudly I can avow, did vengeance take
On my descendants for my parents' sake.
Was I to see my father and my brother
Both slaughtered, from her palace top my mother
Hurled down, and in a single day at once
(Ah, what a ghastly sight!) nigh fourscore[16] sons
Of the King slain—and why? to avenge the death
Of certain prophets whose wild rage of faith
Jezebel punished—and was I to prove
A coward queen, a daughter without love,
A slave to base and profitless compassion?
Should I not, rather, in the same fierce fashion,
Pay murder back with murder, blow with blow,
And to the scions of your David show
That rigour which the ill-starred progeny
Of Ahab suffered? What would my fate be,
Had I not put all weakness by, subdued
A mother's tenderness, and mine own blood
Shedding, as though 'twere water, with this hand,
Thus boldly brought your plottings to an end?
The implacable vengeance of your God, in fine,
Hath broke all bonds that joined your race and mine.
David I hold abominate, and those
Who are the offspring of that monarch's house,
Though of my flesh, are strangers unto me.

JEHOSHEBA (*in a low voice*).

All things have prospered with thee. Let God be
Our witness and our judge!

ATHALIAH.

                This your God, who
Hath long been the sole refuge left to you,—
How are his promises to be fulfilled?
Let him give to you your King foretold, that child
Of David, who should rule the tribes of men,
Your hope, your dream . . . But we shall meet again.
Farewell. I go contented hence. I have
Desired to see, and I have seen.

                  [*Exeunt* ATHALIAH *and retinue.*

ABNER (*to* JEHOSHEBA).

                      I gave
My pledge to thee for his security.
I return what was left in trust with me.

              [*Enter* JEHOIADA *and Levites, armed.*

JEHOSHEBA (*to* JEHOIADA).

Sir, didst thou hear this impious queen?

JEHOIADA.

                      I did,
And pitied thy distress. Ready at need
These Levites and I stood, resolved to die
Too, if we could not succour.
(*To* JOASH, *embracing him*) May God's eye
Watch o'er thee, child, whose courage hath but now
Testified nobly for his sake.
                (*To* ABNER) And thou,
Abner, whose service true I recognize,
Forget not that Jehoiada relies
Upon thee when the expected hour shall come.
    Myself, despite this woman fiend by whom
Our eyes have been polluted and our prayers

Have been disturbed, must to my priestly cares;
But sprinkled by my hands shall pure, fresh blood
Cleanse even the marble where her feet have trod.

[*Exeunt all except the Chorus.*

CHORUS.[17]

One Voice, alone.

What star doth upon our vision dawn?
What for this marvellous child doth fate provide?
He confronted the pomp of pride,
Nor could he be to evil drawn
Though by its deadliest temptings tried.

Another.

While to Athaliah's god
All sacrifice with one accord,
A brave young boy proclaims aloud
That everlasting is the Lord,
And speaketh as Elijah would
To this new Jezebel abhorred.

Another.

Who will tell us the secret, dearest one,
Of thy birth? To a holy prophet art thou son?

Another.

Thus grew up the gentle Samuel
Within the Tabernacle's shade
To be the Hebrews' oracle and hope and aid.[18]
Mayst thou, like him, bring comfort unto Israel!

Another.

Oh, a thousand times should rejoice
The child whom the Lord doth love,
Who from the first hath heard his voice,
And whose instruction God himself is careful of!

Nurtured afar from the world, with all the gifts of the skies
    Hath he been blessed from infancy,
    And no contagion of iniquities
      Came ever near his purity.

All the Chorus.

    Happy, happy that infancy
Which God instructs and shields with his security!

The Same Voice, alone.

    So within a secret vale,
    On the brink of a crystal spring,
    Grows, sheltered from the northwind's gale,
    A tender lily, nature's loveliest thing.
Nurtured afar from the world, with all the gifts of the skies
    'Twas blessed since first it sprang to be,
    And no contagion of iniquities
      Came ever near its purity.

All the Chorus.

    Happy, happy a thousand times
That child whom to obedience the Lord inclines.

A Single Voice.

    Ah me, that with step insecure
Must an innocent youth amid perils proceed!
The soul that seeks thee and would fain be pure—
    What hindrance doth it find indeed!
    What foes assail it from its birth!
    Thy saints, they shall where be hid,
    When sinners cover the earth?

Another.

Palace of David and his city loved so well,
O mount renowned where God himself is wont to dwell,
How have ye on you drawn the wrath of Heaven thus?

Zion, dear Zion, what sayst *thou* to see such things:
  A stranger impious
  Sitting, alas, upon thy throne of kings?

All the Chorus.

Zion, dear Zion, what sayst *thou* to see such things:
  A stranger impious
  Sitting, alas, upon thy throne of kings?

The Same Voice.

Instead of those fair songs and sweet
Which David for his holy raptures found so meet
To extol his God, his Lord, his Father glorious,
Zion, dear Zion, what sayst *thou* to see such things:
  The god praised of the stranger impious,
The Name blasphemed that once was worshipped by thy kings?

Another Voice, alone.

How long, O Lord, how long a time must yet we see
The unrighteous against thee arrayed in their pride?
E'en in thy holy Temple now art thou defied.
They look upon the folk as mad who worship thee.
How long, O Lord, how long a time must yet we see
The unrighteous against thee arrayed in their pride?

Another.

"What availeth austerity?" they say to us.
  "Why must ye needs give o'er
  So much dear pleasure thus?
Ye have naught from your God therefor."

Another.

"Let us laugh, let us sing," this troop unhallowed crieth.
  "With joy on joy, and with flowers upon flowers,
    Let our wishes be ours!
  'Tis a fool on the future relieth.

Of our fast-fleeting years the number is unsure;
Let us hasten to drink of life ere this day dieth.
    Who knows he, till the morrow, will endure?"

All the Chorus.

Then let them weep, O God; let them shake with their dread—
    Those hapless ones who, round thy city shed,
    The everlasting splendour ne'er shall see.
'Tis for us to rejoice, whom thou madest to learn
        Of thy wisdom eterne.
'Tis for us to declare thy gifts and majesty!

A Single Voice.

From all those empty pleasures wherein they delight,
What abides? The same as abides from a dream of the night
    Which the morning proves a mistake.
    When waken they (O despair thus to wake!),
    The poor at thy table by grace
The ineffable sweetness shall taste of thy peace;
But *they* shall drink the cup, fearful and bottomless,
Which thou shalt give them on the day thy wrath shall break
    Upon their guilty race.

All the Chorus.

    O despair thus to wake!
    O dream that flies apace!
    O ruinous mistake!

———————

[*Enter* MATTAN *and* NABAL. *The Chorus do not see them
till* MATTAN *speaks.*

MATTAN.

Go, maidens; to Jehosheba let one
Say Mattan here would talk with her alone.

ONE OF THE MAIDENS.

Mattan! O God in Heaven, may thy might
Confound him!

[Exeunt all the Chorus, hastily.

NABAL.

How now! Scattered in wild flight,
They are gone without an answer.

MATTAN.

Let us press

Onward.
*[As they approach the door at the back, ZECHARIAH appears
between the curtains.*

ZECHARIAH.

Presumptuous man, whither wouldst pass?
Take heed thou dost not overstep this bound.
The Temple's ministers are housed beyond,
Where entrance is forbidden by the Law
To the unconsecrated. Whom dost thou
Seek? On this solemn day my father shuns
The impure sight of all those wicked ones
That serve idolatry; and my mother now
Would fain not be disturbed, for she doth bow
In prayer before the Lord.

MATTAN.

We shall wait here,
My son; no longer vex thyself or fear.
It is thy noble mother unto whom
I wish to speak. From Athaliah I come,
Charged with a message.

[Exit ZECHARIAH.

Nabal.

Their young children, e'en,
Have learned their insolence. But what would the Queen?
Whence in her plans is such confusion born?
Angered by that presumptuous priest this morn,
And in dreams menaced by a child with death,
She planned to sacrifice unto her wrath
Jehoiada, and (thus to crown it all)
Baal's worship in this Temple to install
Under thyself. Thou didst confide to me
Thy joy thereat, and hope was mine to be
A sharer in the spoil. Why hath she grown
Irresolute of will?

Mattan.

I have not known
Her for these two days past. My friend, no more
Is she the bold, clear-sighted queen of yore,
Her timid sex transcending—she that flew
To overwhelm astonished foes and knew
The value of an instant lost. The fear
That springs from vain remorse doth trouble her.
This great soul falters, wavers to and fro—
In short she is a woman. A while ago
I fed with bitterness and gall her breast,
Already by the threats of Heaven distressed,
And she, entrusting her revenge to me,
Bade me collect her guards immediately;
But whether that young child before her led
Who by his parents had been left, 'tis said,
Hath made less great the terror of her dream,
Or whether she hath seen some charm in him,
I have found her wrath now hesitant, now grown

Uncertain; she already would postpone
Her vengeance till the morrow. One design
Wars with another. "Touching the origin
Of this same child I have inquired," then I
Told her. "They boast about his ancestry.
E'en now Jehoiada from time to time
Shows him to the seditious, causing him
To be anticipated by the Jews
As though a second Moses, and doth use
False oracles in his support."

                       It made
Her face flush crimson. Clever lies ne'er had
So swift effect. "Is it for me," she cries,
"To pine in doubt? With such anxieties
Let us have done, have done! Thyself proclaim
My word unto Jehosheba: the flame
Is ready to be lit, the sword is bared,
Nor may they hope their Temple shall be spared
From ravage, if they do not give to me
This child as hostage of their loyalty!"

NABAL.

Surely they will not for a boy unknown,
Whom chance, mayhap, into their arms hath thrown,
Permit this Temple, buried 'neath the sod . . .

MATTAN.

Ah! of all mortals learn thou the most proud.
Sooner than e'er surrender to my hated
Hands a young child whom he hath dedicated
Unto his God, Jehoiada will bear
The ghastliest of deaths. Besides, 'tis clear
They love this boy. If I interpret, then,
Rightly the things recounted by the Queen,

Jehoiada knoweth far more than he
Hath told about his birth. But I foresee,
Whoe'er he is, that he will prove their doom.
They will withhold him, and I shall assume
Charge of what next will follow. Fire and sword,
I hope, will from the sight of this abhorred
Temple set free mine eyes at last.

NABAL.

But whence
Art thou inspired with hatred so intense?
Can it be zeal for Baal that fills thy heart?
Sprung, as thou knowest, from Ishmael,[19] for my part
Not him nor yet the God of Israel
I worship.

MATTAN.

Is there any foolish zeal,
My friend, by which thou thinkest that I could
Be blinded for an idol's sake—for wood
Which perishes, which the worms (do all I may)
Consume beside his altar day by day?
From birth a servant to the God whose will
Rules here within this Temple, Mattan still
Might serve him if the love of eminence
And thirst for power were not at variance
With his strict yoke. Must I recall to thee,
Nabal, the famous quarrel between me
And Jehoiada, what time I dared contest
With him the censership of the high priest?—
My intrigues, struggles, tears, and then despair?
Vanquished by him, upon a new career
I entered, and gave up my soul entire
Unto the Court. Higher I climbed and higher

Into the counsels of our kings, until
My words were hailed as of an oracle.
I searched their hearts; I flattered their caprices;
I scattered on the brink of precipices
Fair flowers for them; I reckoned sacred naught
That clashed with anything they craved or sought.
It was my wont to alter at their choice
Measures and weights. As much as the stern voice
Jehoiada upraised oft gave offence
To their fastidious ears, I charmed their sense
With tact, concealing grim truths from their view,
Gilding their passions o'er with some bright hue,
And lavish most of all with human blood.

    A temple to her newly installed god
At length was built by Athaliah's hand.
Jerusalem wept, seeing herself profaned.
The sons of Levi lifted to the sky
Shrieks of dismay. A lone example I—
Yea, I—set for the timorous Hebrews' eyes,
Forsook their Law, approved the enterprise,
And won the office of Baal's priesthood so.

    Thus made my rival's formidable foe,
I donned the mitre and his equal went;
Yet I confess, howe'er magnificent
My state, the gnawing memory of the God
Whom I abandoned leaveth still some load
Of fear deep in my soul, and this it is
That fans and feeds my rage. O height of bliss,
If, wreaking vengeance on his Temple, thence
I may convict his wrath of impotence
And amid ruin, rapine, death betimes
Lose every qualm through fullness of my crimes.[20]

                              [*Enter* JEHOSHEBA.

But lo: Jehosheba.

(MATTAN *turns to her*) Sent by the Queen
To heal all hate and bring back peace again,
If I have unto thee my words addressed,
Princess, within whose bosom Heaven hath placed
A soul so gentle, do not feel surprise.
A rumour, which, however, I surmise
To be untrue, supports the warning she
Received in dreams, with black conspiracy
Charges Jehoiada, and hence doth raise
Her anger's storm. Touching my services,
No boast I make thee. I know how unjust
Jehoiada hath been to me; yet must
One oppose kindness unto injuries.
I come, in brief, a messenger of peace.
Live; keep your feasts without fear; only one
Pledge of your fealty doth she ask (I have done
All I could to dissuade her, but in vain):
The orphan whom she saith that she has seen.

JEHOSHEBA.

Eliakim?

MATTAN.

Indeed, I feel some shame
For her because of this. Upon a dream
Too much attention she perchance bestows.
But ye declare yourselves her deadly foes
If this child be not yielded to me straight.
The Queen, impatient, doth your answer wait.

JEHOSHEBA.

And this, then, is the peace which she hath given
Unto us!

MATTAN.

Could ye, for one moment even,
Hesitate to accept it? Is so small
Obedience too great a price withal
To pay for it?

JEHOSHEBA.

Very strange, methought, 'twould be
If Mattan, laying aside treachery,
Could triumph over his own evil heart,
And if he could be author of some part
Of good who did such store of ill contrive.

MATTAN.

Wherefore complainest thou? Doth some one strive,
Sent here in fury by Queen Athaliah,
To carry off thine own son, Zechariah?
Who is this other boy so dear to thee?
Such love for him seems in turn strange to me.
Is he a treasure, then, so rich and rare?
Is he a saviour Heaven doth prepare
For you? Bethink thee, not to give him is
But to confirm a rumour that ere this
Hath begun vaguely to be noised abroad.

JEHOSHEBA.

What rumour?

MATTAN.

That he is of noble blood,
And that thy husband rears him for some great
Design.

JEHOSHEBA.

So by this tale which serves his hate
Mattan doth . . .

MATTAN.

Princess, 'tis for thy reply
To draw me from mistake. To every lie
Jehosheba is such a mortal foe
That she would even make choice of death, I know,
Were it needful that, to save her life, her mouth
Should utter one word contrary to truth.
Of this child's origin is there no trace?
Does total darkness shroud his birth and race?
And art thou ignorant thyself, indeed,
By what hands given and offspring of what seed
'Twas that thy husband's arms did first receive
The babe? Speak. I will hear thee and believe.
Render thou glory, by thy truth confessed,
Princess, unto the God thou worshippest.

JEHOSHEBA.

Villain, is it for thee to dare thus name
A God whom thou hast taught men to blaspheme?
His truth—thou canst invoke it even yet?—
Thou, cursed wretch who sittest on that foul seat
Where the Lie reigns and doth its poison spread?—
Thou, in fraud nourished and by treason fed![21]

[*Enter* JEHOIADA.

JEHOIADA.

Where am I? Do I not behold the priest
Of Baal? Thou, David's daughter, sufferest
This traitor to have speech with thee! dost hear,
Dost speak to him! And thou hast felt no fear
Lest an abyss yawn 'neath his feet, wherefrom
The flames shall issue and thyself consume,
Or lest these walls, falling on him, crush thee?
What makes he here? By what effrontery

Cometh God's foe to infect with pestilence
This air we breathe?

MATTAN.

By such great violence
Easy it is for one to recognize
Jehoiada. Yet he should be more wise.
'Twere well to reverence a queen, nor one
To insult whom she hath laid her charge upon.

JEHOIADA.

And unto us what harm would she declare?
What direful hest can such a minion bear?

MATTAN.

I have unto Jehosheba made known
Her will.

JEHOIADA.

Then, impious monster, get thee gone!
Yea, hence, and fill thy cup with crimes at once.
Soon will God join thee to his recreant sons,
Abiram, Dathan, Doeg, Ahithophel.[22]
The dogs to which his hand gave Jezebel
Wait for his wrath to fall on thee,—this day
Are at thy door and clamour for their prey!

MATTAN (*confused and terrified*).

Ere nightfall . . . 'twill be seen if thou or I . . .
Shall . . . Nabal, let us go!

NABAL.

Where dost thou try
To get hence? What confusion overtakes
Thy wits? This is the way out![23]

[*Exeunt* MATTAN *and* NABAL.

JEHOSHEBA.

The storm breaks.
Athaliah in her anger now demands
Eliakim. Of his birth and of thy plans
She hath begun to pierce the mystery.
Mattan did almost name his sire to me.

JEHOIADA.

Who could have told the traitor Mattan this?
He did not learn too much from thy distress?

JEHOSHEBA.

I have done my best to master it; but, sir,
The peril is, believe me, very near.
Preserve this child for some more fortunate
Occasion. While our foes deliberate,
Ere they surround us, hence to ravish him,
Let me conceal him yet a second time.
The streets are open still, the gates still wide.
Must he to desert wilds be borne to hide?
Ready am I. A secret way leads hence
Whereof I know, by which, with never glance
Perceiving us of any human eye,
Crossing the stream of Kedron,²⁴ I shall fly
With him into those wastes where, weeping, once
King David fled from his rebellious son's
Pursuit, like us, for safety. I would choose
Rather with lions and bears . . . But why refuse
The help of Jehu? In that thought of mine
Wisdom may well be found. Let us consign
Our treasure unto Jehu. Ere this day
Be over, one can reach his realm. The way
Thither is short. His heart is nowise grim

And ruthless. David's name hath weight with him.
Yet oh, is any sovereign so fell,
Unless, indeed, born of a Jezebel,
He would not pity such a suppliant's moan?
Must not all monarchs make his cause their own?

JEHOIADA.

What timorous counsels dost thou dare suggest
To me? In Jehu's aid can thy hope rest?

JEHOSHEBA.

Doth God forbid all care and prescience?
In blind assurance is there no offence?
Using mankind to carry out his plans,
Did not the Lord himself arm Jehu's hands?

JEHOIADA.

Jehu, by his inscrutable choice preferred—
Jehu, on whom I see thy hopes are reared,
Pays all his bounties with forgetfulness;
Jehu leaves Ahab's frightful daughter in peace,
Follows the kings of Israel's unhallowed examples,
And of Egypt's vile gods hath preserved the temples;
Jehu, that even dares burn sacrifice
On the high places hateful to God's eyes,
Hath not the upright heart nor stainless hand
To serve his cause and his avenger stand.
Nay, nay! 'tis to God only we must cling.
Let us show forth Eliakim; and as king
Let us, far otherwise than hiding him,
Set on his brow the royal diadem.
I even would advance the appointed hour
Before the schemes of Mattan can mature.

[*Enter* AZARIAH *and other Levites, and the Chorus.*
Azariah, hath the Temple been made fast?

AZARIAH.

Before mine eyes, unto the very last
Door, I have had it barred.

JEHOIADA.

Doth none save thee
Remain here, and thy sainted soldiery?

AZARIAH.

The circuit of the courts I twice have made.
All have gone, to return not; all have fled,
Miserable throng, swept headlong by their fears,
And God no more hath any worshippers
Outside the sacred tribe. Never since they
Escaped from Pharaoh did so great dismay
Seize on this people.[25]

JEHOIADA.

Yea, a craven folk
Bold only against God, born for the yoke!
Let us forward with the work which we have planned.

[*Seeing the Chorus.*

But wherefore have these little ones remained?

A MAIDEN.

Sir, could we leave thee? In God's House are we
Strangers? Our sires and brothers are with thee.

ANOTHER.

If to avenge the shame of Israel
We are not able, as of old was Jael,
To pierce the foreheads of God's foes,[26] we can
At least lay down our lives for him; and when
Your arms shall for his Temple hard bestead
Do battle, we in tears can beg his aid.

JEHOIADA.

Lo now, what champions for thy cause contend,
Children and priests, O Wisdom without end!
But who can shake them if thy power sustain?
From the tomb, if so thou wilt, thou canst again
Call us, destroy and raise up living, smite
And heal. They put no trust in their own might
Or their own worth, but in thy sacred Name
Which hath so often been invoked by them,
In thine oath sworn unto their holiest king,[27]
And in this House of thine inhabiting
That should endure while yet the sun doth shine.

But wherefore comes it that this heart of mine
Thrills as with terror? Is it God's spirit that so
Doth seize me? This it is! I feel its glow
Warm me. It speaks. Mine eyes no more are sealed,
And the dim future centuries stand unveiled!
Ye Levites, with your songs and harmonies
Give aid, and thus enhance mine ecstasies!

THE CHORUS, *singing to the sound of all the concourse of instruments.*

Now let the voice of the Lord be heard of us,
His word divine to our ears be borne,
As, to the tender grass,
Is in the springtime the freshness of morn.

JEHOIADA.

Ye heavens, hear my voice; earth, hearken what it saith!
Murmur no more, O Jacob, that God slumbereth!
Sinners, depart from sight; the Lord awakeneth!
[*Here the music begins again, and* JEHOIADA *at once resumes.*
How is pure gold transformed to lead so vile and base?[28]

Who is this high priest slain within the sacred place?
Weep, O Jerusalem; O faithless city, weep!
Thou that killest the prophets and woes therefor must reap!
Thy God his love for thee doth cancel and efface.
Thy sacrifice doth seem to him but filthiness.

These women and these babes, where lead ye them?
The Lord hath laid the radiant queen of cities waste.
Her priests are captives and her kings to exile cast.
God wills no more that of her feasts should any taste.
Temple, be overthrown! cedars, burst into flame!

Jerusalem, for whom my heart doth mourn,
What hand hath in a day stripped thee of majesty?
Ah, who for eyes will give two founts of tears to me
To weep thy fate forlorn?

AZARIAH.

O holy Temple!

JEHOSHEBA.

O David!

THE CHORUS.

God of Zion, hear!
Remember how of old on her was shed thy grace.
[*The music begins again; and* JEHOIADA, *a moment later,
interrupts it.*

JEHOIADA.

What new city rises there
From the bed of the desert, with light all ablaze,
And a sign evermore on her forehead doth wear?
Peoples of the earth, give praise!
Jerusalem is reborn, more winsome and more fair.
Why seek her from all sides, apace,
These children who within her womb had never place?

Jerusalem, lift up, lift up thy head; be proud.
See all these kings astonished at thy glorious dress.
The kings of earth, each fallen before thee on his face,
          Kiss the dust which thy feet have trod.
The nations by thy radiance gladly walk their road.
O happy he who for Zion's sake is all o'er
          Set aflame with valour's excess!
          Ye skies, shed down your righteousness,
And let the world bring forth her Saviour!

JEHOSHEBA.

Ah, how is this great boon for us in store,
If the kings from whom must descend this Saviour . . .

JEHOIADA.

Bring thou, Jehosheba, the kingly crown
Which on his sacred brow in time agone
David did wear.
     (*To the Levites*) And ye, to arm you, come
With me, to where, concealed within a room
Far from all eyes, are swords and spears high-heaped,
Which in Philistine blood erewhile were dipped,
And which the conqueror David, laden with days
And honours, gave to God, who was always
His shield. Can they to nobler use be put?
Come. I desire myself to deal them out.

          [*Exeunt all except the Chorus.*

CHORUS.[29]

Salome.

O what terrors, my sisters, what mortal dismay!
          All-powerful God, the first fruit is this,
          The incense and the sacrifice,
Which should be offered at thine altars on this day?

One of the Maidens of the Chorus.

What sight to our timid eyes appears?
Can it be that indeed one sees,
Undreamed of, murderous swords and homicidal spears
Agleam in the mansion of peace?

Another.

Whence comes it that, indifferent in her God's defence,
Jerusalem doth give no sign in peril thus?
Whence comes it, sisters, that to succour us,
Not e'en brave Abner breaks the silence and suspense?

Salome.

Alas, in a Court that hath no other laws
Than of force and of violence,—
Where offices and honours choice
Are the prize of a blind and base obedience,—
My sisters, for sad innocence
Who would care to uplift his voice?

Another.

With all in peril and confusion thrown,
For whcm hath been prepared the sacred, kingly crown?

Salome.

At last God deigns to speak his will;
But of what he doth now to his prophet reveal,
Who shall teach us to know the sense?
Doth he arm for our defence,
Or to crush us under his heel?

All the Chorus, singing.

O the hope! O the threat! O darkling mystery!
Both what good and what evil seem here interwove!
How can ever with so much anger be
Made accord so much love?

A Single Voice.

No more shall Zion stand; an implacable flame
Will ravage all her loveliness.

Another Voice.

God will o'er Zion watch! she resteth on, for base,
His word, the changeless same.

The First Voice.

I see her splendour vanish from before mine eyes.

The Second.

I see her shed abroad on every side her light.

The First.

A deep abyss hath swallowed Zion from our sight.

The Second.

Her front Zion rears to the skies.

The First.

What sad abasement this!

The Second.

What glory do I see!

The First.

What cries of grief I hear!

The Second.

What songs of victory!

A Third.

We should not vex ourselves; for the Lord will some day
This wondrous mystery make clear.

All Three.

Let us hold him in fear.
Let us trust in him alway.

Another.

Of hearts that love thee,
O God, canst thou trouble the peace?
I seek, in all, thy will as doth behoove me,
    Nor e'er mine own caprice.
On the earth, in the sky above me,
Can any other happiness rival the peace
    Of hearts that love thee?

[*Enter* JOASH, JEHOSHEBA, ZECHARIAH, *a Levite.*

SALOME.

With proud and stately step beside my mother
Cometh the young Eliakim with my brother.
Under those veils, sisters, what bear they both?
What means this falchion that before them go'th?

JEHOSHEBA.

My son, the dread Book of our sacred Law
Lay on this table reverently; and thou,
Set also here, beloved Eliakim,
By the divine Book, this great diadem.
Levite, it was Jehoiada's behest
That David's sword must by his crown be placed.

JOASH.

Princess, what means this sight—this holy Book,
This sword and diadem? Since the Lord took
And sheltered me within his Temple, ne'er
Have I beheld like preparations here.

JEHOSHEBA.

Thy questions will be answered presently,
My son.

JOASH.

Thou wouldst upon my forehead try
This crown? Ah, do its glory no offence!
Hold the king's memory in reverence
Who wore it. A poor outcast child . . .

JEHOSHEBA.

Let be,
My son. I do what was commanded me.

JOASH.

But I hear sobs burst from thee. Princess, thou
Dost weep. What pity seizeth on thee now?
Must I, as Jephthah's daughter was erewhile,[30]
Be sacrificed this day to reconcile
An angry God? Alas, all that a son
Hath belongs to his father.

JEHOSHEBA.

Here is one
Who will tell thee Heaven's will. Have thou no fear.
We others—let us all go hence.

[*Exeunt all but* JOASH. *Enter* JEHOIADA.

JOASH (*running to* JEHOIADA).

My dear
Father.

JEHOIADA.

Yea, child?

JOASH.

What is it that is prepared?

JEHOIADA.

'Tis just and right that this should be declared
To thee; that ere all others thou shouldst be

Told of the Lord's great purposes for thee
And for his people. Arm thy breast anew
With faith and courage. It is time to show
Alike the zeal and bravery that my care
Was taken deep within thy soul to rear,
And pay the debt thou owest him to thy God.
Canst thou indeed feel such a noble mood?

JOASH.

I feel I would be ready, if he bade,
To give my life for him.[31]

JEHOIADA.

          Thou oft hast read
The history of our kings. Dost thou, my son,
Remember what strict laws are laid upon
A monarch who is worthy of his crown?

JOASH.

Wise kings, we find it in God's word writ down,
Set not their thoughts on riches and on gold,
But fear the Lord and fast in memory hold
His precepts, laws, and judgments stern for ay,
Nor too great burdens on their brothers lay.

JEHOIADA.

But were it needful thou shouldst be like one
Of our kings, which would be thy choice, my son?

JOASH.

David, who loved the Lord unswervingly,
Seems the best model of great kings to me.

JEHOIADA.

Thou wouldst not follow faithless Joram, rather,
Or impious Ahaziah?

JOASH.

Oh, my father!

JEHOIADA.

Speak on! Of them what is it thou thinkest?

JOASH.

May

Those who are like them perish even as they!
[JEHOIADA *prostrates himself at* JOASH'S *feet.*
My father, what is this I see thee do!

JEHOIADA.

I pay to thee the homage that is due
Unto my sovereign. Joash, be of thy
Forefather David worthy.

JOASH.

Joash? I?

JEHOIADA (*raising himself*).

Learn by what signal act of grace God hath
Cheated the purpose of a grandam's wrath.
When in thy breast her knife already stood,
He chose thee, saved thee from the midst of blood
And slaughter. Thou hast not escaped her yet.
With the same cruelty wherewith her hate
Was fain to blot out her son's race erewhile,
Under thy false name she pursues thee still;
But I already have contrived to range
A loyal following, ready to avenge
Thy wrongs, beneath thy banners.
                    (*Lifting his voice*) Enter ye,
Brave chieftains of our sacred family,
Honoured in turn with holy ministering!
[*Enter* AZARIAH, ISHMAEL, *and the other three chief Levites.*

Behold thy champions 'gainst thy foes, O King!
Behold, O priests, the king I promised you!

AZARIAH.

Why, 'tis Eliakim!

ISHMAEL.

The child we knew
And loved . . .

JEHOIADA.

Is Judah's rightful sovereign,
The last of hapless Ahaziah's line,
Who, as ye know, the name of Joash bore.
All the land, like yourselves, hath sorrowed o'er
This flower so fragile and so soon cut down,
Supposing his dead brothers' fate his own.
He was indeed with a disloyal knife
Pierced as were they, but from the seat of life
God turned the stroke, kept his faint spark alive,
And vouchsafed that Jehosheba contrive
To cheat the assassins' eyes, bear him away
All bloody in her arms, and from that day
Conceal him in the Temple with his nurse,
I being sole sharer in this theft of hers.

JOASH.

Alas, how can I ever pay my debt
For such long kindness and for love so great!

JEHOIADA.

'Gainst future years this gratitude store up.
(*To the others*) Behold ye, then, your king, your only hope.
My pains preserved him until now for you;

Servants of God, the rest is yours to do!
The murderous woman born of Jezebel
Shall soon discover Joash liveth still
And come again to plunge him in death's gloom.
Although she knows him not, she seeks his doom
Already. Holy priests, now doth it rest
On you to thwart her rage and end at last
Your country's shameful slavery, vengeance take
For your princes dead, restore the Law, and make
Judah and Benjamin both own their king.
Truly, it is a great and perilous thing
To attack upon her throne a haughty queen,
Who 'neath her standard sees a host of men,
Fierce strangers and unfaithful Jews besides;
But 'tis the Lord who strengthens me and guides.
    Consider: In this child doth Israel live;
E'en now God's wrath makes Athaliah grieve;
E'en now I muster you, despite her care.
She thinks us without arms and helpless here.
Let us crown Joash and proclaim him crowned,
At once; then, soldiers of our prince new-found,
March, calling on Him who giveth victory,
And waking slothful hearts to loyalty,
Within her very palace seek our foe.
    And where is any heart sunk in so low
And vile a sleep that, seeing us come thus,
'Twill not be moved to rally unto us:
A king whom God in his own Temple reared,
Aaron's successor and his priests revered
Leading the sons of Levi forth to war,
And wielded by their hands, that sacred are,
The arms which David offered to the Lord?
    God will send terror on our foes abhorred.

In heathen gore shrink not from bathing; strike
Both Tyrians and Hebrews down alike.
Are ye not from those Levites, famed erewhile,
Descended who, when to the god of Nile
Inconstant Israel in the desert bowed
With sinful worship, in apostate blood
Hallowed their hands, though slaying their dearest kin,
And, by this noble deed, for you did win
The honour, given to none else, to serve
The altars of the Lord?[32]—But I observe
That ye already burn to follow me.
Swear first, then, on this sacred Book you see,
Unto the king whom Heaven this day gives back
To you again, that ye will for his sake
Live, fight, and die.

AZARIAH (*laying his hand on the Book*).
                    Yea, solemnly we here
Both for ourselves and for our brethren swear
To restore Joash to his fathers' throne
Nor e'er the steel our hands have grasped lay down
Till we avenge him on his enemies.
Should any break this oath, great God, let these
Taste of thy wrath; let them with all their seed,
Cast off by thee, be numbered with those dead
Thou knowest no more.

JEHOIADA.
                    And thou, King, wilt not thou
Swear to forsake not God's eternal Law?

JOASH.
Could I be disobedient to his will!

JEHOIADA.

Oh, my son!—thus I dare to call thee still—
Suffer this fondness and forgive the tears
Drawn from mine eyes by too well grounded fears
For thee. Brought up far distant from the throne,
Its deadly witchery thou hast never known,
Nor yet of uncurbed power the drunkenness,
Nor the sweet charm of flatterers' words.[33] Alas!
Soon shall they say that even the holiest law,
Inexorable for lesser folk, must bow
To kings; that his own will restrains a king,
And naught else; that he should let everything
Be sacrificed to make his glory great;
That tears and toil are the appointed fate
Of the common herd; this with an iron rod
Would fain be ruled; if not itself downtrod
Beneath thy feet, sooner or later it
Treads down. From snare to snare, from pit to pit
Thus led, and thy sweet innocence of youth
Corrupted, thou shalt learn to hate the truth
And find all virtue loathsome to thine eyes.
So he of old fell who was the most wise
Of monarchs.[34]
            Swear before these witnesses,
And on this volume, that the Lord's decrees
Shall never cease to be thy first concern;
That thou, the refuge of the good, and stern
Only 'gainst evil, 'twixt the poor and thee
Wilt make God judge, mindful that formerly,
Hid 'neath this linen garb, thyself didst serve,
Orphan and poor like them.

JOASH (*with his hand on the Book*).
                              I swear to observe
That which the Law commands me. Punish me,
O Lord, if ever I depart from thee!

JEHOIADA.
Now with the oil must thou be consecrated.
                    [*He raises his voice, and calls.*
Enter, Jehosheba; thou art awaited.
[JEHOSHEBA, ZECHARIAH, SALOME, *and the Chorus appear.*

JEHOSHEBA (*running to* JOASH).
King! Son of David!

JOASH.
              O my only mother!
Come thou, dear Zechariah; embrace thy brother.

JEHOSHEBA (*to* ZECHARIAH).
Throw thyself at thy sovereign's feet, my son.
[ZECHARIAH *falls at the feet of* JOASH, *who lifts and clasps
      him.*

JEHOIADA.
Children, may you thus ever be at one.[35]

JEHOSHEBA (*to* JOASH).
Thou knowest, then, what sire gave life to thee?

JOASH.
And how from death 'twas thou didst rescue me.

JEHOSHEBA.
Now I can call thee "Joash," thine own name.

JOASH.
Joash will always love thee, just the same.

THE CHORUS (*in unison*).

Why, it is . . .

JEHOSHEBA.

Joash!

[*Enter a Levite, hastily.*

JEHOIADA.

Let us hear this man.

THE LEVITE.

I know not what it is God's foes may plan,
But on all sides the warlike trumpets blare
And 'midst the standards may be seen the flare
Of torches. Surely Athaliah arrays
Her troops. Already blocked are all the ways
For succour; even now the sacred hill
Whereon the Temple stands is ringed with steel
By impious Tyrians, one of whom proclaims
With blasphemy that Abner is in chains
And cannot aid us.

JEHOSHEBA.

　　　　　Ah, dear child, whom Heaven
In vain restored unto me! I have striven
To save thee, daring, alas, all I could!
Thy father David is forgotten of God!

JEHOIADA.

What! Fearest thou not to draw down from above
His wrath on thee and on this king thy love
Holdeth so precious? And even should God decree,
Tearing him from thy clasp eternally,
That David's house should perish, is not this place
The very mountain where in bygone days

The father of the Jews upraised his arm[36]
Obediently, unmurmuring, o'er the form
Of his own blameless son, whom he had put
Upon a funeral pile, though the sole fruit
Of his old age, leaving to God the way
To keep his promises, and leal to slay
For him with this belovèd child the hope
Of all his race, which was therewith bound up?
                    [*Turning to the chief Levites.*

Friends, let us part our strengths. Be Ishmael's care
The side that fronts the east. That of the Bear[37]
Be thine; and thine the west; and thine the south.
Take heed that neither priest nor Levite doth
In the blind fervour of a reckless zeal
Sally forth ere 'tis time, and so reveal
What I have planned. Be not in too great haste.
Let each defend the spot where he is placed,
Even to the death, all of one constant mind.
Our foes regard us in their fury blind
As poor sheep waiting to be slaughtered. They
Look but to meet confusion and dismay.
Let Azariah ever guard the King.
(*To* JOASH) Come now, dear child of a brave line, and bring
New courage to the hearts of those who fight
For us. Come, wear the crown before their sight;
And if it needs that thou must perish, die
At least a king.
                    Follow his steps anigh,
Jehosheba.
(*To a Levite*) Thou, give those arms to me.
(*To the Chorus*) Children, uplift to God your tearful plea.
                    [*Exeunt all except the Chorus.*

CHORUS.[38]

All the Chorus.

Go forth, ye sons of Aaron, go!
A greater and holier cause
Your fathers' zeal did never rouse.
Go forth, ye sons of Aaron, go!
'Tis for your king, for God, ye march against the foe.

A Single Voice.

The shafts are where that would kill,
Great God, in thine anger of yore?
Art a jealous God no more,
Nor a God of vengeance still?

Another.

Where, God of Jacob, are thy bounties shown of old?
In the horror now of our lives
Dost thou hear but the voice of our sins manifold?
Art thou not the God who forgives?

All the Chorus.

Where, God of Jacob, are thy bounties shown of old?

One Voice, alone.

'Tis at thee with single accord
The wicked dare to aim their darts in this affray.
"An end let us make," they say,
"On earth of the feasts of the Lord.
Let us free all mankind from the dread of his frown;
Let us slaughter his saints and his altars cast down;
So of his might, so of his Name
There shall be no longer the fame,
Nor he or his Anointed ever rule us more."

All the Chorus.

The shafts are where that would kill,
Great God, in thine anger of yore?

Art a jealous God no more,
Nor a God of vengeance still?

A Single Voice.

Sad survivor of our kings,
Thou dear and final flower of so fair a tree,
Alas, 'neath a cruel grandam's dagger must we
Behold thee fall a second time, 'mid sorrowings?
Prince belovèd, declare if angels from thy doom
Delivered thee, thy cradle guarding on that day,
Or if, in the night of the tomb,
The voice of the living God hath waked again thy clay.[39]

Another.

Dost thou the sins of father and grandfather hold,
Great God, as his, that 'gainst thee were froward and bold?
Is pity not to be for him while yet he lives?

All the Chorus.

Where, God of Jacob, are thy bounties shown of old?
Art thou not the God who forgives?

One of the Maidens, crying out.

Do ye hear not the trumpet of Tyre,
Dear sisters, resounding so cruel and so near?

Salome.

I can hear the loud shouts of the soldiery dire,
And I shake in my fear.
Away, nor stay! withdraw we now
To seek a safe retreat
Within this dread and holy seat.

[*Enter* ZECHARIAH.

SALOME.

Oh, Zechariah, what news bringest thou?[40]

ZECHARIAH.

Redouble to the Lord your fervent prayer.
'Tis our last hour, perhaps, that draweth near.
Given is the command for battle dread.

SALOME.

And Joash?

ZECHARIAH.

He hath just been crowned. His head
Hath been with holy oil anointed by
The high priest. Ah, what bliss in every eye
To view this king, snatched from the tomb to life![41]
Sister, the mark still showeth of the knife!
His faithful nurse was also to be seen,
Who guarded her dear charge, concealed within
A corner of this mighty edifice,
And for her pains had as sole witnesses
God and my mother. In their joy and love
The Levites wept, mingling the sobs thereof
With their glad cries. Gracious and void of pride,
Amid their ecstasies he fondly eyed
Some of them, and stretched out his hand to others,
Calling them all his fathers and his brothers
And swearing he would let their counsels guide
His footsteps.

SALOME.

Is the secret known outside?

ZECHARIAH.

It hath not passed the Temple yet. There stands
In utter silence one of the armed bands
Formed by the sons of Levi at each door.
All must rush forth at the same time, and for

A battle-cry must shout, "Long live the King!"
But father forbids any hazarding
Of Joash's life, and wills that Azariah
Remain his guard. Meanwhile Queen Athaliah
Laughs at our frail defence of brazen gates,
And with a dagger in her hand awaits
The enginery to shatter them, and death
Breathes and destruction. In a place beneath
The ground, dug long ago, at first some priest
Or two urged that the sacred Ark at least
Should be concealed. "Oh, fear," my father said,
"Base and injurious! What! the Ark which made
Such haughty towers fall, and even did force
The Jordan to flow backward on its course,[42]
And triumphed o'er the gods of many a race,
Flee now before an impious woman's face!"

Beside the King my mother, sore distressed,
With glance on him and on the altar cast
Alternately, silent, and by her fears
Quite crushed, would from the cruelest eyes draw tears.
From time to time clasping her to him, he
Caresses her. . . . Dear sisters, follow me;
And if our king this day must meet his doom,
May the same fate unite us with him! Come!

[*Exit* ZECHARIAH. *A thunderous knocking is heard outside.*
Several Levites hasten across the room, hiding their
weapons as they go.

SALOME.

What rude hand beats amain upon the door?
Why run these Levites wildly thus? Wherefore
Are they so careful to conceal their arms?

[*Re-enter* ZECHARIAH.

Is the Temple forced?

ZECHARIAH.

Give o'er thy vain alarms.

God sends us Abner.

[*Enter* ABNER *from one side,* JEHOIADA, JEHOSHEBA, ISH-
MAEL, *and two Levites from the other.*

JEHOIADA.

Nay, can I believe
Mine eyes, dear Abner! How couldst thou achieve
Thy passage here through the besiegers' lines?
'Twas said that, to insure her cruel designs
'Gainst failure, Ahab's daughter gave commands
To load with shameful chains thy gallant hands.

ABNER.

Yea, my lord, for she feared my piety
And courage; but her rage accorded me
Worse punishment than this, which was my least.
Unto the horrors of a dungeon cast
By her, I was expecting that when flame
Should have consumed this Temple, not yet tame
Nor satiated after such great seas
Of blood, she would vouchsafe to me release
From weary life, and cut short days which woe,
At having survived my kings, should long ago
Have ended.[48]

JEHOIADA.

By what marvel hast thou won
Mercy?

ABNER.

God knoweth the workings, he alone,
Of that dark heart of hers. She had me brought
To her. "Thou seest," she said, as one distraught,

"This Temple, by my troops encompassed round.
The vengeful flames shall burn it to the ground,
Nor hath thy God the power to say me nay.
His priests, however, if without delay
They act, on two conditions can redeem
All: that they give to me Eliakim
And a great treasure which I know is known
To them;—it was amassed in time agone
By your King David and beneath the seal
Of secrecy left with the high priest. I will
Permit, do thou go tell them, at this price
That they shall live."

JEHOIADA.

Friend Abner, what advice
Hast thou for us?

ABNER.

Both all King David's gold,
If it indeed be true that here ye hold
Treasures of David hidden, and all else
Of rich and rare that ye have saved yourselves
From the clutches of this avaricious queen—
Give it! Shall foul assassins enter in,
Would ye instead, to break the altar, burn
The cherubim,[44] against the Ark e'en turn
Their hands presumptuous, and with gore make wet
The sanctuary?

JEHOIADA.

But thinkest thou 'twould be fit,
Abner, that brave hearts should consent to yield
For punishment a helpless child, a child
Whom God himself into my keeping gave,

And with the payment of his life to save
Our lives?

ABNER.

The Lord sees all my heart. Ah, would
To his great power that Athaliah could
Forget an innocent boy and satisfy
Her cruelty with Abner's death, thereby
Deeming assuaged that wrath which threatened her!
But what can possibly avail your care
For him? If ye all perish, will he die
The less? Doth God command that ye shall try
The impossible? Unto a tyrant's will
Conforming, Moses' mother to the Nile
Abandoned him; thus was he given up,
Almost at birth, to doom; but 'gainst all hope
Did God preserve his life and make that king
Himself to rear him.[45] Who shall say what thing
He purposeth for your Eliakim,
And if, preparing a like fate for him,
He hath not now to pity bent the mood
Of the grim murderess of our royal blood?
At least—and even as I Jehosheba
Could so observe—this very day I saw
His aspect move her, saw her wrath grow weak.

Princess, thou dost not in this peril speak!
What! for a child who is unknown to thee
Wilt thou permit thy husband fruitlessly
To let thyself be slaughtered and his son
And all these folk, and flames devour the one
Place on the earth where God would fain receive
Men's worship? If in this young boy did live
The last survivor of our kings of yore,
Thine ancestors—why, what could ye do more?

JEHOSHEBA (*aside to* JEHOIADA).

Thou seest the love he bears the royal line.
Couldst thou not tell him?

JEHOIADA.

Princess, 'tis not time.

ABNER.

Time is more precious than thou thinkest, sir.[46]
While here thou weighest how to answer her,
Mattan at Athaliah's side, on fire
With rage, demandeth slaughter swift and dire.
Must I needs fall before thee on my face?
Oh, in the name of that Most Holy Place,[47]
Open to none save thee, dread place whereo'er
Broodeth God's majesty, however sore
Are the imposed conditions, let us now
Plan how we may ward off this sudden blow.
Give me but time to breathe, and I will take
Measures to-morrow—nay, this night—to make
The Temple safe and to avenge its wrong.
    But well I see that tears and my weak tongue
Are powerless to persuade, nor by them can
Thy rectitude be moved. So be it, then!
Find me some arm, some sword, and at the gate
Of the Temple, where for my return await
The enemy, Abner at least can die
Fighting!

JEHOIADA.

I yield. Thy proffered counsel I
Embrace. Yea, Abner, let us turn aside
These many ills. Truly, there here lies hid
A treasure which may be to David traced.

In my hands hath its guardianship been placed.
'Twas the last hope of the unhappy Jews,
Whence to conceal it, was my care and use;
But since I needs must show it to the Queen,
I will content her. Let her come herein
With her chief captains, through our gates ajar;
But let her from these altars hold afar
The unchecked fury of an alien pack.
Spare me the horror of the Temple's sack!
What harm to her could priests and children do?
Let her with thee decide what retinue
Is large enough. As for this boy so feared,
So dreaded, well I know how much revered
Is justice, Abner, by thy heart; to thee
Will I explain his birth and ancestry
Before her; thou shalt see then if I need
Surrender him into her power indeed,
And I shall let thee be the judge 'twixt her
And him.

ABNER (*joyfully*).

Ah, I already take him, sir,
'Neath my protection. Fear thou naught. I haste
Back unto her that sent me.

[*Exit* ABNER.

JEHOIADA.

'Tis at last
Thine hour, great God, the hour that brings thy prey!
Ishmael, hark!

[*He whispers in* ISHMAEL'S *ear.*

JEHOSHEBA.

As on a former day,
Blind her, O mighty Master of the skies,

With that same veil which was about her eyes
When thou didst let me in my breast conceal
This tender victim from the murderer's steel,
Robbing her of the fruit of all her crime!

JEHOIADA (*aloud*).

Go now, good Ishmael. See thou lose no time.
Obey my weighty hests in everything,
Especially that at her entering
And while she passes hither, all must wear
The look of utter peace.

[*Exit* ISHMAEL.

                                    Children, prepare
A throne for Joash. Let him come at once,
Still followed by the Temple's armèd sons.
Princess, have thou his faithful nurse hard by
Also, and let thy fount of tears be dry.

[*To a Levite.*

Thou, when this queen, with madness of her pride
Made drunk, hath passed the threshold and inside
The Temple stands; when she will nevermore
Be able to go back through yon same door,
See that the trumpet instantly shall blow
And bring a sudden terror on the foe.
The people to their king's assistance call,
Making re-echo in the ears of all
The wondrous tale of Joash saved, restored.
He is here.

[*Enter* JOASH *and his bodyguard.*

                    Ye priests and Levites of the Lord,
Keep hidden, but surround this spot, and letting
Your ardour be controlled by me, bide waiting
Until my voice shall summon you to appear.

[*Exeunt all the train of* JOASH.

King, I believe that thou mayst hope thy prayer
Is heard. Come, see thy foes fall at thy feet.
She who pursued thy childhood with her hate,
To slay thee now is hastening hitherward,
But fear her not; remember for thy guard
Stands the destroying angel by thy side.
Ascend thy throne. . . . But the gate opens wide.[48]
Be veiled one moment by this curtain's fold.

[*He draws a hanging*

Thou growest pale, princess.

JEHOSHEBA.

Ah, can I behold
The Temple filled with murderers again,
Nor blench? What! seest thou not how many men . . .

JEHOIADA.

I only see the Temple's gate once more
Is shut now and refastened. All is sure!
[*Exeunt the Chorus. Enter* ATHALIAH, ABNER, *and retinue.*

ATHALIAH (*to* JEHOIADA).

Thou art there, deceiver, thou the baleful source
Of plots and factions, thou whose one resource
Hath been but strife, wherein thy hope doth lie,
Inveterate foe of sovereign majesty!
On the protection of thy God hast thou
Relied. Does that vain trust forsake thee now?
He yields to me thy Temple and thy life.
Thee ought I on the altar where thy knife
Offers up sacrifice . . . But I must need
Content me with the terms which were agreed
Upon. What thou hast promised me to do,
Forget it not. This child, this treasure too,

Which are to be surrendered to me—where
Are they?

JEHOIADA.
　　　Thou shalt be satisfied—e'en here.
I will show both to thee at once. Appear,
My child, true seed of royal sires!

[*He draws back the curtain.* JOASH *is seen seated on a throne;
his nurse is on her knees at his right;* AZARIAH, *sword in
hand, stands on his left;* ZECHARIAH *and* SALOME *are
kneeling on the steps of the throne; several Levites,
armed, are ranged on either side.*

(*As* ATHALIAH *stands speechless*) The heir,
Queen, dost thou know him, of the holiest
Of monarchs? Thou shouldst recognize at least
Thy dagger's mark. Behold thy king, the son
Of thy son Ahaziah! Every one,
O people—and thou, Abner—know and hail
Joash!

ABNER.
　Ye heavens!

ATHALIAH.
　　Traitor!

JEHOIADA.
　　　　Thou knowest well
This faithful Jewess—seest thou?—at whose breast
He once was nursed. Jehosheba, unguessed,
Saved him from thee; this Temple did afford
Him refuge; his preserver was the Lord.
Of David's treasures, lo, naught else to me
Is left.

ATHALIAH.

Thou false knave, thy deceit will be
Death to the child. Rid me of this vile fraud,
My soldiers!

JEHOIADA (*in a voice of thunder*).
Soldiers of the living God,
Defend your king!
[*The great hangings which covered the apertures at the rear
and on either side are thrown back, and the courts of the
Temple are seen filled with armed Levites, who begin to
pour into the room.*

ATHALIAH.
Why, what place am I in?
Oh, treason, treason! Oh, unhappy queen!
About me are but arms and enemies.

JEHOIADA.

There is no escape for thee. Vainly thine eyes
Search round; for God draws close on every side
The net. Yea, that same God thou hast defied
Gives thee into our hands. Him shalt thou pay
For all the blood wherewith until this day
Thou madest thyself drunk.

ATHALIAH.
What! frozen with fear
Stand my unworthy guards? Into what snare,
Base Abner, hast thou led me?

ABNER.
Queen, God is
My witness that . . .

ATHALIAH.

Leave thy God out of this,
Traitor! Avenge me!

ABNER.

On whom? On Joash? On
My master?
[*He throws himself at* JOASH'S *feet. A confused noise outside
is heard.*

ATHALIAH.

He Joash? He your king? Let one
And all remember, caitiffs, that my power
Still hems you round. I hear a mighty roar
Wherewith my warriors do their queen demand.
Help comes e'en now. Tremble, ye recreant band!
[*Enter* ISHMAEL, *with flashing eyes and drawn sword.*

ISHMAEL (*to* JEHOIADA).

The Temple, sir, hath no more foes; 'tis free!
The Jews submit, and all the aliens flee.
As smoke is scattered by the wind of heaven,
So hath the voice of the Almighty driven
This army hence. Our Levites, high upon
The sacred porches, have proclaimed the son
Of Ahaziah to the multitude,—
Have told how from the sword that sought his blood
He had in infancy been stolen away,
And how the daughter of Ahab hath this day
Fallen into a trap. Loud everywhere
At once hath blown the trumpet; and its blare,
Mixed with the cries in her bedazed array,
The same swift panic spread and wild dismay
As Gideon when he smote the Midianite.[49]

Casting down shields and weapons in their flight,
The Tyrians vanished first on every side.
Certain Jews also made off, terrified;
But the rest, awe-struck at God's grace which spared
Joash, have with uplifted voice declared
For him. Now fired alike, the populace,
Women, old men, and children, all embrace
With joy; all bless the Lord and that one whom
He sends; all hail as risen from the tomb
The son of David. Baal is abominate
Throughout the holy city, and the gate
Lies shattered of his shrine. Mattan is slain.[50]

ATHALIAH.

God of the Jews, thou triumphest! In vain
Have I attempted to deceive me. Yes,
Joash it is. I recognize the place
Where fell my blow. I see the look and port
Of Ahaziah. All recalleth, in short,
A race whom I detest. David hath won,
Hath won; 'tis Ahab is destroyed.
                       Alone
Thy work is this, relentless Deity,
Thou who with thoughts of easy victory
Didst flatter me, and in a single day
Didst twenty times in strife my mind array
Against itself and to confusion turn
My plans, now making pity in me burn
For a child's sake, now dazzling me with hope
Of treasures that I shrank from giving up
To fire and pillage. Let this boy, then, reign,
Thy care and handiwork. Yea, let him stain
His dagger with my heart's gore, and so mark

His coming to his new-found kingdom. Hark:
'Tis thus his dying grandam wishes him
To be—how say I, "wishes"?—nay, I *deem*
That, weary of thy Law's authority,
And true to Ahab's blood, his own through me,
Like to his sire and grandsire, this loathed heir
Of David shall strip off thy honours fair,
Profane thy altar, and take vengeance fell
For Athaliah, Ahab, and Jezebel.[51]

[*Exit* ATHALIAH, *under guard.*

JEHOIADA.

Let her at once outside the Temple be
Conducted, nor profane its sanctity.
Go, and requite your princes' murderer;
Make their blood cease to cry, by slaying her.
Should any dare espouse her cause abhorred,
Let him, too, taste the fury of the sword.[52]

JOASH.

O God, who seest my grief and anxious care,
Her curse avert far from me, that it ne'er
May be fulfilled. Sooner than turn from thee,
Let Joash die!

JEHOIADA (*to the chief Levites*).

Together now call ye
The populace, and show their sovereign
Unto them. Let them come and swear again
Their oath of fealty, on his hands renewed.
King, priests, and people, full of gratitude,
Let us confirm now Jacob's covenant
With God, and for our strayings penitent,

Bind ourselves to him with fresh promises.
    Abner, take by the King thy rightful place.

                    [Enter a Levite.

(*To the Levite*) And have ye punished that unholy one?

THE LEVITE.

Sharp steel hath made her for her crimes atone.
Jerusalem, so long her fury's prey
But free at last from her detested sway,
With joy beholds her weltering in her blood.[53]

JEHOIADA.

By this end, fearful yet to justice owed,
Learn, King of Judah, nor forget thou e'er,
That rulers have in heaven a Judge severe
Who aids the innocent in their distress
And is a father to the fatherless.

NOTES ON ATHALIE

(The line-numbers are those of the French text.)

THE events on which *Athalie* is based are recorded in chapter xi of the Second Book of Kings and in chapters xxii and xxiii of the Second Book of Chronicles. The drama contains many references to earlier chapters of First and Second Kings and of Second Chronicles, and to other parts of the Bible. It is practicable to explain in the Notes only a few such references.

Most of the information about the history and customs of the ancient Hebrews which is really essential in connection with *Athalie* is given in Racine's own Preface to it, and hence a translation of this has been placed immediately before that of the play itself.

1; l. 33. From Aaron, the first high priest, the office descended lineally to Jehoiada.

2; l. 50. Observe how Racine thus at the very outset of the play prepares for its dénouement.

3; l. 114. The field is Naboth's vineyard. See 1 Kings xxi, 1-24. The biblical references for the other "prodigies" which Jehoiada mentions are: 1 Kings xxi, 23, and 2 Kings ix, 30-7; 1 Kings xviii, 17-40; 1 Kings xvii, 1; 2 Kings iv, 18-37.

4; l. 155. Probably nine o'clock a.m. is meant.

5; l. 219. Athaliah, the daughter of Jezebel (originally a princess of Tyre), has a bodyguard of Tyrian soldiers.

6; l. 230. See 2 Kings ix.

7; l. 294. Contrast the prayer of Jehoiada with that of Jehosheba just before it. The two characters are well portrayed in their words. Jehosheba's concern is for the life of the child whom she loves; to Jehoiada the child is but an instrument in furthering God's cause.

8; l. 311. The first chorus is a hymn of praise to God, such as befits the feast-day on which the first-fruits are offered and the gift of the Law is commemorated. The paraphrases of scriptural language are often strikingly beautiful.

9; l. 351. The references in this stanza are to the deliverance of the Israelites from bondage in Egypt (Exod. ii-xv) and to the gift of manna to them (Exod. xvi, 14-36); in the next stanza they are to the passage of the Red Sea (Exod. xiv) and to the bringing of water from a rock by Moses (Exod. xvii, 1-6; Num. xx, 11).

10; l. 450. Mattan's approach is only fourteen lines (in the French) after Hagar goes out to fetch him! Such failures to allow sufficient time for events occurring off-stage are usually confined to Racine's fifth acts. In this instance he has sought to mask the impossibility by Athaliah's command that Mattan shall come "in haste."

11; l. 472. The picture which is here given of the brilliant success of Athaliah's reign is Racine's own invention. The seas referred to are the Red Sea and the Mediterranean. During the reign of Athaliah's husband, the kingdom of Judah suffered fearfully at the hands of the Arabs and the Philistines. "The Syrian monarch," Hazael, is the "strong neighbour" before whose attacks Jehu "quails"; Racine imagines these attacks to have been instigated by Athaliah to prevent Jehu from pursuing even against her the vengeance on the whole race of Ahab which God had enjoined him to take.

12; l. 506. See 2 Kings ix, 33-7.

13; l. 616. See Note 5.

14; l. 642. This is evidently what Joash has been told by Jehoiada and Jehosheba. It is figuratively true, and he has taken it literally and so repeats it.

15; l. 661. From this point, Athaliah's questions are put with a view of discovering whether treason is being hatched against her in the Temple. She asks what is the substance of the Law which is being taught within its walls, and how those who dwell there occupy themselves. She counts upon the fact that, as she has said to Mattan, a child's naïve answers are likely to reveal the truth.

16; l. 714. In the Bible the number is given as seventy. See 2 Kings x, 1, 6, and 7.

17; l. 751. The Chorus sings of the wisdom of the wonderful child, and develops the thought that "the prosperity of the wicked, like a torrent, soon runs dry."

18; l. 766. See 1 Sam. i and ii.

19; l. 917. Ishmael was the son of Abraham and Hagar, and the ancestor of the warlike nomadic tribe bearing his name. See Gen. xvi, 11, 12.

20; l. 962. Many critics have considered Mattan's frank revelation of his vileness unnatural. The parallel which those who defend its psychology draw with the self-revelation of Shakespeare's Iago is not wholly satisfactory. Iago most fully unveils his character in soliloquy. His custom of cynical speech to others was not such as to forfeit their confidence; only Roderigo was permitted to glimpse his real depravity, and he despised Roderigo as a fool. It is perhaps harder to believe that Mattan would confess his secret fear of Jehovah than his outright wickedness.

21; l. 1018. This terrific denunciation of Mattan has all the more force in coming from the "gentle" Jehosheba. That she is delivered from the perils of Mattan's searching inquisition by the purely fortuitous entrance of Jehoiada at this moment, is one of the few defects which can be found in this play.

22; l. 1037. Abiram and Dathan revolted against Moses in the desert (Num. xvi). Doeg betrayed the priests who befriended David when he was fleeing from Saul (1 Sam. xxi, xxii). Ahithophel, who had been David's chief counsellor, joined the revolt of Absalom (2 Sam. xvii).

23; l. 1044. Mattan in his panic tries to escape by the wrong door.

24; l. 1060. The brook Kedron flows on the east of Jerusalem, and separates it from the Mount of Olives. The wastes referred to are the desert of Engaddi, the rough, mountainous country between Jerusalem and Jericho. It was through this region that David fled from Absalom.

25; l. 1106. The reference is to the terror of the Children of Israel when they found themselves apparently trapped between the Red Sea and Pharaoh's pursuing army. See Exod. xiv, 10.

26; l. 1114. See Judges iv, 17-22.

27; l. 1126. David.

28; l. 1142. The gold transformed to lead is Joash himself, who later in his life forsook Jehovah and had Zechariah "slain within the sacred place." The rest of this prophetic speech of Jehoiada refers to the taking of Jerusalem by Nebuchadnezzar, the captivity of the Jews, and the destruction of the Temple. In his next speech Jehoiada foretells the rise of the New Jerusalem, the Christian Church. The children "who within her womb had never place" are the Gentiles.

29; l. 1187. The third chorus sings of the foreshadowings of bane and blessing which are so strangely mingled in the prophecy of Jehoiada.

30; l. 1260. See Judges xi, 29-40.

31; l. 1274. Jehoiada's words have only strengthened the suspicion of Joash that he is to be sacrificed.

32; l. 1368. See Exod. xxxii.

33; l. 1390. Cf. *Phèdre*, l. 1325-6.

34; l. 1402. Solomon.

35; l. 1416. Jehoiada has just seen with the eye of prophecy the death of Zechariah at Joash's hands. Is he able to remember his vision, now that the hour of divination is past?

36; l. 1440. According to tradition, Mount Moriah, on which the Temple stood, was the spot on which Abraham attempted to sacrifice Isaac (Gen. xxii, 1-19).

37; l. 1447. The Bear is the constellation of the "Great Bear" (the "Great Dipper"). Hence the north is meant.

38; l. 1463. The fourth and last chorus is a war song, speeding the Levites to battle.

39; l. 1497. The members of the Chorus were not present when Jehoiada explained to his five chief subordinates how Joash had been preserved.

40; l. 1510. Observe that this line rhymes with a line in Salome's preceding speech in choral stanza form. Thus the continuous nature of the action, without act pauses, is shown.

41; l. 1517. In the rest of this speech, Racine strangely loses his grasp on the dramatic situation. That Zechariah, a boy some twelve years old, can be so completely diverted from his intense anxieties of just three lines earlier, and that at such a time he can prattle on and on enthusiastically about the spectacle presented by Joash, is incredible. He has evidently ceased to be a character, temporarily, and has become merely a "Messenger." Only after the apposite question of Salome, "Is the secret known outside?" does he resume his own rôle.

42; l. 1546. The allusions are to the fall of the walls of Jericho (Joshua vi, 1-21) and the miraculous crossing of the river Jordan (Joshua iii, 9-17).

43; l. 1574. Racine devises cleverly: Athaliah's treatment of Abner somewhat palliates his subsequent breach of faith with her, the most dubious point, ethically, in the conduct of her adversaries.

44; l. 1594. The cherubim were two winged angelic figures of gold which spread their wings over the Ark. See Exod. xxv, 18-20; I Kings vi, 23-8.

45; l. 1612. See Exod. ii.

46; l. 1629. Abner overheard Jehoiada's answer to Jehosheba, which was not whispered as her question had been.

47; l. 1634. The Holy of Holies. See Racine's Preface.

48; l. 1699. The time which Racine allows for Abner to go and deliver Jehoiada's message to Athaliah and to return with her after her retinue has been selected, would of course be too short in actuality, but the interim is so full of bustle and action that verisimilitude is not obviously impaired.

49; l. 1756. See Judges vii.

50; l. 1768. The events narrated in this lengthy recital have all occurred between the closing of the Temple door and the entrance of Ishmael, a space of forty-one lines in the French text! Cf. my translation of *Phèdre,* Note 36.

51; l. 1790. Athaliah is before all else the daughter of Jezebel. Her mother's name is the last word on her lips.

52; l. 1796. Doubtless the zealot Jehoiada would not have spared even Abner if he had interfered in behalf of Athaliah; but it was indeed a time when that captain could more honourably have laid down his life than have preserved it. He was thoroughly justified in transferring his allegiance to Joash when he beheld that rightful heir to the throne; he may reasonably have felt that Athaliah deserved to die; but he should have recognized that she had been trapped through her trust in his representations, made as her officer, and that he was hence in honour bound to protect at least her life at any cost.

53; l. 1812. Another and still more glaring instance of hurried action. In the French text only eleven lines are between Athaliah's exit and the entrance of the Levite announcing that she has been slain and that Jerusalem rejoices to behold her weltering in her blood! Cf. Note 50.